Wildlife of Eastern Australia

Northern Quoll with her young

Stanley & Kay Breeden

Wildlife of Eastern Australia

TAPLINGER PUBLISHING CO., INC. NEW YORK

Printed in Hong Kong

First published in the United States in 1973 by
TAPLINGER PUBLISHING CO., INC.
New York, New York

Library of Congress Catalog Card Number: 73-7256

ISBN *0-8008- 8332-2*

Contents

Male Lace Goannas fighting

Illustrations

Preface

IN THIS BOOK an attempt has been made to look, in some detail, at the wildlife of Australia's east coast and in the context of the plants' and animals' natural environment. Australia's eastern seaboard has a great range of habitats from the true tropics of northern Queensland to temperate Tasmania. But for its full 2,000 miles length the area is dominated by just two geographical features, the Great Dividing Range in the west and the Pacific Ocean in the east. In the following pages we discuss the major land habitats that lie between the Divide and the ocean. For reasons of space marine and freshwater habitats are excluded. Even within the indicated limits it is possible to give only an impression of the vast diversity of life and life histories. Much remains to be discovered.

We spent four years gathering information. Our time was about equally divided between recording the wildlife in its natural surroundings and studying the available literature. Most of the information about the wildlife on the following pages is therefore based on what we saw, but modified and qualified by previously recorded observations.

Each field trip to gather fresh material was a new experience—more forests were destroyed, more illicit and large scale plundering of animal and plant life had taken place. Irresponsible use of fire, ravages caused by introduced animals from feral cats to pigs, the spread of introduced plants, all had eaten further into the east coast's subtly beautiful landscapes.

This leads to the question of conservation which wrongly has become synonymous in many respects with natural history. Natural history is the study of an area's natural life in its own right. Conservation is the wise use of natural resources by man; two distinct and separate approaches.

This book is about natural history, about the living environment, how to appreciate and enjoy it and perhaps understand it a little. Had we taken a strictly conservationist point of view and constantly referred to the many disasters which have overtaken Australian wildlife and the dangers that constantly face it, the quality of the living environment would have been submerged. The special problems of conservation are therefore discussed separately in the final chapter.

Our aim is to convey the atmosphere and significance of the region as a whole. Emphasis has not been placed on those species which are well known; our concern is with a species' importance in shaping the environment.

Published information on the region's natural history is scattered through numerous scientific journals published in many countries. We found no single work which described in detail the full spectrum of life of a particular habitat. To piece a story together, material had to be drawn from many sources and supplemented with our own observations. But a few works stand out and these were of great value as they gave us a basic understanding of the major habitats. Most important were P. W. Richards' *Tropical Rainforest*, M. R. Jacobs' *Growth Habits of the Eucalypts*, and the ecological papers on rainforest by L. J. Webb and on eucalypt forests by R. G. Florence. Some of the other published works which were consulted are listed in a selected bibliography at the back of this volume.

The information gathered in the field and in the library fell into two basic categories. One was concerned only with scientific study and analysis. The other is less easily defined but has to do with appreciation of growing, living things and their impact on us. Both aspects are essential to a total understanding of the environment. To reflect this duality some chapters have been divided into two parts, but not always in the same order. In one section we use the basic knowledge gained from published work and field observations to analyse a particular habitat—the effect of the soil and climate, the way a eucalypt regenerates or a glider behaves. In the other section we put all the pieces together and present it as a totality which can then perhaps be better appreciated and be better understood. We hope these two approaches to the same situation reinforce each other. We are trying to communicate what it means to experience the living Australian environment and perhaps to stimulate the reader to set out on his own journeys of discovery.

Each section looks closely at a habitat or group of similar habitats, not by giving an itemised list of its inhabitants, but by endeavouring to demonstrate how the various groups interact and by seeing how every niche created by climate and soil is filled by plants and animals best suited to it.

Originally this text, in a slightly different form, appeared in Vols. 1 and 2 of *A Natural History of Australia*.

WE COULD NEVER have seen the great variety of wildlife nor found many of the places of special interest, had it not been for the ready help we received along the way.

For both the guidance they gave us in the field and for their friendship we thank Don and Helen Gilmour, Ian and Dale Straughan, Kevin and

Gep Sparkes, all members of the Roberts family of Shipton Flat, Dick and Greta Verhey, Eric and Jess Palmer, Percy and Mabel Grant, John and Marion Simmons, Bob Green, Jim Napier, Hardy Buzzacot, Cyril and Fay Webster, Bill and Robyn Cooper, Bill Dunmall, Don Taylor, Colin Limpus, Dane and Robyn Wimbush, David Corke and Mr and Miss Nason.

For information about and help in tracking down particular plants and animals we gratefully acknowledge the aid given by L. J. Webb, J. G. Tracey, B. P. M. Hyland, Ian Bevege, John Calaby, Bob Warneke, Peter Dwyer, John McIlroy, Peter Temple Smith, V. C. Mullett, and I. F. B. Common.

We owe a particular debt to Ted Wixted for his encouragement throughout the four years and his constructive criticisms of the text.

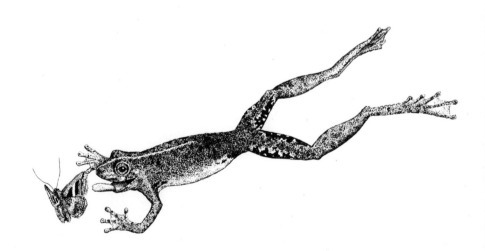

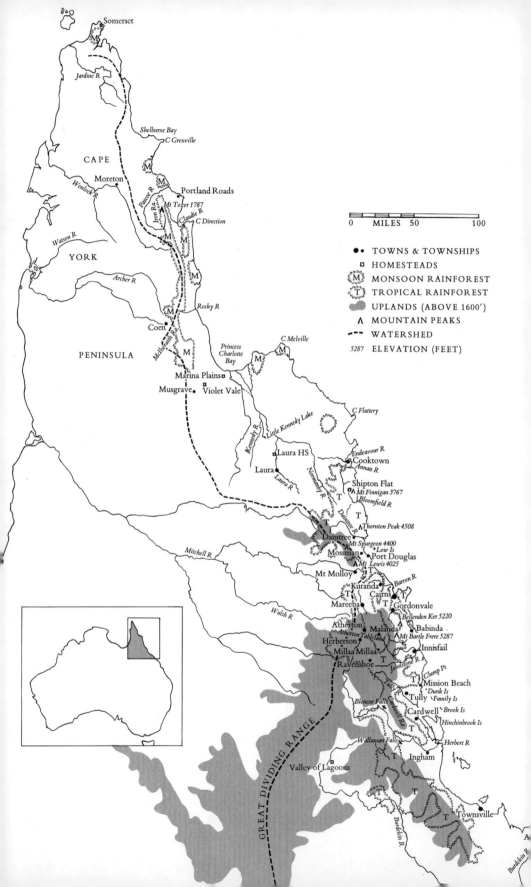

Somerset

M

Jardine R

CAPE

Shelburne Bay
C Grenville

Moreton

M
Wenlock R

M
Portland Roads

M
Mt Tozer 1787
Claudie R
Iron Rd
Pascoe R
C Direction

YORK

M

Watson R

Archer R

M

Rocky R

PENINSULA

M

Coen
McIlwraithR

M

Princess Charlotte Bay

C Melville
M

M

Marina Plains

Musgrave

Violet Vale

Kennedy R
Little Kennedy Lake

C Flattery

Endeavour R
Cooktown

Laura HS
Annan R

Laura
Normanby R
Laura R

Shipton Flat
Mt Finnigan 3767
Bloomfield R
T

T

Mitchell R
Daintree R
Thornton Peak 4508
T

Daintree
Mt Spurgeon 4400
Low Is
Mossman
Port Douglas
Mt Lewis 4025
T

Mt Molloy
Kuranda
Barron R
Cairns
Mareeba
T
Gordonvale
T
Bellenden Ker 5220

Walsh R
Atherton
Malanda
Babinda
Atherton Tableland
Mt Bartle Frere 5287
Herberton
Innisfail
Millaa Millaa
T
Ravenshoe
Johnstone R
Clump Pt
Mission Beach
Dunk Is
Family Is
Blencoe Falls
Tully
T
Cardwell
Brook Is
Tully R
Herbert R
Hinchinbrook Is
Wallaman Falls
T
GREAT DIVIDING RANGE
Valley of Lagoons
Ingham
T
Burdekin R
T
T
Townsville
Burdekin R

0   MILES   50   100

● ● TOWNS & TOWNSHIPS
□ HOMESTEADS
Ⓜ MONSOON RAINFOREST
Ⓣ TROPICAL RAINFOREST
▨ UPLANDS (ABOVE 1600')
∧ MOUNTAIN PEAKS
- - - WATERSHED
5287 ELEVATION (FEET)

I EAST OF THE GREAT DIVIDE

A CHAIN of mountains and hills runs down the entire eastern half of Australia, from the tip of Cape York Peninsula to southern Victoria. This backbone, known as the Great Dividing Range, is never far from the coast and has a profound effect on the continent's climate and consequently on its plant and animal life. The range is a watershed separating two distinctly different environments. To the west of it are dry, flat plains clothed in open eucalypt woodlands, acacia thickets and grass. On the Divide itself and to the east of it is land with higher rainfall, and in places covered with dense rainforests and tall eucalypts. The great forests of Australia are east of the Great Divide.

The wildlife which lives between the crest of the Divide and high tide mark on the ocean shore is the subject of this volume. Tasmania, which can be regarded as an extension of the Divide separated from it by an inundated valley, is also included. The Divide though more or less continuous shows great variation in height and in distance from the coast. In one place in particular the Range sweeps a long way inland; at this same point it is of slight elevation. Just southwest of Bundaberg (Queensland), the Divide begins to bend away from the coast till roughly at the Tropic of Capricorn; it is more than 300 miles from the sea. Then it bends back in a northeasterly direction to return almost to the seafront near Townsville. This combination of low elevation and inland direction forms a distinct gap in the Divide's continuity and in effect allows the dry inland plains to bulge out right to the coast. It forms a drier climate band across the east coast and separates its wildlife in two distinct regions. For the purposes of this book this is a convenient division and allows us to examine the two regions separately and in greater detail. One area, in the north, is tropical and its essential feature is rainforest. The other, southern, area is subtropical and temperate; eucalypt forest is its most distinctive characteristic. By making this north and south distinction it appears that a 450-mile gap, between Townsville and Rockhampton, is left out altogether. But in fact this stretch of country has very few habitats that are not found to the north or the south of it. Most of the country is similar to that discussed in the chapter, Tropical Woodlands. Only around Mackay is

Map 1: Tropical Queensland

there substantial rainforest, and it does not differ greatly from that of southeast Queensland.

In many respects this dry belt of country has more in common with the plains of the inland than with the true coastal habitats which are our theme. So rather than a hiatus we would consider it a zone of transition between the tropical and the subtropical-temperate east.

Before delving into details it is of value to take a bird's-eye view of the region as a whole. First the northern section then the southern.

The northern region begins near Townsville and stretches 700 miles north to the tip of Cape York Peninsula.

AS THE NAME IMPLIES *tropical* rainforests are constantly wet places. But high rainfall is only one of several requirements for its establishment. Good soil and an even, warm temperature are also essential. In Australia all three conditions of rainfall, soil and temperature exist together in only one place—along its northeast coastline. There are other areas which are as warm, but they are also dry; further south it is wet but cold and there are only subtropical and temperate rainforests which are far less complex in structure and have fewer species of plants and animals.

True tropical rainforest of the kind that exists in Australia's northeast corner is the most luxuriant, diverse and complex plant community on earth. It supports a wide variety of animals as well. For example there are more than twice as many species of frogs in northeast Queensland than in the state of Victoria and there are more species of butterflies in the tropical northeast than in the whole of the rest of Australia. Rainforest therefore is the chief reason for the region's rich variety of wildlife which is unparalleled by any other Australian region. Rainforest is also the most truly representative of tropical Queensland. It is the region's essential feature, one that distinguishes it from all others. As we shall see in later chapters, this quality is further reflected in the unusually large number of species which are unique to this comparatively small part of Australia.

The 700-mile-long coastal strip is, however, not the endless tract of impenetrable rainforest it is sometimes imagined to be. Nor are the rain-forests all the same—there are many different kinds. A convenient way to show both the extent and variety of the region's rainforests is to take two sections through it. The first section from north to south shows the overall extent of the rainforest and its relation to the open woodlands. The second, taken from east to west, shows many of the habitats in greater detail. It also demonstrates how seasonal fluctuations, altitude, soil drain-age and fertility produce several distinct kinds of rainforests. The area is treated as it would have appeared before settlement.

In the overall north-south view of the entire region the rainforests appear as two separate chains of dark green islands in a yellow-brown sea of open woodlands. These woodlands of widely spaced paperbarks or eucalypts with a ground cover of grasses and sedges, isolate the rainforests in much the same way as the sea does islands. Both sea and woodland are equally effective in stopping the spread of plants and animals from one group of 'islands' to the next.

The most northerly of the two chains of rainforest 'islands' runs along the east coast of Cape York Peninsula from a little south of Cape Grenville to a little north of Musgrave, a distance of about 160 miles. But the rainforest is only fifteen miles wide at the widest point and on average much less. This narrow band of rainforest is the habitat of the cuscus, Palm Cockatoo, Yellow-billed Kingfisher and others which are today isolated from the rainforests further south by a 140-mile-wide 'sea' of open woodlands stretching to Cooktown. Separate from the coastal strip is an isolated, 30,000-acre tract of rainforest at the very tip of Cape York Peninsula. Even from the little it has been studied this unusual area is known to be of great botanical and geographic interest.

The other chain of 'islands' makes up the largest single area of rainforest in Australia, 300 miles long from Cooktown to Townsville and in places fifty miles wide. Included is the Windsor Tableland, one of the most rugged places in Australia and one few people have crossed. As in the northern rainforests many life forms are isolated by open woodlands from other rainforests. The tree kangaroos, three kinds of ringtail possums, the Golden Bower-bird and many others are unique to these southern 'islands' of rainforest.

There are a number of species such as the catbird and fruit pigeons which are common to both chains of 'islands' of rainforests and there is evidence that at some stage in the geological past the two were connected. But generally speaking the north–south pattern is two isolated areas of rainforest, each with its distinct flora and fauna, encircled by open woodlands and the sea.

The section from east to west gives some impression of the variety of habitats. As is to be expected on a 700-mile strip of land the east–west succession of habitats varies greatly from point to point. Between Daintree and Cooktown, for example, mountains covered with rainforest plunge straight into the sea. Further north open tea-tree woodlands or even grassy plains sweep to the water's edge. But let us look now at the general picture between Cardwell and Cairns and follow the changes travelling from the sea to the plains on the far side of the Great Dividing Range.

In the wide river and creek estuaries and wherever rocky outcrops trap sufficient mud and silt, mangroves grow in thick forests. The few areas with extensive sandy beaches are usually fringed with casuarina and paperbark trees. Behind the mangroves and the beaches lies a more or less continuous coastal plain of varying width. This plain has mostly infertile soils which are poorly drained and swampy for most of the year. Despite the warm and humid weather rainforests cannot grow here—this is a strip of open woodland; stands of paperbark trees with a ground cover of sedges and heath. The further we move from the coast the more drainage and fertility improve and gradually eucalypts become more numerous among the paperbarks. Then, sometimes very abruptly, the open forest is replaced by dense stands of palms in swampy soil. One of these is the striking Fan Palm. The infertile plains and Fan Palm swamps are penetrated in places by fingers of rainforest spreading along the fertile floodplains of the rivers and creeks.

Beyond the swamps the soil continues to improve and eventually the open forests are replaced by lowland rainforests. In some places there are deep, red soils of basaltic origins where tropical rainforest reaches its highest development in Australia. These forests are the most complex and luxuriant. Next in the succession are the eastern slopes of a plateau, the Atherton Tableland. The average height of the escarpment is about 2,500 feet but in a few places, such as on the granite massifs of Bartle Frere and Bellenden Ker it rises to over 5,000 feet. Rainforest covers the whole of the escarpment up to its highest points, but as the altitude increases the forests become less and less complex, with fewer and fewer species of trees.

The Atherton Tableland has mostly good soils and it supports rainforest. Pockets of more open eucalypt and casuarina forests dot the plateau in spots of poor soil or where fire has wrought changes in the vegetation patterns. The Tableland is twenty to thirty miles wide and on the western side where the slopes begin to dip down towards the plains of the inland, rainforest is quite suddenly replaced by sparse eucalypt woodland. The western slope of the Tableland is at the maximum only 50 miles from the east coast but it is quite dry and sparsely vegetated.

The reason for the sudden change is the decrease in rainfall as one moves west. Innisfail on the coast has 142 inches of rain per year while Herberton, about 45 miles to the west in a direct line, and on the western escarpment of the Great Divide, averages only 44 inches per year.

So far we have discussed the area as it was before settlement but it must be stressed that most of the rainforests that once covered the coastal plain and the Atherton Tableland have been cut down. They have been re-

The White-tailed Kingfisher embodies the
colour and excitement of Australia's tropical rainforest

placed by dairy farms, canefields and more recently by cattle stations. Extensive rainforests now occur only on the mountain slopes and on the Windsor Tableland.

THE ONLY SEASONAL CYCLE is wet and dry. The temperature is a little lower in winter, but not low enough to make any difference to the plants and animals; their whole seasonal rhythms are determined by only one factor, the 'wet'. The wet and dry seasons are most pronounced in the monsoon region north of Cooktown—usually there is no appreciable rain there from May to November. South of Cooktown, with the exception of a few dry months in spring, there is rainfall all the year round but here too, from January to April or sometimes May, there is a distinct wet season when rain is extra heavy and may last for days on end.

Each season has its particular vivacity. During the wet from January to March frogs and many kinds of insects, particularly beetles, are at the height of their activity; ground and swamp plants flower and grow profusely. In early March before the wet is quite finished waterbirds and many seed-eaters begin to build their nests and will raise one brood after another until the water recedes and grass seeds become scarce. This may be as late as June. At the same time many rainforest trees have put out flowers and are covered with colourful shoots of new leaves. Butterflies flit all around. Then in September when the open forests have turned brown, the insect- and fruit-eating birds of the rainforests south of Cooktown begin nesting and continue frantically till the wet sets in once more.

The wet season pattern frequently has a violent element—so violent in fact that it leaves permanent scars on the rainforests of the lowlands. This is the cyclone. Cyclones sweep in from the Coral Sea any time between December and June but usually in January, February or March. They sometimes bring winds of over one hundred miles per hour and in the area between Cairns and Tully blast along natural corridors between parallel north–south mountain ranges. The large trees are uprooted, branches are ripped off and trees are stripped of nearly all their foliage. Torrential rain lasting several days usually accompanies the winds. The sodden ground further weakens the root systems of the trees and they are more easily blown down. Creeks and rivers choked with silt and leaves tear down the hills and sweep logs and branches down with them. The cyclone may rage for several days, though the maximum wind force usually lasts less than one day. After the weather has settled, the forests are devastated and strangely quiet. Fallen trees lie heaped together, the stark leafless branches of the survivors jutting up through the jumble. Animals have difficulty in finding food and move to the higher ground and shel-

Resting on its rump and anchored by one broad hind foot, with the other three feet tucked under, is the typical sleeping position of the Green Ringtail

OVERLEAF Map 2: Australia's southeast

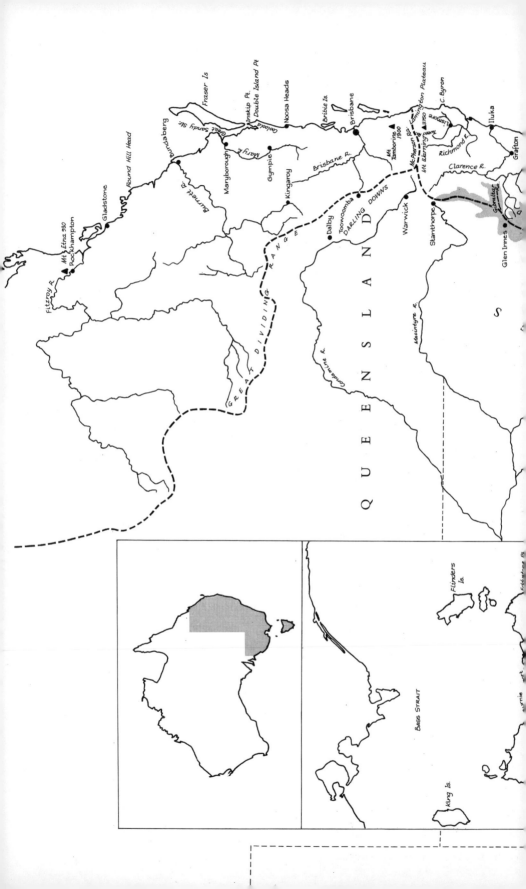

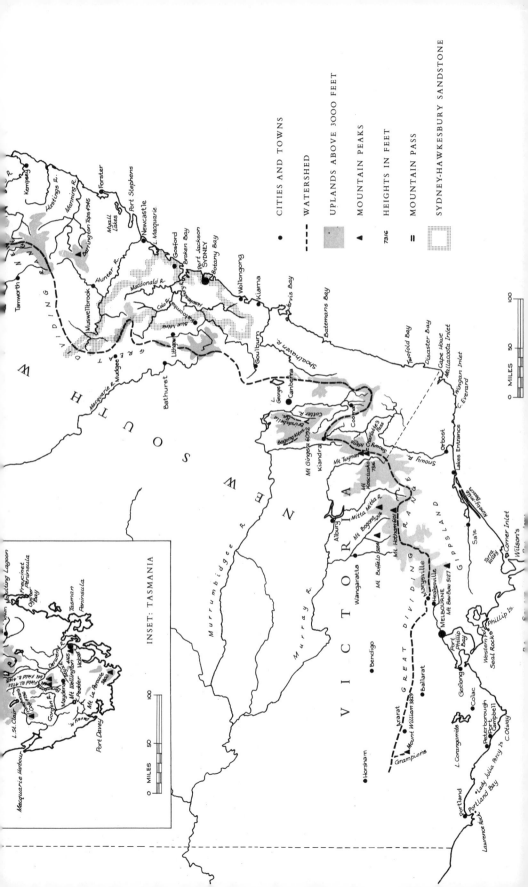

tered gullies that escaped the full blast of the cyclone. Many fruit- and leaf-eating animals starve. Within two weeks after the catastrophe startling changes take place. Trees still standing and the stumps of those snapped off are sprouting new leaves and shoots. Vines also respond quickly and begin to cover the debris. But cyclones are frequent on the lowland and forests never outgrow their effects. They have a low, uneven canopy smothered with vines. Here and there a tree that has withstood the wind blasts towers over its surroundings and these emergents too are heavily draped with vines.

Within recent years the most severe cyclones were in 1918 and in 1956 and in the 'corridors' between Tully and Cairns their effects are clearly visible to this day.

The southern section is much larger in area and has greater variety of habitats. Its plants and animals are in an area of mountain ranges and coastal flats that stretch 1,200 miles south from Rockhampton to Wilson's Promontory, and from there—still along the Great Divide—another 250 miles west where the range comes to a full stop at its last outlier, the Grampians. Tasmania, 150 miles across Bass Strait is also included.

The southern half of the range before it stretches westwards is the most mountainous and most rugged area in the whole of Australia. Only here, in parts of the Great Divide in the New South Wales-Victoria border regions and in parts of Tasmania, do true alpine lands occur. Where they do occur they are most extensive.

The dominant geographical features, mountains and seashores, are both overshadowed by eucalypt forests as the landscape's most distinctive element.

In Australia 90 per cent of the forests are composed solely of eucalypt trees, i.e. trees belonging to the genus *Eucalyptus*. This is a large genus of trees with close on 600 species and varieties. Each one is sensitively adjusted to a particular combination of climate, soil, aspect and cover. Even within short distances it is possible to see a great variety of eucalypt forests—from those dominated by pink-trunked Spotted Gums and rough, dark ironbarks with an understorey of hard-leaved shrubs, to others where wattles, ferns and soft-leaved shrubs grow under glistening, clean-trunked trees over 200 feet tall. The complex patterns of forest types is one of this region's most characteristic features and one unparalleled in other parts of the world.

The variety of forest patterns is partly explained by the fact that there are widely differing climatic conditions. The region ranges from sub-tropical climates with summer rains, balmy winters, and warm to hot summers, to temperate zones which have winter rains, a distinct cool season and warm dry summers with occasional extremely hot and dry days. The temperate climate's most distinctive feature is its changeability. A hot dry morning can change to a cold wet afternoon with a temperature drop of 11°C (20°F).

The temperate and highland winters are severe enough to make many birds flee its rigours. Robins, fantails, parrots, honeyeaters, Rainbow Birds, kingfishers and others regularly leave Tasmania, Victoria and southern New South Wales in autumn and spend the winter in the subtropics and tropics. In spring they return to the south to nest.

Eucalypts dominate the vegetation, but the region is not an unbroken tract of eucalypt forests. These are the major component in a patchwork which also includes heaths, paperbark thickets, banksia woodlands, rainforests and alpine habitats. Large expanses of what once was bushland have been cleared for agriculture and for the development of cities, and add, in this, the most populous and densely settled part of Australia, yet another kind of environment. The artificially created environment is not considered in this volume.

Superficially Tasmania appears very much like the mainland. There are eucalypt forests and the animal life is of a similar composition. Viewing the island closely, however, there are significant differences. The temperate rainforests are more extensive, have larger, more ancient trees than their counterparts across Bass Strait. One tree of rainforest and mountain slopes, the Deciduous Beech, *Nothofagus gunni*, is the only winter deciduous tree in the Australian flora. It is a pointer to Tasmania's colder climate. Mountains, though generally not as high as those of the Australian Alps, are generally more rugged and because of the colder climate have true alpine lands at lower altitudes. Snow may fall there at any time of the year. A large proportion of Tasmania's highland plants are restricted to the island. Other habitats also have many endemic plants and together give the land a characteristic flavour and atmosphere quite distinct from the mainland.

The endemic animal life, as we shall see in later chapters, reinforces this special quality of the island's wildlife.

For mammals in particular Tasmania is a very important place; it is the last refuge for many kinds long since extinct or fast disappearing on the mainland. The Thylacine and Tasmanian Devil for example once occurred over most of Australia, but are now found only in Tasmania. Other animals and plants, on the other hand, have either disappeared from south of Bass Strait or have never crossed it. Of the five species of glider only one, the Sugar Glider, occurs in Tasmania; no tree-creepers grace the island's eucalypt forests. But the gaps in Tasmania's wildlife, when compared with that of the mainland, are more than adequately filled by the endemic species of both plants and animals. The rugged, often cold, island has many charming qualities entirely its own.

So far the wildlife has been mentioned in only the broadest terms. To feel the real impact of the Australian bush, such as the moment of flashing beauty as a White-tailed Kingfisher flies through the undergrowth of a tropical forest, or the intimate details of animal life such as the relationship between a Grey Kangaroo and her joey, it is essential to look and to listen in the one place for longer periods. These more detailed observations form the basis for the next chapters.

A Common Wombat emerges from the burrow
it has dug underneath a eucalypt

II FORESTS

1 Rainforests — Mostly Tropical

IMAGINE A PLACE where the normal restrictions to plant growth do not exist; where there are no frosts to eliminate sensitive species, no droughts to stunt development. A place where the only limiting factors are soil and the competition between the plants. Such a place is warm and humid and green. Rain or mist is frequent. The plant life is overwhelming, profuse and dense. Trees are crowded close together, their crowns interlocking, pushed aside in places by the light-hungry vines coiling up out of the gloom below. The trees themselves are covered with other plants; mosses, ferns and orchids cling to their bark with probing roots. Not only is the vegetation dense, it is on a gigantic scale, ferns the size of trees thrust their twenty-foot crowns high above the undergrowth, others shade a swift flowing stream with fifteen-foot long fronds. Cycads, including the world's tallest, compete with palms in the lower levels.

The slender trees grow in several size classes, each class constituting a well defined layer. There are the emergents, giants that spread their branches high above the next level, the trees making up the general canopy. Below this canopy there are several more layers of trees. Some of these are specially adapted to the lower light levels. Others are dormant waiting for a catastrophe, such as the falling of an emergent or some other break in the light-filtering canopy, when they will shoot up to take their place. Below that are the ground plants, a mere handful with specialised habits to survive in the permanent gloom. This is *tropical* rainforest, where forests grow within forests, plants upon plants; where every available niche is saturated with plants. There is no other formation on earth with as many different life-forms.

Tropical rainforest gives the impression of uncontrolled growth, of vegetation rampant; but competition and other factors ensure that mature rainforest is an ordered formation, the result of complex sociological progression. Not only is tropical rainforest the richest in species, these species live together in the most complex relationships.

TROPICAL RAINFORESTS OCCUR where all conditions for plant growth are not just favourable but optimum. These conditions have already been mentioned in general terms. Specifically it has been shown that there must be 60 or more inches of rainfall per year for rainforests to be established. But the quantity of rain is not the only necessity; it must be evenly distributed throughout the year. Temperatures must be at least a 19°C (66°F) monthly average without great daily fluctuation. Soils are also of the utmost importance and must be well drained as well as fertile; rainforests do not grow in places which are waterlogged for long periods.

The above rainfall and temperature figures are the lower limits for tropical rainforests. Always providing they are evenly distributed over the year there are no upper limits but there is considerable fluctuation within the limits and between the climatic and edaphic elements. Every fluctuation alters the forest in some way.

For example, high rainfall with a lower temperature such as exists on mountain tops results in the distinctive montane forests or mossy thickets; dense stands of stunted trees only 20–50 feet tall. Clouds envelop these 'elfin' woodlands for long unbroken periods and for part of almost every day. The constantly moist atmosphere is ideally suited for the growth of epiphytes; the trunks, branches, twigs and even leaves of the trees are festooned with trailing growths of mosses, lichens, leafy liverworts and filmy ferns.

A prolonged dry spell even in areas with high annual rainfall also creates changes. The plant species are fewer in number and their relations are less complex. Only the hardiest epiphytes survive and many trees are deciduous. These are the characters of the monsoon forests of Cape York Peninsula where the mean temperature is 24°C (75°F) and the rainfall about 70 inches a year, nearly all of which falls between November and May; a typically monsoon climate. In these monsoon forests the canopy height is 30 feet or less with occasional taller emergents to about 100 feet. A large proportion of the emergents drop their leaves in the dry season.

Although both rainfall and temperature may be optimal the soil may be poorly drained and swampy for long periods. As we have already seen this often excludes rainforest altogether, but where it does grow it is as palm swamps, which are dominated by only a few tree species and is probably the simplest of all rainforest communities.

The variations between the three main forces which control rainforest are legion and they produce a number of distinct rainforest types, a far greater number than are mentioned here. But the boundaries between them are never clear-cut, unlike the sharp division between rainforest and open woodland.

In the eucalypt and other open woodlands of Australia there is a fourth natural and potent ecological force which determines the composition and variety of plant species; fire. The plants in these forests are adapted in many ways to regenerate after apparent devastation by fire. But in rainforests this force plays no part naturally as it is excluded by the general humidity in the forests and the dampness of the ground litter. Rainforest trees have very thin bark and are poorly adapted to withstand fire. On rare occasions of drought the edges of rainforests adjoining grassland or eucalypt forest, are burnt. All the rainforest plants are then killed. The careless annual burn-off of grasslands in north Queensland in the driest parts of the year kills a small strip of rainforest where grass and rainforest meet. Where the rainforest is killed it does not grow again; the area is invaded by the fire resistant grasses, paperbarks and eucalypts. So, year by year, the area of rainforest shrinks due to fire. Along forest borders where fire is excluded, the reverse takes place; the rainforest margin slowly advances.

Only in the equatorial regions of the world are all conditions necessary for maintaining tropical rainforest met in full; in Central and South America where the Amazon basin is the major area; in the Congo basin of Africa and in the Indo-Malaysian region. The rainforests in the last region are found in parts of India, Southeast Asia, Indonesia, New Guinea and its nearby islands.

Each of these three major areas of rainforest has distinctive elements to its flora. Bromeliads occur only in the American rainforests. The Indo-Malaysian rainforests are particularly rich in orchids of which there are few in the African rainforests. Trees of the family Dipterocarpaceae dominate large tracts of the Indo-Malaysian forests. By contrast, some groups, like the ferns, are well represented in rainforests the world over.

The origins and affinities of the tropical rainforests of northeast Australia are not entirely clear, but botanists and ecologists are generally agreed that they are closest related to those of the Indo-Malaysian region. Both Australian and Indo-Malaysian forests are rich in species of fig trees and lawyer vines. However, Dipterocarpaceae so typical of Indo-Malaysian forests are entirely absent from Australia where the families Myrtaceae, Proteaceae and Rutaceae are particularly well represented and make up a large number of the tree species. These latter families have strong Australian affinities. Broadly speaking Australian tropical rainforests are allied to those of the Indo-Malaysian region but have a strong endemic element.

None of the north Queensland rainforests have a truly equatorial climate. There is a short but distinct dry period in spring and temperatures are slightly lower in winter than in summer. The lowland rainforests between Tully and Babinda, with a mean annual temperature of

23°C (73°F) and a rainfall of 142 inches are nearest to the equatorial type particularly in the areas of deep, red basalt soils. In nature and appearance there is little difference between these forests and the equatorial rainforests of other parts of the world. The species diversity is as wide, there are as many vines and epiphytes and plant relationships are as complex. These are the highest developed rainforests in Australia. They cover only a few square miles of Australia's total area of nearly three million square miles.

Mature tropical rainforests all over the world have a very distinctive appearance. They are dominated by trees of an average height of 100 feet with an occasional giant of 150 feet or more. The trees' evergreen crowns interlock, reaching out in competition for the life-giving light. Almost every square foot of canopy is utilised in this struggle and as soon as a tree or even a branch falls, new growth to take its place appears within weeks. So dense is this canopy of leaves, supported by the tall trunks, that two separate realms are created—one at tree-crown level and another on the ground. Even though these worlds are on an average only 125 vertical feet apart each has a completely different climate, or more correctly, microclimate. Measurements have been made of these microclimates in rainforests, both in Australia and overseas, and are much the same for any tropical rainforest.

The tree top level is one of brightness, fluctuation and often violence. There are long periods of hot sunshine with temperatures of 32°C (90°F) which drop at night to 21°C (70°F); humidity fluctuates from 90% at night to about 60% in warm sunshine. Rain is frequent, often in the form of turbulent storms. On ground level, where most of us see the rain-forest, everything is quiet and calm, in places even gloomy. There is barely any wind; humidity is about 90% night and day and the temperature fluctuates only about 6°C (10°F). Rain which lashes the tree tops reaches the ground only in trickles along the tree trunks and in drips from the leaves. Light intensity is on an average only 1/100th of that in the canopy. This low level of light is the reason for the scarcity of ground plants.

It is often so gloomy that there is only enough light for specially adapted plants to photo-synthesise; some mosses, ferns and herbs and the cycad *Bowenia spectabilis*. There are also a few plants such as orchids and fungi which are parasitic or saprophytic and obtain their energy from other organisms and do not need light as an energy source. Because of the scarcity of shrubs and herbs and ground plants, undisturbed mature rain-forests are easy places to walk about in; there are few obstructions. The luxuriant masses of intertwining and impenetrable vegetation, popularly thought of as rainforest or 'jungle' only exist along the edges of the forests, along river banks and in places where the rainforest has been disturbed by such upheavals as cyclones or clearing operations.

The distinctive appearance of the rainforest and the creation of its own climate are not entirely shaped by the ecological forces considered earlier in this chapter. It is a plant's adaptation to the struggle for light which largely determines its shape and the niche it will occupy in the forest. The typical atmosphere and feel of the rainforest is therefore not only the result of such tangible forces as dampness and heat but more of the plants' reactions to competition for their energy source, the light. The trees— tall, slender with spreading crowns and without low branches—derive their shape from ever pushing their leaves to the light. In rainforests there is also a preponderance of thick woody vines, strangling trees, and epiphytes, plants whose whole mode of life is adapted to finding a short cut to a place in the sun. All these elements taken together separate rainforests from all other vegetation formations.

Climbing plants are much more abundant in rainforests than anywhere else. About 90% of all climbers occur in the tropics and in some rainforests one out of twelve of the flowering plants may be a climber. Woody vines, or lianes or monkey ropes as they are sometimes called, as well as being the most characteristic kinds of plants in the rainforest, are also among the most impressive. Their thick flexible stems, sometimes as thick as a man's thigh, hang down from the tree tops like gigantic ropes, or twine around tree trunks in tight loops.

Vines use trees for support and therefore do not need to grow thick woody trunks of their own to hold the weight of their heavy crowns. The climbers' thin stems grow rapidly and reach the light much more quickly than the trees which must spend so much energy in building a solid foundation for their leaves and branches. But often the vine's journey is a long circuitous route; the stem of one climbing palm was measured at 700 feet long. The average length, however, is much less—about 220 feet. When a vine reaches the light it spreads out into a wide crown, smothering and misshaping the trees that provide its foothold; it has no leaves or branches below tree top level. Growth of the vine may become so profuse that it becomes too great a burden for its support and the whole mass, tree branches, vines and all, crashes to the ground. If the climber is not killed it immediately grows up again and in time regains its place in the tree tops. A tangle of rope and wire-like loops will then be the only evidence of the mishap. Lianes of a mature age have woody but still flexible stems. Apart from their roots in the ground they are attached only high up in the canopy. From the ground they look completely unsupported, as though they made their own way up by some magic Indian rope trick.

These vines are very old and their original supporting trees may have died, or the climbers may have kept pace in growth with their supports and been taken aloft in their crowns.

Stranglers, mostly fig trees, are more ruthless in their fight for light. Their seeds, which are distributed by birds, germinate in a fork high up in a tree. The seedling then sends down roots along the trunk and through the air to the ground. Growth is vigorous. The roots multiply and branch, at the same time thickening and becoming woody. Soon the supporting tree is completely enmeshed by the roots which are by now well established in the soil. The crown of the strangler has kept pace in growth and has become large and heavy. Cut off from much of the light by the strangler's crown, and slowly strangled by its network of roots the host tree in time dies and eventually rots away; the strangler, with a hollow trunk but firmly rooted in the soil, has usurped its place and its light. Strangler figs grow to be among the tallest trees in the forest.

We have shown how trees, lianes and stranglers—large woody plants—compete for light. While the rainforests are dominated by these giants, there is a number of species of smaller plants. But as it is too dark on the rainforest floor, most of them are forced to grow on the trunks and high branches of the trees and on exposed rock faces. The ground layer of mosses, ferns and small flowering plants of other forests has moved to the tree tops in rainforests, the only place where they can get enough light. These small plants are wholly dependent on the trees, but only for a foothold, they do not live off the larger plants' sap; they are not parasites but epiphytes. Epiphytes sometimes festoon the trees in large numbers—one average-sized tree in a north Queensland rainforest was covered with fifty species of plants, sixteen were ferns and orchids, the others mosses, lichens, liverworts and algae. Trees heavily covered with epiphytes are found only in rainforests.

Epiphytes usually attach themselves to tree bark or even bare rock with a network of clinging roots. This life away from the moisture and nutrients of the soil presents serious difficulties for them. They must collect all their water and nutrients in the tree tops. For this purpose they have many adaptations. A group of ferns called staghorns and elkhorns are probably the most successful in trapping food and water. They have two kinds of leaves with different functions. One kind is broad and rounded and several together form a rosette around a tree trunk, branch or rock. Shaped like a basket, the rosette collects falling leaves and bark. These decay and provide food for the growing plant and also soak up and hold sufficient water for the fern to grow. The amounts of humus that these and other ferns of similar shape and size collect may be so great that earthworms, centipedes and other organisms usually found only in the soil, live in them. Some large clumps of ferns when full of water may weigh half a ton or more. Frequently they become too heavy for their supporting branches and crash to the ground.

The second kind of leaves of the staghorn fern are narrow and darker green. These carry out most of the photosynthesis which provides the plant with the energy to utilise the food released by the humus collected in its basket. The narrow leaves also carry the spores.

Orchids are another major group of epiphytes in the rainforest and they have adapted in other ways to life away from the soil. Water storage is probably the most important aspect, for it is obvious that the bark of trees cannot hold water as the soil does. To store water, many orchids have fleshy leaves and bulbs. Many can also store water in their roots. These roots when dry look greyish-white, their outer cells being filled with air. As soon as rain falls, these cells soak up water like a sponge and become translucent; the roots then look green as the chlorophyll inside them becomes visible. Food is even more difficult to come by for the orchids because the bark of trees is as poor in mineral nutrient as it is in water. Somehow the orchids are able to live and multiply on the minute quantities of minerals found in rainwater and in the bits of decaying leaves and bark trapped amongst their tangled roots.

The epiphytes are well adapted to live under precarious conditions of food and water but to maintain their lofty foothold their spores and seeds must be specially modified. Obviously if these plants had even moderately heavy seeds these would inevitably fall to the ground where they could not grow. A few species such as the strangler figs which begin life as epiphytes, and Umbrella Trees, *Brassaia actinophylla*, have fruits which are eaten and dispersed by birds but most have very light seeds which are scattered by air currents. The spores of mosses and ferns are microscopic in size and easily carried by the wind. Orchids have immensely numerous and tiny seeds that are so light that they float in the slightest breeze. A single orchid seed pod may contain as many as three million tiny seeds. At least some will lodge in places where they can germinate and grow.

Slender trees closely spaced together, a large number of woody vines, trees covered with epiphytes, are all distinctively rainforest characters. But the single most characteristic feature of all rainforests under optimal conditions is the diversity of species of trees. Seldom are two of the same kind found standing side by side or even very close together—a sharp contrast with eucalypt forests where hundreds of acres may be dominated by a few species. Between Townsville and Cooktown alone there are more than 600 species of rainforest trees. On one quarter-acre plot of rainforest on the Atherton Tableland, 164 different species of trees were counted. Sumatra and Borneo rainforests have 3,000 species of trees which grow to a trunk diameter of one foot and over. This diversity is probably the result of favourable conditions and the long-stable environ-ment of the equatorial regions. Drought, frost and fire have not elimin-ated sensitive species. Palms for example can only survive under these beneficial conditions. They do not have reserve buds as do most other trees, they have but one growing tip, the 'cabbage'. If this is killed in some way the whole plant dies.

This great diversity is at first glance not at all apparent for the trees tend to look very much alike and it seems that the forces shaping them gave them the same characteristics. Their bark is mostly smooth or covered with fine flakes; the trunks are straight without branches below the crown. Flowers are mostly small and pale, though there are enough ex-ceptions to this rule to make an occasional burst of colour amongst the dark green crowns and on the ground beneath when the flowers fall.

The characteristic uniformity even extends to the leaves. At least 80% of the leaves in tropical rainforests are of what botanists call mesophyll size, that is, between three and ten inches in length. The mature leaves are deep green in colour, leathery and shiny in texture and elliptical in shape. The tips of the leaves are particularly interesting as about 80% have what are known as 'drip-tips'. These are drooping elongated points on the end of the leaf and are thought to drain the leaves of moisture during rain and heavy mist. This is of obvious advantage since dry leaves can photo-synthesise more efficiently than wet ones. Tree ferns, palms, cycads, and pandanus however, have very different shapes and relieve the sameness in the appearance of the trees.

The similarity of tree bark and leaves tends to give the rainforest a certain uniformity. Yet it is never monotonous. Many characteristics typical of rainforests are startlingly different from those of any other en-vironment. Most impressive are the gigantic plank buttresses which flange out from many of the large tree trunks. The buttresses are huge thin slabs of wood roughly in the shape of a right angled triangle growing from the trunk to a horizontal root lying close to the surface of the soil. The hypotenuse of the triangle is the top edge of the buttress. Some tree species in all major families have well developed buttresses which suggests that they are a characteristic of rainforests rather than of certain families or trees. The only thing that buttressed trees have in common is a shallow root system spreading out widely in a horizontal plane and without a tap root. Some buttresses are huge, starting at a height of twenty feet and sloping down to a point on the ground the same distance from the trunk. Much has been written and speculated about the function of the buttresses and it was thought for a long time that they were developed by the plant to take strains and stresses and support the tree's weight in shallow soil. This theory is now generally rejected—just as many buttressed trees as others are blown down in gales. The exact use of these spectacular growths is not known, but it is generally agreed that it is a root development rather than a trunk development and may be related to soil drainage.

A flowering characteristic known as cauliflory is, like tree buttresses, found only in rainforests. In most trees flowers develop at the tips of the branches or on the small twigs but in cauliflory, flowers develop on the trunks and thick branches of the trees. One of the most interesting examples of this is a small tree known as *Archidendron lucyi* which has large bunches of white flowers all along its trunk and main branches from a few inches above the ground to forty or fifty feet high. The trees look even more striking when the fruit is ripe. The large coiled bright red beans then split open and show the yellow inner sides studded with black seeds. In the gloom of the rainforest their brightness stands out like a beacon.

The fresh new leaves of rainforest trees have a similar brightening effect and are just as typical of rainforest. The new leaves are often red in colour—mostly a brilliant red. A few trees have white or a pale yellow new growth. These fresh leaves hang down limply for a few weeks before they become rigid and a typical dark green. Some new shoots are always to be seen in the rainforest, but in the right season many trees will unfold their new growth simultaneously and the rainforest canopy becomes a blaze of colour.

The shape of the trees, predominance of vines and epiphytes, buttress roots, cauliflory and other phenomena all are a part of the appearance and feel of the rainforest, but they are not the whole essence. Certain groups of plants, the palms—including the lawyer vines—the cycads, the epiphytic orchids, the fig trees and the ferns give the final touch to the rainforest's special atmosphere.

The ferns are worthy of particular mention. Of 10,000 species of ferns in the world only 250 are found in Australia, but out of these, 205 are found in the tropical rainforests of northern Queensland. Though on a worldwide basis there may be few species in Australia, they include a wide variety of forms and some of unusual interest.

In the rainforests ferns cling to rocks and trees as epiphytes. Some of these are tiny plants growing like a mat over their support. Others, like the birds' nest and basket ferns, are huge plants which trap falling debris in their rosettes of fronds and accumulate their own supply of humus. Ferns grow as trees with wide crowns and trunks up to 30 feet high. Along the swift flowing streams in sheltered dimly lit spots delicate maidenhair and coral ferns unfurl their fronds. *Angiopteris evecta* one of the largest ferns in the world, perhaps *the* largest, also grows along creeks and rivers. It has fronds fifteen feet long, the stems of which are four inches in diameter at their base.

Angiopteris is of a very ancient lineage, being one of the few genera of the family Marattiaceae still living today. The Marattiaceae were a large and important family in the forests of the Carboniferous period about 300 million years ago. Some of the forests of that period, compacted and compressed by the gigantic upheavals and stresses of the earth's crust have been preserved in the form of coal. Fronds and other parts of the Marattiaceae preserved as fossils in the coal do not differ greatly from *Angiopteris evecta* growing in north Queensland's rainforests today.

Most of the major groups of ferns contain one or two species that can live outside rainforest. But the filmy ferns (family Hymenophyllaceae) are exceptions. All of them are epiphytes which can live only in the dampest spots in the rainforests; in the cloudy zone of the mountain tops and around waterfalls where the spray of the rushing water keeps the air saturated with moisture. Filmy ferns, of which there are twenty-four species in Australia, are the smallest and most delicate of ferns with fronds so thin that they are translucent. The edges of the fronds are only one cell in thickness. The thin leaves have little resistance to water loss; even the smallest amount of drying, an amount that does not affect any other plant, makes them shrivel. This curling up for short periods does not harm the plants; it is their adaptation to dry conditions, though they cannot survive long without moisture or withstand extremely dry winds. Unlike other epiphytes filmy ferns have no methods of protection from drought and no provision for storing water.

When they are curled up after a short dry spell they respond quickly to any increase in moisture. Dew at nightfall, a gust of spray from a waterfall or mist from a passing cloud are all enough to revive them. In fact during relatively dry periods of the year the moisture from the dew every night is sufficient to keep them alive. This quick recovery is possible because the plants can absorb moisture over the whole leaf surface as well as through their roots.

WE HAVE SHOWN WHAT FORCES shape the rainforest and how these forces acting on the plants produce a distinctive formation. It is a highly efficient and complex community that makes greatest possible use of the

Light striking a fallen tree reveals the gap it has left in the forest canopy. The dead tree decays rapidly and the gap is soon filled by seedling trees and vines

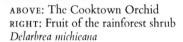

ABOVE: The Cooktown Orchid
RIGHT: Fruit of the rainforest shrub
Delarbrea michieana

BELOW: A thick growth of lichens on the trunk of
an Antarctic Beech in the Tasmanian rainforest
BOTTOM RIGHT: The twisted bean-shaped pods of
Archidendron lucyi split open exposing the black seeds

energy from the sun and nutrients in the soil. Before equilibrium is reached, an area goes through a series of gradually changing patterns of vegetation, the climax of which under the conditions outlined is tropical rainforest. It is estimated that it takes 500 years to reach this condition (most mature rainforest trees are 300 years old) but that once it is reached it remains essentially the same and is then self-perpetuating. This is supported by findings in Trinidad where fossil deposits dating back twenty million years to the Miocene period showed that rainforests of that era were essentially the same as those growing there now.

The next question that arises is—how does the climax community maintain itself? At least part of the answer is to be found in the turnover of organic matter called the litter cycle. Simply stated it is this: the leaves, twigs, branches and whole trees which fall to the ground are decomposed by millions of soil organisms, mostly microscopic ones. In this process of decay the litter is broken down to humus and its original mineral components which return to the soil and are then re-used by the roots of the living plants. This is a never ending cycle. Some of the nutrients are lost through leaching or are washed away into streams but in undisturbed rainforest on relatively level ground, this amounts to very little. Analysis of stream water in such a forest in tropical Africa revealed it to be virtually distilled water. Any minerals that are lost are soon replaced by fresh weathering of the parent rock underlying the soil. The litter cycle is remarkably efficient. In some parts of Queensland rainforest grows in pure sand, which apart from the topmost inch or so, contains no nutrients to support trees of any size. These rainforests which always occur on coastal sand-dune areas are completely self supporting. It is thought they first became established in areas where the sand was enriched by shell debris.

As well as being efficient the turnover of litter in tropical rainforest is rapid. In rainforests nearly all nutrients contained in the plant matter of a given area are contained in the living plants. The turnover is so rapid that little is lying about on the ground in the form of dead leaves, branches and logs at any time. In pine or eucalypt forests by contrast, as much nutrient may be contained in the litter on the ground as is contained in the living plants.

The breakdown of organic matter takes place mainly in the litter and in the top few inches of the soil, a hidden world where microscopic organisms, bacteria, fungi and protozoans live in constant and fierce competition. These microscopic plants and animals are the chief agents of decay; they cannot be seen with the naked eye. The ones that can be seen are the snails, slugs, earthworms, millipedes and larger insects but these are mainly responsible for breaking the litter up into ever smaller particles which are then eventually broken down to their end products by the micro-organisms. This process is perhaps best understood if we take a close look at what happens when a large tree, say a fig, is blown down in a storm, a frequent occurrence in rainforest.

The night after the tree has fallen, large grey beetles with red spots and huge black antennae, nearly twice as long as themselves, land all over the trunk. These *Batocera boisduvali* and other longicorn beetles lay their eggs on the still-fresh bark. Within two weeks the eggs hatch and the larvae burrow into the trunk where they live on the woody tissues for up to two years before emerging as the next generation of beetles. Microscopic fungi and bacteria immediately attack the outer bark and green leaves. These first micro-invaders are extremely numerous but decompose only the easily digested substances such as the sugars. They exclude other organisms from benefiting from this ready food source first of all by sheer numbers and secondly by excreting an antibiotic which is poisonous to their competitors. But plant tissues are mainly built up of the very tough and stable substances, cellulose and lignin, which the unspecialised early colonisers cannot attack. These have soon exhausted their food, produced spores and other reproductive or resting stages and are ready to invade any other freshly fallen litter. All that remains after only a few weeks is the trunk, branches and skeleton leaves. Now the hardy cellulose and lignin are attacked almost exclusively by fungi, the chief causes of decay in all timber. They are more specialised than the previous groups of organisms and are able to digest cellulose and lignin with special enzymes that break them down. Some fungi decompose only lignin, leaving white strings of cellulose behind. This is white rot. Others are cellulose decomposers leaving soft cubes of brown lignin behind which is known as brown rot.

Because of their method of growth, fungi are well able to decompose large volumes of wood like the trunk of a large fig tree. The fungus network, called mycelium, spreads over the surface of the wood and absorbs its food as it grows. The growing points of this network furthermore can penetrate the hardest wood by a combination of mechanical force exerted by forward growth and the secretion of the wood-dissolving enzyme. This process is very much slower than the breakdown of the non-woody tissues and logs may lie on the forest floor for three or four years before they are completely decomposed. In eucalypt forests, where through lack of moisture the process is even slower, logs sometimes lie on the ground for a hundred years.

The main reason for the slowness of the process is that the enzymes can dissolve only the cellulose of cells with which the fungi are in actual contact. They cannot penetrate far into the wood. The dead tree is decomposed cell by cell. But here other, larger organisms come to play a significant role. After the outer surface of the trunk and main branches have been softened by the first wave of fungus attack, many different kinds of beetles and their larvae will burrow into and live on the rotting wood. One group in particular hastens the breakdown. A group of weevils, known as Ambrosia Beetles actually deposit a fungus, growing on the surface of the wood, into their burrows which they tunnel into the trunk. These burrows are only shelters, the larvae feed on the fungus the beetles have introduced. The fungus spreads and penetrates further and quicker into the wood. Millipedes, cockroaches and other invertebrates also dig into the softening trunk. The result of all this burrowing, gouging, digging and chewing is the breakdown of the wood into ever smaller pieces and the smaller the pieces the quicker they are decomposed. The leaves too are decomposed more rapidly if they are broken down in smaller particles and one organism in particular, the amphipod, plays an important part in this breaking up process. Studies of the ground litter in subtropical rainforest near Sydney showed that these crustaceans chewed up 25% of the $7\frac{1}{2}$ tons of leaf litter that was incorporated into an acre of soil every year. It was found that the amphipods attacked the litter about six weeks after it fell to the ground at which stage the early colonisers had already moved to fresher leaves and twigs.

The breakdown is helped even further by the larger animals that are predators on the beetles, millipedes, amphipods and other invertebrates. Jungle Fowl turn over the ground litter with their powerful feet while looking for insects. Striped Possums excitedly rip the rotting trunk to pieces searching for beetle larvae. There is one lizard, *Tropidophorus queenslandicus*, which is so specialised to fit into this pattern that it can live only in the damp, dark tunnels in fallen rotting trees. *Tropidophorus* lives there on the insects and other small animals that are hollowing out these trunks.

The final breakdown takes place in the soil and here the earthworm is the vital link. The masses of partly decayed leaves and pieces of trunk that fall to the ground have to be worked into the soil before this final breakdown can be effected. The earthworms drag all this material down into their burrows and partly digest it and at the same time break it down into smaller particles. In the process they thoroughly mix and aerate the soil. So thoroughly do they work that nearly all the soil to a depth of several inches has passed through the alimentary tract of an earthworm at some stage.

When the earthworms have dragged the organic material down, bacteria, fungi, nematodes and other micro-organisms immediately set to work. These microscopic beings live in the moisture saturated atmosphere between the soil particles. The larger organisms, the mites, millipedes, centipedes, earthworms and various kinds of insects, all of which contribute to the process at some stage, live in the air spaces between the clumps of soil or in burrows of their own making. It must be emphasised that most of the activities discussed overlap and many occur simultaneously.

The soil organisms and their predators are constantly active and the topsoil and litter layers of the tropical rainforest are among the fiercest animal battlegrounds. Little of this is apparent because most of the combatants are microscopic, but evidence of their ruthless efficiency is shown by the speed and volume of the turnover of the ground litter. In a South American rainforest, for example, it was found that the annual turnover of organic matter is 100 tons per acre. Another pointer to the efficiency of the turnover is that litter never accumulates on the rainforest floor. The basic reasons for this efficiency are the high level of nutrients in the litter and the tropical climate. High rainfall spread evenly around the year ensures there is always enough moisture for the soil organisms to live and the year round high temperatures mean that they can multiply rapidly without a period of inactivity during cold months, while the high nutrient status of the litter ensures that there is an adequate supply of energy and nutrients for the very active populations of organisms.

At the end of several years the fig tree has been reduced to humus and the original mineral nutrient components. Humus, a dark brown substance, is the end product of decomposition and is made up of microscopic, structureless plant particles together with the remains of dead soil organisms. These nutrients, necessary for plant growth, are rapidly absorbed by the roots of the living trees. The process is all the more rapid as rainforest trees nearly always have their feeding roots close to the surface and even in the decomposing litter itself.

The extra light let in through the gap in the canopy and the decrease of root competition in the soil result in a sudden upsurge of plant growth. The light demanding species, particularly vines, soon fill the empty space with an impenetrable dense stand of vegetation. A frequent invader of these spaces is the lawyer vine—a scrambling palm that attaches itself to the supporting trees with thin flexible trailers studded with recurved hooks. These hooks support the vine as it scrambles up to the light. The stems of the climbing palms are studded with sharp spines for much of their length and these plus the whip-like, hooked trailers and the general

density of the plants make progress in these cleared spaces most unpleasant as well as difficult. Unfortunately this is the popular image of
tropical rainforest or 'jungle' as it is sometimes called. But as stated at the
beginning of this chapter these conditions occur only where there has
been a disturbance—be it a cyclone, fallen tree, or bulldozing for farm-
land. Inside mature, undamaged rainforest only the coils of a fallen vine
may make walking in the forest occasionally difficult.

At first it appears that the plants in the newly created clearing have just
run riot but a pattern emerges and it becomes clear that the formation
of the gaps by the death of old trees is an essential part of the regeneration
of rainforest.

To establish how this pattern fits together is not such a simple matter
and it has taken scientists many years to unravel.

When the large fig tree crashed to the ground a community of light-
tolerant seedlings and saplings already existed. These are of trees such as
the *Eugenias* and some members of the family Lauraceae which generally
have large seeds containing food reserves for the seedlings. In undisturbed
rainforest the seedlings of these trees grow slowly and can withstand long
periods of suppression, as long as twenty years, in the gloom of the
understorey. During this period they have thin trunks with only a small
bunch of dark green leaves at the top but a well developed root system.
The suppressed trees may take as long to grow to a stem diameter of two
inches as it will take them to grow from two inches to eight inches stem
diameter in later life. At all times these spindly saplings have the power
to put on rapid growth when given full light. Saplings not smashed by
the fig tree immediately begin vigorous growth, and may eventually
reach tree size.

Not all rainforest trees have large seeds; many such as the Red Cedar
and the various species of the genus *Flindersia* have small, winged seeds.
The seedlings of these trees grow even faster than those of the previous
group, but cannot withstand suppression in low light intensity and the
seeds are viable for only a few months. Unless seeds of this type fall and
germinate in areas flattened by a fallen tree, or a gap is formed within
months of their germination, they die. In the area flattened by the fig
tree, seeds of these kinds of trees germinate and then grow so rapidly that
they catch up to the slower growing species.

But there is a third group of seedling trees that grows even faster, and
is perhaps the most remarkable of all. Seeds of these species, which
include the Sarsaparilla, *Alphitonia petriei*, the stinging trees, *Dendrocnide
moroides* and *D. cordifolia*, and a wattle, *Acacia aulacocarpa*, lie stored in the
soil where they remain viable for many years. When a gap is formed, and

only then, these seeds germinate and the trees grow more rapidly than any other. The stinging trees' natural habitat is in these clearings.

Vines too invade the gap, put on unbelievably rapid growth and are soon the dominant feature. They grow in a wild tangle over the seedlings and saplings.

Within a few years the gap is a dense thicket of saplings with vines trailing from them. From now on numbers decline. First to go are the naturally short-lived species; these are mostly the kinds that grew the fastest in the early stages. The stinging trees, which initially grew so fast that they overshadowed the other plants, have reached their maximum height of about fifteen feet. Several crops of fruit have been produced and their life cycle completed by the time the canopy closes above them.

Many of the less vigorous saplings have succumbed to the pressures of competition for light and soil nutrients. Other short-lived trees such as the Sarsaparilla and perhaps the wattle have completed their life cycles in thirty to forty years and made way for longer-lived and shade-tolerant trees growing underneath them. So one by one the invaders and original inhabitants of the gap die till in time it is once more occupied by one large tree with an understorey of suppressed saplings and seedlings.

The bewildering variety of leaves, flowers, fruits, buds, shoots, bark and wood of the rainforests support, directly or indirectly, all the animal life. Together plants and animals form a stable but dynamic integrated entity. As we have seen, rainforests the world over are very similar in appearance even though the individual plants may be very different. The animal life in the north Queensland rainforests on the other hand is unlike that of any other part of the world; it is unique. We shall have a look at some of these animals in the following chapters.

Subtropical and temperate rainforests differ in many important ways from those of the tropics. Moving southwards the rainforests become progressively simpler in structure: robust woody vines become fewer and fewer; epiphytic orchids and ferns diminish in variety; trees belong to fewer species and occur in progressively simpler patterns; the size of the leaves of the principal shrubs and trees gradually decreases. The change is from the highly complex plant communities of tropical rain-forests to the quite simple communities of the cool temperate rainforests of Tasmania. Between these two extremes is subtropical rainforest.

It occurs in pockets, some large, some small, along the eastern scarp of the Great Divide and other coastal ranges from Mackay in central Queensland to just south of Kiama in New South Wales. Lowland rain-forest was once extensive on the coastal plains of southern Queensland

and northern New South Wales. Virtually all of this type has been destroyed.

IN SPITE of the differences from tropical rainforest, the subtropic forests are of the same basic structure. The difference between the two types is one of degree. On the other hand temperate rainforests, particularly the cool temperate ones of Tasmania, are vastly different. There are no plank buttresses, no stout woody vines, no epiphytic orchids and the trees belong to only a few species. The leaves of the main shrubs and trees vary from small to minute. The most common tree, the Antarctic Beech, for example, has leaves only a quarter of an inch long. This is in sharp contrast with the tropical rainforest where trees commonly have leaves from seven to ten inches long.

The animal life is also low in number of species present. Among the vertebrates at least, there are none which are found exclusively in rainforest as all occur too in the wet sclerophyll forests, which can be described in most cases as an association of rainforest and eucalypts.

Cool temperate rainforest is so different from any other Australian rainforest that an experience of the actual living environment cannot be compared with that in any other habitat.

The extensive rainforests of western Tasmania receive up to 100 inches of rain annually—rain received directly from the Southern Ocean and accompanied by cold blustery winds. Rainforest on the higher slopes, up to 3,500 feet, can be subject to very cold spells even in summer. Some of the most interesting rainforests are found on these slopes, such as those in the Cradle Mountain district. The dominant tree there is the Antarctic Beech. Though these trees have ancient thick and shaggy trunks, in the higher altitudes at least they are not tall. In spring this tree's new leaves have a bright orange-red tinge.

Two other large trees grow in association with beeches; these are the King Billy Pine, and the Celery-top Pine. In places these are joined by Sassafras, but this tree does not grow to the massive proportions of the beech and the pines. Below the four main species of tree that form the canopy grows an assortment of shrubs and smaller trees. Most interesting in appearance is *Richea pandanifolia*, a tall palm–like plant which usually grows as a single, unbranched stem 15 feet tall. Another beech, *Nothofagus gunni*, grows as an understorey shrub in the higher altitude forests and in places such as exposed rock faces, even as dense, low pure stands. It is winter-deciduous, the only tree in Australia with this characteristic. In autumn its leaves turn golden-yellow before they fall.

The ground in the rainforest is strewn with the remains of trees that collapsed from old age long ago and with branches fallen off the living trees.

Most striking of all the features of this rainforest is the thick covering of vivid green mosses and lichens over everything except the pine trunks. The flaky brown bark of the beeches is at times completely obscured by a lace-like covering of blue-grey lichens studded with orange dots. In other places green soft mosses envelop the trunks. The heaped ground litter, too, is densely covered with a coat of mosses.

A wealth of unique plants and animals gives tropical rainforests the richest variety of species of all Australian land habitats; an outstanding chorus of bird song makes the subtropical rainforests one of the most musical of all habitats; temperate rainforests impress mostly as over-whelmingly green places where plants reign supreme. But these impressions are only highlights in a whole range of forces interacting to create the vibrant communities known as rainforest.

Rainforest snail

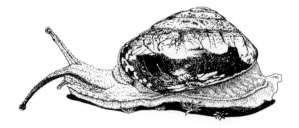

2 *Night in a Northern Upland Rainforest*

IT IS DUSK. A soft mist swirls down over the tree tops and there is a constant 'drip-drip' to the ground below. In the brief twilight the eerie miaow of the Spotted Catbird is the last of the daytime sounds. A few bats, the first of the nocturnal hunters, already weave and dodge amongst the trees, hawking after insects on silent wings. A pademelon thuds along his track to his feeding ground in a small clearing. He grooms himself as he waits for darkness to fall.

With darkness, the mist intensifies to drizzle and a strong wind stirs the crowns of the trees. In the lower levels this changes little—it has become a little cooler, and the drips are more frequent, but the wind is hardly felt. After about an hour of darkness the night animals have emerged from their hiding places and the forest is alive with their activity. They do not advertise their presence like the more flamboyant day animals. There are no birds singing; no bright butterflies fluttering about; no colourful skinks scuttling underfoot. The sounds are quieter, the 'clop' of a possum jumping on to a tree trunk, the slight rustle of a rodent pushing through the ferns, the quiet chirp of a cricket. Only the frogs raise their voices. From under a dead leaf a Microhylid frog tinkles, along the streams the larger tree frogs quack in less musical tones. The few nocturnal predators are also on the move. A Sooty Owl cocks his head as he listens carefully from the low branch of a tree for the faint rustlings of small animals below. He pounces on a tree rat, accurately guided entirely by his hearing. A Brown Tree Snake finds his way in the darkness not by hearing but by a sense of smell and touch; he feels his way through the leaves along the branches with flicking movements of his tongue. His huge, orange, doll-like eyes pick up the slightest glimmer of light. Slowly he moves through the branches, stalking tiny sleeping birds. Predatory activity however is only slight, particularly if it is compared with rainforests in other countries. For the larger animals, at least, the uplands constitute a gentle, benevolent world.

Two to three hours after sunset most of the animals are out of their hiding places. The bats hang from low branches, resting and grooming after their first insect hunting session. Shiny brown crickets, four inches long, come from hollow logs and cavities in rocks. These insects make prodigious leaps. If it had been one of the rare moonlit nights the white joints of their legs could have been seen flashing in the dim light.

The three species of ringtails unique to the tableland are late risers. The first signs of activity of these possums are the sounds of their feeding; leaves being ripped from the trees and twigs falling to the ground.

Such debris is crashing and floating to the ground from the top of a Sarsaparilla Tree. A sweep of the spotlight reveals first one pair of brilliant yellow-green reflections then three, four, eight pairs distributed through the interlocking crowns of a clump of the trees. The brilliant lights are the eyes of a group of possums reflecting the spotlight's beam. They are interrupted while feeding on the fruits and leaves of the trees. The possums are dark brown all over, as large as a domestic cat, and have long tails, bushy to their very tips. They are unmistakably Brush-tipped Ringtails. A male sits lower in the tree than the rest of the group and the strong spotlight reveals his features. He has broad, well muscled shoulders covered in a mantle of inch-long silky fur, much silkier than that of any other possum. His large dark brown eyes too are different from those of most possums; they are set more to the front of the face. His broad naked nose and deep jaw gives a chunky look to his profile. A little higher a female pulls a branch towards herself and eats some of the fruits. She is identical in colouring, but smaller and slimmer than the male. Both have a patch of short crinkly fur on the rump on which they rest when curled up asleep.

The whole group of Brush-tipped Ringtails spends hours quietly munching in the tree tops. Not a sound is uttered. Sitting in one place the possums reach out with their short but powerful arms and pull branches towards themselves. Some hold the branch with one hand and rip the fruits and leaves off with the other and push the food into their mouths. Others pluck the leaves with dainty bites, wrinkling bare noses and lips.

Two of the females in the group have well grown young. The joeys make short exploratory trips while their mothers keep eating. But the youngsters are still unsure of themselves and at the slightest rustle rush back to the safety of their mothers.

A dark form flaps overhead and the band of possums is immediately alerted by the movement. For an instant they freeze, look and listen. They sit with one foot raised, arrested in grasping for a fresh leaf or with a half eaten leaf sticking out of their mouths, the only movement in the group is the twitching of tiny ears. But soon the interruption is over and feeding resumes. It was not an owl, one of the possums' few enemies, but a flying fox searching for a fruiting tree.

Close by a dead, rotten tree trunk collapses and crashes to the ground. This time the peace is completely shattered. The possums throw the half-eaten leaves to the ground; the joeys rush back to their mothers, climb on their backs and hold on with claws and teeth. The group scatters. Some streak along a horizontal branch and leap into the leafy canopy of a smaller tree. Others leap onto the trunks of trees and gallop into the high crowns. Still others leap daringly from branch to branch, from tree to tree. Within seconds all the Brush-tipped Ringtails have disappeared into dense foliage. No other possum leaps as far and as gracefully, and in this the Brush-tipped Ringtails' behaviour differs sharply from that of the other two ringtail possums of the uplands.

Sounds of tearing leaves come surprisingly loud through the clear night air. They come from low in a large Candlenut Tree. The beam of the spotlight flicks from one clump of leaves to another and comes to rest on a boldly patterned black and white possum tearing pieces out of a heart-shaped leaf. As the light finds him he sits 'frozen' his bare, mauve, moist nose and bright chestnut eyes peering from above the green leaf he holds in his hands. His tiny ears are almost hidden in the fur and are only apparent because their insides are pink and hairless. His tail is black but tapers to a thinly furred white tip. The underside of the tail is bare for three-quarters of its length. The fur in an irregular pattern of what at first appears black and white is dense and glossy, but under the very strong light what appeared black is really a very dark umber. Sitting confused but unafraid in the light beam is a Herbert River Ringtail Possum.

When the disturbing light is gone, the Herbert River Ringtail continues to forage in the Candlenut Tree and slowly moves along the branches away from the trunk. Droplets of condensed mist glisten on his pelt. Eventually he reaches the thin outermost twigs which bend under his weight. Now in a series of easy, fluid and controlled movements he flows along the branch and into the canopy of another tree. When he reaches the end of a branch he briefly anchors himself with his prehensile tail and his hindfeet while the front feet reach out for the twigs of the next tree. These he pulls towards himself until he has enough to support his weight, then in the one smooth unhurried action he releases his hold with his tail and swings across. The fresh support momentarily bends under his weight then with a slight rustle of leaves he is gone. Unlike the Brush-tipped Ringtail, he does not leap. At first the Herbert River Ringtail's actions seem slow, though never awkward, until it is realised just how quickly and silently he can melt out of view.

In rainforests where the trees and vines grow so close together that their branches interlock there is never any possibility that a possum cannot find an escape. Sometimes a Herbert River Ringtail finds himself on a low branch some distance below the intermeshed leaves and twigs of the canopy. This is a situation fraught with difficulty for him. Even when frightened he will not leap wildly for another trunk or branch. Instead he moves back towards the trunk. If he is frightened away again he runs out to the furthest, thinnest branches. He throws himself forward hanging on with tail and hindfeet, his short arms frantically windmilling to grab for a handhold. None is found. He goes slightly back again, the branches springing up when his weight has shifted. Instead of reaching across he now reaches up, pulls himself up onto a higher branch, speeds along it towards the trunk, climbs quickly into the crown and races out to the thin branches and disappears amongst the foliage of the next tree. His movements are easy, fluid and controlled, his legs so short that his underside brushes the branches as he runs along. But still he takes a comparatively long time to get out of a situation that the Brush-tipped Ringtail would have escaped from in one leap.

The mist has cleared momentarily and the strong beam of the spotlight probes far into the forest. It picks up two red glowing reflections moving amongst leaves of a low vine. The light approaches closer and closer and the reflections resolve themselves into the eyes of another possum. He is larger and much lighter in colour than either the Herbert River Ringtail or the Brush-tipped Ringtail. The light has caught him crossing from one tree to another along the loops of a thick vine. He pauses as he tries to adjust to the dazzling light.

His pelt is dense and of an even length, without guard hairs projecting through the underfur, which gives him a rounded appearance. The colour of the fur is mainly a yellow-green, the only marsupial with this unusual colour. It is the Green or Striped Ringtail. His face, turned towards the light, is grey with touches of white at his ears and eyes. He has three irregular frizzy grey stripes down his back and is pure white underneath. At the base his tail is very broad but it tapers gradually to a thin white tip.

Soon he is used to the light, ignores it and continues his search for leaves to eat. Slowly and placidly he walks along the vines and then climbs through the trees; he moves in the same branch-hugging fluid actions as the Herbert River Ringtail. He stops frequently and investigates his surroundings, twitching his pink bulbous nose and black wire-like whiskers in all directions. Both nose and whiskers are sense organs. By scent and by touch he finds his way and his food in the dark forest. The choice of edible leaves is endless; he eats a great variety.

When he finds a leaf to his liking he plucks it, exposing the broad orange-pink palm of his hand. The large fig leaf drips with a milky white sap and he holds it between the second and third fingers. Like all ringtails, he uses the first and second fingers as two thumbs opposing the other three fingers. Next he rips a bite out of the leaf and chews noisily. He eats only half the leaf before he flings it to the ground and picks a fresh one. After an eating bout of several hours he selects a spot on a horizontal branch, or more often a vine looping between two trees, to take a nap. He anchors himself to his support with one clamp-like hind-foot, brings his tail forward between his legs and wriggles backwards until his ample rump is comfortably settled on the branch. When he is completely comfortable he tucks his other three feet underneath himself and rests them on the tightly curled tail. With a final sleepy look around he tucks his head in till it too rests on his tail. Now, a globe of green fur, he sleeps. But at the slightest vibration of his supporting branch he raises his head to assess if there is any danger. Usually there is not, it is just a sudden gust of wind or another possum moving about. And the ringtail again closes his large brown eyes and dozes off.

Gentlest and most imperturbable of all Australia's possums he is not easily frightened but when he is he speeds away, and despite his greater bulk is even faster than the Herbert River Ringtail.

The three ringtail possums with their graceful fluent ways hardly make a sound as they move through the entangled vegetation. A crashing gallop among the ground litter followed by a bark-scrabbling tree ascent must, therefore, be made by another animal. Once more the light beam scans the trees, pauses on a tree trunk, sweeps along a branch then comes to rest on a puzzled-looking possum staring down from the fork of a tree. He is a little larger than a fox terrier, has large ears and a tail which is black and bushy to its very tip. His fur is soft and dense and shines in the strong light. On the back he is silver grey suffused with copper and a warm red brown underneath. It is the Coppery Brushtail.

The strong light does not hold his interest for long and with a last inquisitive glance he bounds along a branch, runs head first down a tree trunk, jumps to the ground and ambles bowleggedly away to resume his search for beetles, fallen fruits and other tidbits.

Where the elegant ringtails move swiftly through the foliage, hardly making a sound, the tough brushtail barges through using sheer strength.

The other nocturnal mammals apart from the placid possums are small rodents that scuttle away nervously whenever a twig snaps or a leaf rustles suspiciously. They are found in all the rainforests, high and low altitudes, and we shall meet them in another chapter.

Mammals are not the only vegetarians living on the infinite variety of plants; insects suck their juices, bore into the tree trunks, eat the leaves and fruits and suck nectar from the flowers. Most of the insects sit on the underside of leaves, behind bark or otherwise hide themselves, waiting motionless for the return of daylight. But many crickets, beetles, butterfly larvae and an almost unbelievable variety of moths are now active. They attract predators; praying mantises stalk amongst the foliage; spiders build silken snares; scorpions creep amongst the leaf litter. The soft-skinned geckoes are also hunting insects and other small animal life.

Two kinds of geckoes live in these highlands. On the tree trunks lives the Leaf-tailed Gecko. In day-time he is a mere mottled green smudge as he lies flattened against a giant tree trunk and is virtually invisible. His fringed sides and broad tail do not even cast a tell-tale shadow and his huge lidless eyes are a maze of green and black squiggles which also match his surroundings. No bird or other predator has sight keen enough to detect him. As long as he does not move he is safe. At night the large ten-inch gecko becomes active—he no longer looks like a flake of bark. Head facing down he raises himself on his thin front legs surveying the tree trunk for insect prey. As he spots a movement he rushes forward and snaps up a moth or beetle in his strong jaws.

The other gecko, *Carphodactylus leavis*, is of almost equal size but lives on the ground. He too is difficult to see for his dull brown colour blends with rocks and litter. When hunting, his tread is jerky, slow and deliberate, his movements punctuated by the swaying of his carrot-shaped tail raised above his body. When he is ready to pounce on his prey he moves swiftly and accurately.

By day the frogs sit perfectly still on a leaf or branch or hide in a hollow. At night they come out to catch insects and spiders. In the trees, shrubs and ferns live the tree frogs. Mostly green species with large discs on their toes, they sit in wait for their quarry on a large leaf or a branch. Their eyes can detect only moving prey and as soon as something stirs within reach, perhaps a small moth slowly fluttering by, the hitherto immobile frog lunges forward. With its large mouth wide open it catches the moth on its extended sticky tongue. When it darts forward like this it usually remains anchored with its hind feet and immediately returns to its former sphinx-like pose, but sometimes it will leap right off its perch and catch a passing insect in mid-air.

The ground-living frogs are of a general brown pattern with, in some species, patches of gold, yellow and black. The largest, most striking of these frogs is the Northern Barred Frog which grows to a stout six inches. When fully alert, watching for the give-away movements of potential prey, he sits bolt upright, his front legs fully extended and back legs folded under him in readiness for a leap. In this way the sturdy frogs expose their cream coloured undersides and are conspicuous even in the dim moonlight of the forest floor. But at the merest suggestion of a disturbance they squat down and flatten themselves on the ground. Now they are hardly distinguishable, their backs having the same colour and the same intricate pattern as the partly decayed leaves on the ground.

Activity gradually slows with the approach of dawn. Bats fly to their roosts in hollow trees, Herbert River Ringtails curl up in the huge 'baskets' of staghorn ferns, Green Possums curl up and merge with the green foliage. Tree frogs tuck their legs under their bodies and seem to become part of a leaf or a mossy branch. Leaf-tailed Geckoes once again flatten themselves on the tree bark. Ground animals seek the shelter of a hollow log or a tumble of rocks.

Just before first light there is a brief moment when all is quiet; with light there is birdsong. The Toothbill's powerful voice is usually the first. Soon a catbird miaows, a riflebird screeches and warblers twitter in the undergrowth. The forests belong to the day animals once again.

A typical night in the upland rainforests of the Atherton Tableland has come to an end.

THE RAINFORESTS of the Atherton Tableland and the adjoining uplands at first do not seem to differ sharply from those of the lowlands. The vegetation changes are indeed slight and subtle; the trees are taller and the leaves of the plants generally smaller in size with an increase in altitude. But the climate and animal life, however, are quite different. On the uplands the air is cooler and except for the dry spring months the forests are shrouded in mist and receive a drizzly rain for long periods. Sometimes the sun does not shine for weeks on end. There is a difference in the chorus of bird songs, in the kinds of lizards that bask in the dapples of sunlight, in the insects that bustle all around, in the mammals that live in the tree tops.

Many animals are so critically attuned to the upland's special conditions of temperature and humidity that if they are taken away they quickly die. A Great Barred Frog, *Mixophyes schevilli*, taken from the uplands to the lowlands, for example, dies in a matter of hours. Some animals are even further specialised—they can thrive only in high altitude rainforests growing on soils of basaltic origins. This specialisation has resulted in an unusually high proportion of the upland rainforest animals being unique to the area.

The specialisation can best be illustrated by further considering the four possums described earlier in this chapter.

The Brush-tipped Ringtail, *Hemibelideus lemuroides*, and Herbert River Ringtail, *Pseudocheirus herbertensis*, occur only on the Atherton Tableland at misty altitudes of 3,000 feet and over. In a few isolated spots on these heights where the forests grow on basalt soils, these two possums are quite common. They have very rarely been seen at lower altitudes or in the rainforests of the northern parts of the tableland which are on soils derived from granite.

The Green Ringtail, *Pseudocheirus archeri*, and the Coppery Brushtail, *Trichosurus vulpecula johnstoni*, are much more common at lower altitudes between 2,000 and 3,000 feet where the forests are a little drier and the skies clear for longer periods. But neither the Brush-tipped Ringtail nor the Herbert River Ringtail occur in these lower and, to humans, more comfortable forests. The reasons for this are still obscure. Maybe the Brush-tipped and Herbert River Ringtails need constant mist and drizzle on their glossy coats to thrive or perhaps some of their essential food trees are missing at the lower altitudes, although Sarsaparilla, *Alphitonia petriei*, and Candlenut, *Aleurites moluccana*, both grow there.

The Green Ringtails are the most adaptable of the four possums. There are records of them from areas as low as 300–400 feet above sea level, and as high as 4,000 feet and from forests growing on most soils. Still the densest populations of Green Ringtails are at 2,500 feet altitude in forests on basaltic soils.

A fifth possum is a strikingly coloured subspecies of the Herbert River Ringtail. It occurs only in the upland rainforests behind Mossman fifty miles to the north of the Atherton Tableland—one of the wettest areas in Australia. In anatomy this possum is identical with the typical Herbert River Ringtail, but it has a gentler disposition and except for a dark brown stripe down its head is of a uniform pale caramel colour instead of the typical black and white pattern.

Because of this restricted and inaccessible habitat, *Pseudocheirus herbertensis cinereus* remained undiscovered until 1937. Since then it was not recorded until we found and photographed one in November 1967.

The other upland possums were first recorded by Carl Lumholtz during his ten-month expedition to north Queensland in 1882–1883. He collected specimens which he either shot himself or which were brought to him by Aboriginal hunters. He had no experience with the living animals. Since Lumholtz' days quite a number of expeditions, from Sweden, the United States and other countries as well as from Australian institutions have collected specimens of these possums. Yet none of these expeditions resulted in an increase in the knowledge about the living animals. To this day there is no accurate information on the habits of the

possums; what kind of leaves they eat, whether they include insects in their diet; whether they feed on the nectar of flowers; when the young are born and how long they stay with their mothers; it is not known whether they live solitary lives or congregate in small groups or perhaps family parties. These and many other questions remain unanswered.

THE UPLAND RAINFOREST at night is a silent world alive with the activities mostly of mammals and insects but also of a small number of geckoes and frogs. With the coming of day these animals melt away into forests and their places are taken by the more vocal birds. Innumerable insects and a few reptiles also come out of hiding and add to the colour.

The base of an *Angiopteris evecta* plant—each stem is about four inches in diameter

3 Day in a Northern Upland Rainforest

A DAY IN LATE SPRING. The first grey light creeps amongst the tree tops, so faint that it does not penetrate to the ground below. Most of the night animals have long since retreated to their sleeping places. Only a Lumholtz Tree Kangaroo moves in the crown of a tall tree. He shuffles along a horizontal branch on his thickly padded, black feet and feeds on a branch which he has pulled towards him with his powerful arms. He eats first the leaves then rips off strips of bark with his strong teeth. He is sombre coloured; his round face, limbs and underside of the tail are black, his back is grey with patches of orange-fawn on the flanks, arms and underside. While eating he squats low on the branch, a powerful dark figure in the shadowless early light.

He moves on, leaps nonchalantly ten or twenty feet from branch to branch, his long tail, which is not prehensile, streaming behind him for balance. The tree kangaroo crashes through the vegetation. There is no finesse in his climbing skills; he is rough and tough. He descends a tree trunk backing down tail first and browses on seedling trees and shrubs on the ground.

In this peaceful early morning he goes about his business slowly. But if he is pursued or when worry about intruders changes to panic, he leaps to the ground from great heights, as much as sixty feet, or comes down a thick vine like a fireman down a pole and then thuds away along the ground. He seldom tries to make his escape through the tree tops.

When necessary he can gallop up a tree quickly too. He jumps up and embraces the trunk with his arms, then he kicks with both strongly clawed feet together and embraces the tree again higher up. Alternately embracing and kicking in rapid succession he soon disappears into the crown of a tree. The tree kangaroo is not entirely nocturnal. It is some time after sunrise before he ascends a large tree, settles himself comfortably on a branch and sleeps.

The sun is not yet over the horizon but some light has penetrated to the forest floor, the signal for the small Musk Rat Kangaroo to stir himself from his slumbers. He is one of the very few Australian mammals that are completely diurnal—he sleeps in a hollow log or under a rock all night. At first light he awakes and begins his search for food. He stands only ten inches tall and is the smallest of the kangaroo tribe. Apart from his preference for daylight, he has many other unusual features. His tail is completely bare, like polished leather, and scaly. His hind foot has five toes, the first is small and clawless and is like a possum's. None of the other members of the kangaroo tribe has this first toe.

With the first glimmer of light the rat kangaroo yawns, scratches himself a few times and hops out of his hollow log. Another yawn and a luxuriant stretching and he walks off into the forest. His first stop is under a Candlenut Tree where he snuffles around looking on the ground for any fruit that may have fallen overnight. Several green fruit litter the ground—as they fell they burst open and the rat kangaroo fastidiously picks out the nuts with his slim but strong brown hands. He gnaws for a while on the very hard shell of the nut then holding it in both hands eats the kernel. His dark chocolate brown form merges with the leaf litter and brown rocks of the basalt soil. Periodically he peers around through almost black, bright shining eyes. Soon he has finished one nut and throws the empty shell amongst the thousands of others under the tree—each has a neat round hole in it. The few nuts, three in each fruit, are soon eaten and the rat kangaroo moves on, this time looking for insects. He fossicks amongst the gravelly rocks, tossing some aside dexterously or probing amongst the leaves with his long roman nose. Now and then he pounces on a beetle, cockroach or longhorned grasshopper which is quickly eaten.

The first rays of sunlight filter through the foliage. Sombreness changes almost instantly to liveliness—not only as a result of the sun's brightness but mostly because of the vigour and energy of the birds. Early morning in the upland rainforest is a pageant of birds. There are brightly coloured ones and species plumaged in subdued browns and greens; some are noisily vocal, others whisper quietly; some feed on the flowers of the tree tops, others flit through the ferns of the undergrowth.

Birdsong carries far through the fresh morning air. In places the continuous outpourings of songs of particularly powerfully voiced species are ear-splitting at close quarters. The non-stop song of the ground-dwelling Chowchilla drowns out all other sounds near it. In another part of the forest the Toothbill's clear notes overwhelm almost all other sounds. The male Toothbills sit over their playgrounds, small clearings in the forest decorated with 50–80 large leaves placed upside down on the ground, and sing in long unbroken bursts of clear far-carrying notes. Usually three or four other males have their playgrounds within 100 yards, their songs sounding like echoes of the nearest bird. But this species' songs are so varied and intricate that each bird has a slightly different one. The one bird may even have different songs on different days.

From higher in the trees the clear, full song of the Stripe-breasted Thrush pours down.

As well as these continuous outpourings of loud songs, there are many birds whose 'song' is a short, penetrating but nonetheless melodious call; the rhythmic whistle of the pitta, a soft single-note whistle followed by a resounding 'choo' comes from a whipbird. Softer notes are the creaky drawn out 'miaow' of the catbird and the bell-like notes of a pair of Grey-headed Robins chasing each other amongst the trees.

But not all sound is bird song. From low in a fruiting tree come slapping sounds; the clapping together of wings made by courting Brown Pigeons. One bird lands on a thin branch that sways slowly under its weight; with a berry in its beak and wings spread it fans its long tail. Others land near, wing-slapping as they land. The first one immediately rises, again slapping its wings. In this way the birds tumble over and around each other rising and landing from swaying branch to swaying branch. Now and again a small brown feather floats slowly to the ground.

On the higher parts of the region, at altitudes of 3,000 feet and over, the uplands' most brilliantly coloured bird, the Golden Bower-bird, starts the day with some careful attention to his bower. After the first inspection the male bower-bird flies off to a special tree, *Melicope broadbentiana*, and picks off one of the opened seed pods. These pods are star-shaped, about an inch across and when opened show off-white insides—this is what attracts the bird. With one of these opened seed pods in his beak the male flies down to his bower on the ground. The first rays of sunlight glint off his glossy brilliant golden-yellow plumage. He lands on the display stick of his bower and with great care places the *Melicope* seed pod with others beside a few large white flowers at the base of the smaller of two pyramids of sticks. This pyramid is about two feet high and was built by the bird around the base of a small tree. After some more adjustments to the decorations of flowers and seed pods the bird flies off again in a flash of gold. Within a few minutes he returns, this time with his beak full of yellow-green lichen, plucked from the high branches of the trees. This lichen is placed on the opposite end of the well worn display stick at the base of a larger pyramid at least $3\frac{1}{2}$ feet high and built around another tree. The two piles of sticks are about four feet apart and joined by the display stick which may be a vine or a small fallen tree a few inches to a few feet off the ground. The bower-bird, dwarfed by his immense structure, for a while hops along his display stick adjusting a few decorations here, some sticks there. A leaf fallen near the decorations overnight is carried away. Eventually the bower seems to be to the bird's satisfaction and he flies to a branch about ten feet above his playground, and begins his unusual song. With his feathers fluffed out he weaves strange harmonies out of sweet whistles, soft whisperings and harsh chatterings. Now and again he pauses, catches an insect that ventured near, or with angry calls chases a bird that has accidently strayed near his bower.

The whole impressive performance of building, singing and chasing is for only one purpose—to attract a female. She is a uniform nondescript grey-brown, a little lighter and greyer underneath than on top. She is as plain as her mate is brilliant. She does visit the bower, but infrequently, and it is not known if the male displays to her on the bower itself.

As the morning warms, the bird songs and displays become less and less and eventually only an occasional call resounds through the ranks of tall trees. The birds are now busy feeding, nest building and looking after their young. They are busy at all levels of the forests from the highest tree tops down to the ground.

Late in spring a few trees are in flower: *Oreocallis wickhamii* has dense bunches of orange-red flowers; here and there the white flower spikes of the Bull Oak dot the canopy; Umbrella Trees project their gracefully curved bunches of deep red flowers above the tree tops. Lower down in the forest a *Eugenia* is covered with star bursts of white flowers. Small birds with sharp, slightly down-curved beaks chatter amongst the flowers; the Lewin, Yellow-streaked and Mountain Honeyeaters, ever active, hop from flower to flower gathering nectar with a quick succession of dabs with their sharp beaks. They pause occasionally to make sorties after flying insects which are also attracted to the rich flow of nectar.

Besides flowering trees there are many in fruit. Wompoo Pigeons feed on figs in the highest part of the canopy. A flock of Topknot Pigeons, large heavy pigeons, are feeding on bunches of black berries of another tall tree and with wing flapping and tail fanning try to balance on the thin twigs. Often the branches cannot support the birds' weight. The flapping and balancing of forty grey birds is a lively, noisy occasion. The ripe berries are pulled off and swallowed whole in an almost feverish haste by the pigeons whose red-brown crown feathers vibrate every time they jerk their head back to swallow a fruit. Within a short time the pigeons have eaten their fill and fly to the topmost branches of an emergent tree and rest.

Brown Pigeons and catbirds feed on the red fruits of a Piccabeen Palm. The catbird mashes some of the fruit in its strong beak and flies off to feed the pulp to its young.

Many of the insectivorous birds hunt in the lower strata of the forests. A Pied Flycatcher strikingly marked in black and white hops and hovers around a large tree trunk. He clings to the tree probing behind the bark for insects with his sharp beak. With wings and tail spread and white neck-ruff raised he hops all over the tree minutely investigating every flake of bark, every crevice in which an insect might hide. He turns himself in all directions hanging sideways or even upside down in the concentration of his search.

The Stripe-breasted Thrush catches its food amongst the leaves and minutely examines the undersides for moths, beetles, caterpillars, cicadas and a host of other insects.

Honeyeaters, flycatchers and thrushes are all lively birds incessantly on the move after their food. Amongst the tree-buttresses and lower trunks lives a bird of quieter habits. A Grey-headed Robin sits motionless and grave on a tree buttress or the side of a trunk. Now and again in a single precise movement he cocks his head to direct his large eyes towards a stirring amongst the leaf litter. Something is spotted and he glides down amongst the trunks, his wings showing bars of a startling white against the warm brown of his back. He lands on the ground and with a few deft strokes of the bill parts the leaves and uncovers a millipede. He takes it to his nest and feeds it to his single tiny young. For a while the bird stands on the nest rim on his long pale legs, adjusts some of the lining of the nest and then settles down to brood his young—he wiggles his body from side to side but with his head never moving and his eyes ever watchful, till he is comfortably settled. It is a busy morning for the robin, he has to hunt to feed himself and his young and had to distract the attention of a hungry goanna. Loudly calling his alarm call of 'teck-teck' and fluttering seemingly injured and helpless on the ground, he lured the hunting reptile away from his nest. His partner in the meantime kept watch over the nest and uttered a soft, ventriloquial 'ping-ping' apparently a signal for the nestling to keep perfectly still and quiet.

On the ground the search and competition for food is intense. Every square foot of this basalt soil is raked over by the birds. The litter decomposition is rapid and the layer of dead leaves is very thin. There are so many birds looking for the invertebrates of the litter that it is difficult to understand how they all find a meal.

Largest of the soil rakers are the Jungle Fowl and the Scrub Turkey. The first is about the size of a domestic fowl, warm brown in colour with a small crest and orange-yellow legs, while the Scrub Turkey is a little larger, black all over except for its naked and bright red neck and head, and a yellow wattle at the throat. Both birds have very large and powerful feet with which they turn over the soil and litter. When they are feeding they first of all scrape off the debris covering the soil, throwing heaps of leaves behind them with powerful, alternate strokes of the feet. After each scrape they closely inspect what has been uncovered. They move slowly when foraging.

Next most thorough are the Chowchillas which are only about half the size of a Scrub Turkey. Chowchillas are dark brown birds, round in shape but also with very strong feet and legs. The male Chowchilla has a white throat, that of the female is orange. Chowchillas move in small groups and turn over the litter with energetic sideways swipes of the legs. If they get into an area of deep litter they dig down so far that they disappear from view.

Whipbirds are even more zestful in their search for soil animals. They are slimmer than the Chowchillas, dark green all over except for a white throat and black head which is topped by a jaunty crest. They have no particular way of getting their food, they chuck leaves about with their beaks, rake the ground with their feet and even crawl under the dead fronds of a staghorn fern rustling noisily as they chase beetles, spiders and cockroaches.

The Fern Wren and Yellow-throated Scrub Wren, both ground dwellers, are small birds—too small to be able to rake the ground. They use their size to advantage and move right underneath the fallen logs and between the larger rocks creeping about like mice and seeking out prey that the larger birds cannot uncover.

By mid-day it is warm and humid. It is not too hot for a pair of small skinks to fight and chase each other in a small patch of sunlight, but the birds fly to their favourite waterhole for a bath. They approach the water carefully, moving slowly and constantly looking over their shoulders as they move down from the trees. When they reach the water they flutter in a series of quick splashing dips, never lingering for long. After a few splashes they move back into the cover of the trees to preen themselves.

The smaller birds are uneasy. These waterholes are the hunting grounds of their greatest enemy. If they relax their vigilance for one moment they could be struck down by a grey and white fury. The Grey Goshawk can often be seen perched at a vantage point overlooking a pool. Watercourses are much easier hunting areas for him, here he can manoeuvre his large grey wings without entangling himself in the dense foliage of the forest. Also, few of the birds which come to drink and to bathe can match the goshawk in speed. Even so the stern-looking hawk catches his prey by surprise attack not a fast pursuit.

It is warm and quiet in the upland plateau's rainforest and the last wisps of cloud evaporate from the mountain slopes. The morning mist which enveloped just the very peaks of the mountains has covered everything there with a film of moisture. In the topmost layers of the forest this soon dries but the ground remains wet.

For a period it is calm and warm on the peaks—a state not in keeping with the surroundings which show the effects of the violence of the elements. The trees are short and stunted and leaning in the direction of the constant southeast winds. The moisture of almost continuous cloud cover has stimulated the growth of all kinds of epiphytes. The long trailing growths of lichens, mosses and bryophytes in the lower reaches still drip from the morning's mist and drops catch the sunlight as they fall. Rocks and tree branches are carpeted with dense coverings of orchids, ferns and mosses. *Bulbophyllum* orchids cling to the bare rock faces with intricate root systems and in the less turbulent spring weather open small, pale flowers amongst the fleshy green leaves. Larger orchids, such as *Dendrobium fusiforme*, have taken root in small depressions and small spaces between rocks. Their fragile flowers carried on long spikes are shredded by the wind in the more exposed situations. *Agapetes meiniana* hides $1\frac{1}{2}$ inch-long, deep pink flowers amongst its dense foliage. The Mountain Honeyeaters and spinebills push themselves through the closely packed leaves like lizards to reach the blossoms and twist themselves to reach the nectar deep in the tubular flowers.

But the peace of the mountain tops is short lived. Soon the sun begins to go down, the temperature drops and a wind springs up. Clouds once more gather round the peaks as the voice of a Toothbill in the forest below marks the beginning of the afternoon bird chorus. A flock of Topknot Pigeons sweeps up the mountainside in powerful flight and lands in a tall dead tree just under the cloud canopy. The last yellow rays of light illuminate their grey breasts and high helmets of rufous feathers.

Down below, the chorus continues till dusk. A small marsupial mouse emerges from a hollow in a tree to begin its nocturnal hunting of insects and small birds. A pair of warblers even smaller than the mouse have a nest not far away and twittering agitatedly mob the little creature in an effort to drive it off.

Dusk is brief and soon it is dark.

THE PAGEANT OF BIRDS can be experienced in any of the upland rainforests growing on basalt soil, between Mt Spec in the south and Cooktown in the north. Forests growing on less fertile soil have fewer numbers of birds, they are quieter and their ground litter is much less disturbed. The only indication that the day described took place on the

Atherton Tableland was the presence of the Lumholtz Tree Kangaroo. It is found only in a few spots on the Tableland and perhaps on the uplands immediately to the south. The Musk Rat Kangaroo occurs throughout the rainforests, lowland and upland, from Cardwell to Cooktown.

It has been discovered that the two mammals together with the nocturnal species have a profound effect on plant regeneration in the rainforest. Firstly they eat the seeds of many species, not just the fruit, but the actual kernel of the seed itself. Under trees like the Candlenut and the Kauri Pines and others which are palatable, the entire seed crop is often devoured by the mammals. The ground may be strewn with many thousands of the nuts fallen to the ground but many unprofitable hours can be spent looking for an undamaged seed or a seedling tree. No seedlings will be found and if a nut is found intact it is either freshly fallen or sterile. Rodents and Musk Rat Kangaroos are mainly responsible for the eating of the seed crop. Any seeds that escape are usually those within fruits eaten by birds, which digest only the outer covering, and are then more widely scattered and so may escape the attention of the gnawing mammals. But frequently these seeds are also found and attacked—the Musk Rat Kangaroo has been seen picking out and eating fruit kernels from the droppings of Cassowaries. The tree kangaroo and pademelon, *Thylogale stigmatica*, affect regeneration in another way; they browse on the young trees and seriously impede their growth or even kill them.

So far we have only considered what takes place on a certain day in forests on basalt soil. However, large tracts of the uplands between Townsville and Cooktown have granite derived soils. Nearly all the high mountain peaks are granite.

There are many such peaks along the coast between Mossman and Cooktown. On the seaward side they are covered with rainforest from high tide mark to the topmost granite boulder but on the inland side there are patches of open forest on the lower slopes. These mountains are quite inaccessible and must be one of the least spoiled areas in Australia, an area where there is no direct evidence of man and where it is possible to get completely absorbed in and captivated by the natural surroundings.

In ascending one of these granite peaks, about 4,000 feet high, from the western side one passes through a variety of habitats. To remain unspoilt and free from the desecration of orchid collectors this peak must remain nameless.

At the base of the mountain are mainly eucalypt woodlands crossed by bands of rainforests along the streams originating in the mountains. One tree, the Messmate, *Eucalyptus cloeziana*, or Dead-finish as it is known locally, dominates these lower forests. These are huge trees with rough flaky bark on the trunk but with smooth cream-coloured branches. The ground cover is sparse, mainly short grasses. At the height of a few hundred feet the gentle slope becomes steeper and rocky. Gradually the eucalypts disappear and their place is taken by the needle-leaved *Casuarina torulosa*. Fire, which is deliberately lit each year on the more accessible places, is rare in this remote area. Its exclusion here has given a completely different character to the casuarina forests, its original character, which is now non-existent in the closer settled parts of north Queensland.

The trees are old, covered with thick corky bark. Needles fallen from the trees have lodged on this bark and over the years have built up to give the trunks a shaggy covering. Needles also carpet the ground. The warm brown of bark and fallen needles contrasts pleasantly with the blue-green of the plume-like foliage which weeps down from the mature trees and pushes upward from the young plants on the ground. No stock has grazed here and the ground cover is undisturbed. Young rainforest trees have taken root in the soil enriched by many generations of decomposed leaves and compete with young casuarina trees in the undergrowth. If fire is kept out long enough the more vigorous rainforest trees may eventually suppress the young casuarinas and replace the trees that die of old age. But this is an extremely slow process.

Epiphytic orchids flourish. Huge clumps of *Dendrobium fusiforme* grow in the forks of the trees and on rocks low to the ground, a sure indication that the collectors have not yet found the area. The trunk of a leaning tree is a hanging garden of *Oberonia* orchids, mosses and ferns, the vivid green of their leaves a bright spot in the brown forest.

Continuing up the mountain the lowest point of the cloud zone is soon reached and here the casuarinas give way to rainforest trees. The slope is steep, with more and more rocks and boulders. The rainforest is at first rather open with trees to sixty or seventy feet in height. In the gullies between the ridges radiating from the summit the vegetation is denser with many tree ferns along the streams. The water in these streams, cold and crystal-clear, cascades over and between rocks covered with green moss.

The higher one climbs the denser the forest becomes, but with an ever lower canopy. It is a highly characteristic community called montane forest or, with reference to the delicacy of the trailing epiphytes, elfin woodlands.

Suddenly tall granite spires rise 30–50 feet sheer out of the ground with here and there a passage between them. It is possible to weave in and out between these towers without realising that the summit has been reached.

This is only clear when one of the spires is climbed, by scrambling over a covering of damp orchids, ferns and mosses, and one stands perspiring in the wind on the top. A view of the sea stretches to the east and more rainforest covered mountains in all other directions. The mountain top is granite, its solidity broken up by gigantic cracks and fissures. It is in these fissures that the trees grow, their crowns filling the spaces between the towers. Because of the constant wind the crowns do not project above the rocks but form a densely matted canopy so dense that it is possible to walk over the tops of these trees from one granite spire to another without climbing thirty or fifty feet down to the ground and then up again. One of these trees is *Agapetes meiniana* mentioned in the first half of this chapter. Another interesting plant of these mountain peaks is the red flowered *Rhododendron lochae* which flowers during the wet season when these peaks are completely inaccessible and there may be no break in the cloud cover for many weeks on end.

To drink the nectar from the inch and a half flowers of *Agapetes meiniana,* this Eastern Spinebill has to turn its head almost upside down

4 Lowland Tropical Rainforest in November

ALL DAY THE CAMP of the Spectacled Flying Foxes has been a noisy, squabbling place. But just before sunset there is a general quiet. Thousands of the giant fruit bats hang clustered from the branches of the trees, their bodies now wrapped in their black leathery wings as they sleep. Then just after sunset, when the landscape is already dark but the sky is still bright with yellow light, wave after wave of the large bats fan out to fly to the feeding grounds.

Twilight is brief and by the time the bats reach their favourite quondong, fig, palm, White Cedar or other fruiting tree, it is dark. The warm night in a Cape York monsoon forest is mostly silent. Apart from the shrieks and gurgles of the flying foxes in the fruit trees, and high-pitched trills of insects, the nocturnal animals are secretive and shy. The only signs of their existence are soft rustling, scratching, gnawing, ripping and scuttling sounds. Sound and hearing, scent and attracting chemical substances secreted by many species guide the nocturnal animals to their food and to their mates. The animals are mostly colourful or strongly patterned, yet sight for most is of secondary importance as a sense organ, used only to detect movement.

While the flying foxes squabble, the lowland rainforest's staggering variety of nocturnal insects comes out of hiding. A Spiny Cricket feels his way with his long antennae across the dead leaves and rocks on the ground. Deep in the rotting mound of leaves in which the Jungle Fowl incubates her eggs, a Rhinoceros Beetle has just split his pupal skin and pushes his way to the surface. He is jet black. He climbs to a vantage point and turns his horned, shiny head in all directions then slowly lifts his hard wing cases, unfolds his transparent two-inch long wings and with a deep humming sound he is airborne and lumbers off in search of a mate. Other beetles emerge at night. In a decaying log a longicorn beetle makes his way through a tunnel to the outside world. His antennae, which may be as much as three times as long as his body, sense the air for danger, but more importantly, pick up the scent of the female.

A soft persistent sawing, scratching noise from the branches of a small tree draws attention to a six-inch-long cocoon ingeniously spun between the leaves of a small twig. The noise is made by an insect sawing its way out of the nut-hard cell that protected it during its pupal stage. Soon the hole is made and a furry warm-brown body stumbles out. Its wings are stubby and as yet useless. The insect climbs to a thicker branch and then remains still, the wing stubs hang limply down. Slowly, almost imperceptibly, the soft wings expand as the insect pumps liquid into them. After about ten minutes the wings have reached their full size. Each pair measures seven by four inches and are of the same warm-brown colour as the body except for a tear-shaped transparent window in each wing. The soft, floppy wings soon become dry and rigid. A female Atlas Moth, one of the largest moths in the world, has just emerged. A sudden flutter of the sail-like wings and she dances slowly off amongst the leaves and tree trunks, her body already heavy with eggs.

She broadcasts her presence by exuding a chemical which has an overpowering attraction for one and only one creature—the male Atlas Moth. Most other animals cannot detect the chemical and none but male Atlas Moths are attracted by it. After fluttering aimlessly about for some time the female moth settles on a tree trunk. Before long she is joined by a male. He is several inches smaller in wingspan, has a much smaller body and his back wings taper into elegant tails. He also has just emerged. He picked up the female's scent or perhaps other radiation with his huge feather-like antennae which are four or five times as large as the female's. They mate.

The female flies off in search of a suitable tree to lay her 80–100 eggs. She flies from tree to tree, her wings becoming ragged, until she finds one of the six or eight kinds of trees the caterpillars will eat and grow on. She will not lay her eggs on any other. After hatching, the blue-green caterpillars grow rapidly till they are about ten inches long. Then they spin their cocoons to emerge as moths several months after first hatching from the egg.

Egglaying completed, the female Atlas Moth will not live much longer—she has no mouthparts and therefore cannot feed. Once the fat stored in her body is exhausted she dies.

This rainforest at night abounds with insects, but by far the greatest number are beetles and moths. Crickets, earwigs, cockroaches and others combined are only a small fraction of all the flying, hopping and burrowing multitudes that provide food for the insect hunting animals. Tree frogs hunt amongst the leaves of shrubs as well as the tallest trees in their typical method of motionless patient waiting and sudden tongue-darting attacks. The most striking species is the eight-inch Giant Green Tree Frog, the largest member of its world-wide family. From time to time during the night the frog will move to another vantage point—not in the hopping motion so characteristic of the ground living frogs, but in slow, walking, stretching and clinging movements of his long legs and large-disced toes.

Other insect hunters move purposefully among the dead leaves and fallen logs on the ground. A Banded Gecko makes a sudden wriggling dash at a small beetle and engulfs it with his cavernous mouth. He continues his hunt. He freezes, one thin front leg raised and his white tail elegantly curved over his body as he watches for the smallest movement. His foot is slowly, carefully put down and the next one raised—thus step by step the gecko stalks amongst leaves, rocks and branches. Only when prey is within range does he rush forward.

The brown coloured marsupial mouse on the other hand is all nervous energy. He has just emerged from his hiding place amongst the buttress roots of a large fig tree. Sniffing and scratching he seeks his prey out from under leaves, stones and bark—he does not wait for any tell-tale movements; he goes in after it fearlessly. In jerky, darting movements sometimes too quick for the eye to follow, he feels in cracks and hollows with his front feet, pushes aside leaves and bits of bark with his nose. Suddenly he rushes up a tree trunk to pounce on a cockroach. A quick bite and the insect is dead, then almost as quickly it is fastidiously dismembered and eaten. All insects, scorpions, spiders and centipedes are tackled no matter what their size. A centipede eight inches long, as long as the marsupial itself and equipped with a strong pair of pincers that can inject a poison, is quickly despatched in a furious whirlwind attack. With eyes tightly closed the pouched mouse darts in, biting and grappling with the thrashing centipede.

An intense honey smell is traced to a hollow in a tree—the daytime sleeping quarters of a black and white Striped Possum. Sometime after dark the possum wakes up, grooms himself and then leaves his hollow for the night's feeding. He is a most striking marsupial and unlike any of the other possums. As he comes out of his hole he rushes along a branch then stops suddenly and slowly curves his long bushy tail over his back—then a quick flick of the white tail tip and he disappears into the night. His actions are quick and his temperament excitable; he is of a lanky, slim build. All these are un-possum-like characteristics. Most possums are placid, heavily built animals with an inclination to sit and stare for long periods.

But the Striped Possum is not still for a moment; he leaps and sprints among the branches pausing briefly to nibble at a fruit here, a leaf there. Then he finds a dead, decaying tree riddled with the tunnels of insect larvae. First the possum runs about sniffing all over the dead wood and finally settles down to a particular spot. He sniffs at the entrance to a small tunnel in the decayed trunk and in a series of rapid, excited actions sets to work. His sense of smell has told him an edible insect lives at the end of the tunnel. Immediately the sharp teeth rip into the soft wood— but the tunnel is deep and winds through the old tree trunk. Quickly the elongated, slender fourth finger is inserted in lightning quick stabs. The depth and direction of the tunnel thus established, another rip with the teeth and a beetle larva lies exposed, is grabbed and eaten while the possum hangs upside down, suspended only by his hindfeet. He never uses his tail when climbing but holds it elegantly upright. The complete operation took only a few seconds. Eventually the whole tree may be torn apart—the cracking and splintering of the wood resounding through the quiet of the night as the Striped Possum feeds on cockroaches, beetles, millipedes and insect larvae.

The two species of Cuscus, the Brown and the Spotted, like the Striped Possum, have a strong scent, a musky odour in their case, but there is no further resemblance. Cuscuses are typical possums, and the largest and strongest of all. They have spent the day rolled up, a ball of fur in a secluded clump of dense vegetation or on occasions a hollow tree. Large, round faced, round bodied, they spend the night ponderously moving through the tree tops. Slowly and placidly they pull leaves and fruits off the trees to eat. Often they hang upside down from their bare, rasp-like tail and their hindfeet while reaching out with the front feet for a particularly delectable young leaf or ripe fig. Their rounded heads with the ears completely hidden in the fur and the yellow bare face are very monkey-like in appearance. This has led, no doubt, to the frequent but erroneous reports of monkeys from the rainforests of Cape York Peninsula.

The placid, slow witted appearance of the cuscus is misleading to some degree. When he is threatened by an enemy, the Amethyst Python for instance, the cuscus in his panic puts on a remarkable and unexpected burst of speed. If cornered he barks and snarls and slashes at his adversary with his sharp front claws. At close quarters he bites savagely and both teeth and claws can inflict serious wounds. Yet these weapons are seldom effective against the python. He too seems slow at first as he moves through the trees or along the ground, or lies motionless in ambush, but when he strikes, his coils are around his victim so quickly and so tightly that it can neither bite nor scratch. This of course is the only way the python can survive for he attacks mostly flying foxes, possums and small wallabies, all of which have the teeth and the claws that could kill a python. From the scars on some of the large pythons, they must sometimes misjudge their strikes and give a possum or flying fox enough room to counter-attack.

From high in the trees comes the sound of strong teeth gnawing and cracking a hard woody substance, a different sound from the Striped Possum's splintering of soft decayed wood. A Giant Tree or White-tailed Rat is feeding on the nuts of a Black Walnut Tree. No other native animal has teeth large enough and strong enough to crack these extremely hard seeds. The tree rat is not a marsupial, but a true rodent, the largest of the forty to fifty species native to Australia. His most characteristic features are his long bare tail, the first half dark brown, the other white, and his great size for a rat—about the size of a rabbit. This Giant Tree Rat will eat practically anything and will go anywhere to get it. On the forest floor he fossicks for insects and fallen fruit; along the creek bank he catches frogs; with his large pink feet and gripping tail he moves easily through the trees where he catches small birds and steals their eggs and young and looks for fruit. His nose is ever active and nothing is safe from his great powerful slashing and gnawing teeth.

Another tree rat, the small and gentle *Melomys* about half the size of a house rat, also lives in the rainforests. Superficially he looks like the marsupial mouse but there are some striking differences. The marsupial has a pointed snout and rows of tiny needle-sharp teeth ideal for his insect diet. *Melomys* on the other hand has a typical rodent head—a blunt chunky snout with a set of large gnawing incisors for his predominantly vegetable diet. *Melomys* also has a longer tail which is hairless and shiny and used in climbing. The marsupial mouse never uses his shorter hairy tail to grip a branch or leaf. Further, the marsupial mouse is all nervous energy, darting and leaping in quick jerky actions: *Melomys* walks and runs in fluid continuous motions. This small tree rat with his short but dense soft red-brown fur lives mainly on the ground and small shrubs where he feeds on fruits and young shoots and leaves, bark and an occasional insect. In disposition he is one of the gentlest of all animals, rarely biting or scratching even when cornered—a sharp contrast to the aggressive, bullying Giant Tree Rat. Both rodents are common in the rainforests, much more so than any of the marsupials, yet they are rarely seen. This is because they are shyer and generally more aware of danger. At the mere suggestion of a suspicious noise or scent they rush silently out of sight.

The comparative rarity of the marsupials, the shyness and suspicion of the rodents, the immobility and quiet stealth of the insect hunters all give the impression of an empty, even deserted forest at night, an impression

A Striped Possum stops to investigate a hole in a rotting log. The elongated fourth finger is used to probe for insects behind bark and in tunnels bored in wood

TOP: With quick stabbing movements of the extra-long finger the possum ascertains if an insect, usually a beetle or wood cockroach, lives in the hole

MIDDLE: If an insect is detected, the rotten wood is ripped open with the teeth

BELOW: The freshly caught prey is soon devoured. The whole sequence of events is executed in a series of lightning quick movements

partly erased by the noisy flying foxes. To discover the full spectrum of animal life, an observer must learn to interpret every little noise and examine closely every tree and every square foot of forest floor.

Well before first light, the Striped Possum has returned to his hollow, the cuscus is rolled up in sleep, the Atlas Moth clings motionless to a tree trunk, tree rats are in a hollow or small cavity between some rocks, the tree frogs squat low on a large leaf. The day animals have not yet stirred. Only the Red-legged Pademelon, a small wallaby, enjoys this time of the day. This is the time of their greatest activity, when they wrestle with each other, when the joeys leave their mothers' pouches and frolic around them; until the sun is above the horizon even the serious business of eating is momentarily forgotten. As it becomes light, some of the pademelons move to a small clearing or to the edge of the forest ready to soak up the first rays of the sun. The rich chestnut colour of their flanks and glossy grey and black of their backs shines in the bright light. They sit bolt upright, their broad triangular ears pricked up, their pink noses constantly twitching, on the alert for danger. Soon the sun becomes too hot. With heads bent low, tiny front feet tucked right under, the small wallabies bound in short hops back to the cool of the forest.

THIS HAS BEEN a typical night in the monsoon forests of Cape York Peninsula. Of the animals mentioned only two, the cuscuses, are unique to the area. All the others occur in rainforests to the south. These animals are comparatively rare on the cooler uplands where the mammals have thicker pelts and are certainly more characteristic of the lowland rainforests, but south of Cooktown there is now very little rainforest of this kind left.

The lowlands between Cooktown and Townsville are noteworthy for their rainforests which constitute the most diverse and complex plant community in the whole of Australia. The conditions of the rich, well drained basalt soils, rainfall of over a hundred inches per year and a constantly warm temperature are the optimum for plant growth. The result is a vegetation pattern where plant species are the most numerous and varied per unit area, where the relations between them and the equally rich fauna are the most complex, where the vines are the densest and the epiphytes occur in the greatest variety of forms.

It is the habitat for many unique day animals.

THESE DAY ANIMALS begin to stir themselves at first light, when their nocturnal counterparts are already in their shelters and pademelons play and wrestle. It is the beginning of a day late in November when bird

An adult Cassowary in the background, with two
well-grown chicks photographed in a rainforest gully

activity is at its peak. Birds are busy courting, nest building or rearing young. At sunrise this is manifested in song and display. The powerful clear voices of the Rufous Thrushes ring through the air almost drowning out the more sedate 'pree-pree' of the Spectacled Flycatchers. Other flycatchers and robins also join in with their subdued songs. There is a constant undertone of 'coos', 'ooms' and 'hoos' of the numerous pigeons.

A scratchy penetrating 'yah' startling in its suddenness announces that a male Queen Victoria Rifle Bird has arrived on one of his display perches, which usually is the top of a dead tree. The male is a velvet jet black. The iridescent green on his head, throat and tail sparkles in the first rays of the sun. With beak wide open, yellow colour flashing from the inside of his throat, he screeches another challenging 'yah'. A female in a plain flecked red-brown plumage is attracted by his call and lands nearby. The male launches into his display. He spreads his wings and rocks gently from side to side now clapping his wings together in front of him, now spreading them wide. The female flies to his perch but lands some distance away. Excitement mounts and the male hangs upside down, tail fanned, wings spread, from his perch. In a series of hops the female moves towards her prospective mate. In an instant he is upright again, his head with the scimitar beak held high, chest gleaming in the light and wings still spread. The female moves closer until she is encircled by the male's wings. He taps her gently first with one wing then the other. Suddenly the female flies away and the display is over. The male shakes himself, utters another 'yah' and also flies off into the forest, his plumage rustling like heavy silk.

As the morning progresses, song and display lessen; it is time for feeding. The fruit trees are filled with pigeons, parrots and Shining Starlings. There is a constant twitter of the birds in the tree tops and a constant patter of falling fruit on the ground. Lower down in the forest flycatchers, honeyeaters, thrushes and robins swoop and dive on insects. Jungle Fowl, whipbirds and pittas scratch amongst the leaves for snails and centipedes.

Noisiest and busiest of this great number of birds are the Shining Starlings. They came to these rainforests from New Guinea back in August and ever since have been busy at their nesting trees. Shining Starlings construct their nesting colonies in a tall tree projecting above the general canopy, the same one year in year out. Immediately upon arrival the starlings start on their bulky nests in a state of feverish excitement. Each pair selects a spot to build and for the first two days bring only a few straws or vine tendrils, most of their time being spent in singing and bickering for positions. But once the position has been decided, nest building begins in earnest. The birds fly off singly in search of their favourite nesting material, a strong woody tendril of a particular vine. As they arrive with the precious material at the partly completed nest they are met by a loud chattering call and greeting display from their mates. For a while the birds are beak to beak; their large red eyes blaze with excitement; metallic purple, green and gold reflections glint from their feathers in the sunshine; their hackles blow in the breeze; their wings shake like those of young birds begging for food. When the excitement abates the bird winds the nesting material round and round a branch. At this time of the year when they begin their nesting cycles the starlings look their best. From close up it seems as if each individual feather were dusted with gold. A little later in the season they have already lost some of their lustre.

At times during the exciting early days a sudden frenzy will seize the colony. As if at a sudden signal all the birds are silent and, after a short pause, simultaneously leave the tree and hurtle in a tight formation amongst the trunks and branches of the surrounding forests. Just as suddenly they return and continue to chatter and build their nests. There is a great deal of stealing of nesting material; if one pair neglects to guard the partly built nest they will find it ransacked on return.

Sometimes a bird will bring a long trailing piece of nesting material, perhaps four to five feet long. Immediately he is tackled by other starlings trying to wrest at least some of it from their enterprising neighbour. This kind of squabble has sometimes been misinterpreted as co-operation, for superficially it looks as though a number of birds are together carrying a particularly difficult piece of material. But actually they are fighting over it. On arrival at the nest, several birds often become so incensed that they become locked together. Screaming and pecking they flutter to the ground. At other times twenty or thirty starlings may suddenly turn their frenzy on one unfortunate pair of birds and in a chattering flapping horde pull their laboriously built nest to pieces.

In spite of everything nests are completed and by the end of August forty to fifty of the large globular nests are complete. More and more are added as the season progresses; we are viewing it in November and the tree has about 300 nests; the branches of the tree are bent by their great weight. Underneath the tree there is a tangle of broken twigs and old nests, the aftermath of an earlier catastrophe when the weight of too many nests broke the support. A sprinkling of pale blue eggshells on the ground means that most nests contain young. To feed this new generation—flight after flight of chattering starlings comes and goes all day, ferrying between feeding area and the nests. The starlings favour fruit but will eat almost anything. A flowering Black Bean Tree is full of the noisy starlings gathering nectar from the large orange blossoms, their shining metallic coloured heads dulled with orange pollen. They also eat insects which are attracted to the nectar and will try to eat anything new. When they find a fruit they have never eaten before they take one, swallow it, then bring it up again. Three or four times the fruit goes down and is brought up. Finally it is either discarded or every fruit within reach is quickly eaten.

Nesting in large noisy colonies with no attempt at concealment of the nests means that the starlings frequently suffer at the hands of predators. The birds often fly around chattering helplessly as a tree snake or climbing goanna imperturbably moves from nest to nest robbing it of young or eggs. A Grey Goshawk often takes possession of the nest-tree while the whole colony scolds him from the leafy protection of a neighbouring tree. The Goshawk is not after the young—he attacks the adult starlings.

Torres Strait Pigeons—majestic white birds—are also regular migrants and came from New Guinea at about the same time as the starlings. They arrive in the lowland rainforests each morning to eat fruit, departing again in the evenings to their nesting grounds on off-shore islands. Their story is in a later chapter.

A third migrant between these lowlands and New Guinea is the White-tailed Kingfisher. These kingfishers are always late comers and have only just arrived. They waste no time in their nesting preparations. Within a few days of his arrival the male calls with a series of insistent notes from various low perches near the ground in his territory. As he flies from one perch to another, his red beak glints in the dapples of sunlight, his blue wings spread in flight uncover a white rump; the ten-inch tail feathers stream behind, scintillating against the subdued browns and greens of the forest litter and shrubs. As he lands he flicks his long tail a few times till he is balanced, then he resumes his call. For hour upon hour he does the rounds of his territory, and continues day after day till he has wooed his mate. She is slightly smaller with a shorter tail but her colours are equally brilliant.

When a mate is found the nest is excavated out of a termite mound. These conical mounds are about two feet high and are built on the ground. Using their heavy red beaks the kingfishers first dig a six-inch long tunnel in the cardboard-like substance of the mound. Next a nesting chamber six to seven inches in diameter is excavated. No lining is put in the chamber; the three to four white lustrous eggs are laid straight on the floor. The termites in the meantime have sealed off the galleries the kingfishers exposed. It will be early January by the time the young hatch.

The female who does most of the incubating makes most trips to the nest to feed the young. Her long tail feathers become frayed and bent from long periods in the small nesting chamber but the male is still as brilliant as ever. He does catch worms, insects, snails and spiders for the young and even feeds the young himself, but sometimes he passes the food on to the female and lets her make the trip to the nest.

Many birds have nest hygiene of some kind but not the kingfishers—droppings and bits of food accumulate in the nest chamber. On a hot humid day the nest can be smelt some distance away. A partial and on occasions efficient nest hygiene is effected by the larvae of a fly which feed on the droppings.

At the end of January the young leave their smelly nests and by early April are ready to make their first trip to New Guinea. The termites will now re-occupy the cavity and by the next November the kingfishers will have to dig out new holes for their nests. As we shall see later, various kinds of predators take a heavy toll of birds' eggs and young but only a few of these affect the White-tailed Kingfisher in the safety of its termite mound. Their breeding success is very high. Yet their numbers are limited by another factor, the nesting site. Suitable termite mounds are comparatively rare in the lowland rainforests and in some localities there are more pairs of birds than termite mounds. The kingfishers will not nest in any other situation, such as a tree hollow, or move to the more extensive upland rainforests. Some birds must forego nesting.

As the morning warms, most bird songs taper off to an occasional call—only the pigeons continue in full chorus. All around may be heard the 'coos' and 'ooms' of the Green-winged and Purple-crowned Pigeons. These calls provide a continuous undertone for the strange 'bock-bock-cahooo' of the Wompoo Pigeons—the first two notes are a gobbling sound like a turkey's, followed by the booming 'cahooo'. Torres Strait Pigeons add their strong 'roo-cahoo'. The pigeon calls boom through the forests all day long, yet from the ground the birds, except for the terrestrial Green-winged Pigeon, are difficult to see in spite of their brilliant plumage. The small Purple-crowned Pigeon, besides the brightly coloured cap his name suggests, has patches of pink, yellow and grey. His wings and tail are an intense green and he has bright yellow eyes. The Wompoo, one of our largest pigeons, much larger than the Purple-crowned species, is equally brilliant. His head is a pearly-grey, his wings and tail green; the underside is purple and yellow. The main reasons for the difficulty in seeing them are their shy quiet movements high in the trees and their habit of staying motionless when suspicious of sounds or movement. November is the height of their breeding season and those pigeons which are not busy calling are either sitting on the nest or gathering food for young. The nests are ridiculously flimsy structures. Both the Purple-crowned and Wompoo Pigeons do no more than put a handful of sticks roughly together. On this platform their single white egg rests precariously and later the young spends the first month of his life on it. The Green-winged Pigeon builds a more substantial platform for its two eggs.

The feeding of the flying foxes at night, of the pigeons and starlings during the day, the action of the wind and the natural ripening process, send a constant rain of fruit to the ground. In places it may be blue with quondongs or red or yellow with innumerable other kinds of fruit. These fallen fruit are the major food item of the rainforest's largest creature, the Cassowary.

Black feathered and flightless, the stocky giant strides through the forest in search of food. He eats enormous quantities of fruits of which he seems to digest very little. In areas where Cassowaries are common their characteristic piles of droppings are everywhere. Even old droppings are immediately recognisable since in many the undigested seeds of the fruits have germinated and show as small bunches of green leaves. In spite of their size and the brilliant blue and red colours of their bare head, neck and wattles, Cassowaries are also surprisingly difficult to see in the forest. More often they are heard. To people moving quietly through the forest the presence of these tall birds can evoke frightening feelings. They can be heard walking and quietly booming and rumbling, seemingly only a few yards away, usually behind, and no matter how hard one tries they are impossible to see.

The five-foot-tall, heavy birds can be quite dangerous and are known to attack with hard, straight kicks of the long sharp nails on the inside toe when defending their eggs or young. In spite of their bulk of 120 pounds or more and flightlessness they can run and manoeuvre with great speed even in the densest, thorniest vegetation. When they run they stretch their neck forward and slightly downward. The strong hard feet move also forward but upwards so that the toes are right under the chin. In this way the densest undergrowth is crashed downwards with the feet and pushed upwards by the hard, horny helmet on top of the head and can be penetrated by the bird with comparative speed. In November the Cassowary has young, as many as five, which have already grown out of their brown and cream striped, downy stage and are now feathered in a glossy chestnut brown. The pea green eggs were laid on a bed of dry leaves back in July.

Like the Cassowary, the Jungle Fowl is terrestrial and more often heard than seen. Its trumpeting call is one of the most characteristic of the rain-forest and may be heard anytime—even during the night. The Jungle Fowl can fly though it does so infrequently and awkwardly. Despite its comparatively small size, Jungle Fowl build the largest structures made by birds. These structures are huge mounds of soil and decaying ground litter as high as fifteen feet and up to forty feet in diameter. Not all the mounds are as large as this and it takes a number of seasons for the birds to build one of this size. The Jungle Fowl constructs the mound entirely by scraping and scratching with his huge orange feet.

The mound is used as an incubator for the bird's eggs; the heat for in-cubation is generated by the decaying organic matter. During November when thunderstorms bring heavy rains the bird is constantly in atten-dance carefully regulating the heat. Every few days when conditions are suitable the birds dig a hole eighteen inches to three feet deep in which the female then lays an egg. Over thirty eggs may be deposited in the mound during a season.

Pigeons, Cassowaries, Jungle Fowl—all shy birds that are usually only sighted when surprised—give an air of mystery and majesty to the forests. The smaller birds, the robins, flycatchers and warblers, fearless and living in the shrubs near the ground add to the forests the quality of charm.

A trilling 'pree-pree' and a Spectacled Flycatcher, skeleton leaf in his beak, flies to his partly completed nest. The outside, decorated with living green moss is already completed. The lining is now put in. As the fly-catcher arrives he gives the leaf to his mate who carefully places it under herself then sits in the nest and wriggles from side to side, readjusts the leaf, wriggles some more till everything seems to be to her satisfaction. Meanwhile her partner has returned with more nesting material—a spider's cocoon which he weaves amongst the moss on the outside of the nest. The two birds, in identical plumage of orange, black and grey build their nest only about eight feet above the ground, neatly fitted in the fork of a small tree.

A pair of Lesser Lewin Honeyeaters chase each other wildly and noisily through the branches of a tree. A tiny green and yellow bird flies by, trailing a long piece of dry grass. It is a female Black-throated Warbler flying to her almost finished nest suspended from a twig—and as is characteristic—right beside the nest of a kind of large and aggressive wasp. From its neat, bark decorated nest set amongst the spines and prickles of a lawyer vine, a Pale Yellow Robin tilts her head and peers down at a small lizard running amongst the dead leaves on the ground.

Only about a foot above the ground, suspended in a clump of ferns hangs the nest of a pair of Lovely Wrens—the only ones of the uniquely

Australian fairy wrens to live in the rainforest. The males of the fairy wrens are extremely colourful in shining blue, black or red patterns, but the females are a dull brown—except the female Lovely Wren. Compared with the brilliance of the male her colours are subdued, but the delicate blues of her head and tail could never be considered dull.

The Lovely Wrens have two well grown young in the nest which keep up a constant, penetrating, sibilant call. The parents are never far away. Within a radius of perhaps fifty yards they search every patch of moss, every fern and every leaf and catch the small insects that abound there. At intervals of a few minutes one of the parents returns with a small grasshopper, moth or other insect. The parents take turns in feeding the constantly hungry young. One will fly to and fro with food for the young for about twenty minutes while the other preens, feeds itself or just rests—then the roles are reversed. At times both birds will arrive at the nest together making a tiny spot of intense colour on the sombre forest floor.

Moths, cockroaches, cicadas, hoppers, beetles, flies and countless other invertebrates, large and small, sustain not only birds but a great many spiders and lizards as well. Spiders snare their victims in webs—some webs so large that they are spanned with golden threads between trees, others so small that they span only a small cavity in a tree trunk.

Large, shiny skinks slither from their hiding places in hollow fallen logs to catch ground insects, snails and centipedes. Tiny brown skinks with splashes of orange, yellow and blue scuttle amongst the leaves, running after ants and minute beetles. Spotted yellow and grey goannas walk over the forest floor with swinging steps feeling with their pink forked tongues for insects under leaves and in hollows. Immobile, the green Rainforest Dragon clings to a tree trunk. His large red-brown eyes are ever watchful. If an insect walks or flies within range, the lizard darts out his sticky tongue and swallows its prey. Large prey is first crunched with sharp teeth. Like so many dragons, the Rainforest Dragon when threatened by a predator or otherwise frightened often stands his ground hissing and puffing in a spectacular display of bluff which is frequently successful.

The first part of the Rainforest Dragon's display is to inflate himself as much as he can, trying to appear larger than he really is. If this does not impress an attacker he inflates his brilliant yellow throat as well. When fully provoked he will raise himself on his feet, open his wide mouth showing a surprisingly large expanse of pink and a row of sharp triangular teeth. Crest with bluish 'teeth' erect, yellow throat inflated and mouth wide open, the fifteen-inch lizard does indeed take on a terrifying aspect that makes even the ruthless Black Butcherbird think twice about driving home his lightning attacks.

But at this time of the year, the breeding season, lizards are comparatively safe from the attacks of Black Butcherbirds and to some extent from their other enemies, snakes and rats. These predators now feast mainly on the eggs and nestlings of birds. It is very difficult to assess just how many they do take and just which animals take the heaviest toll. But a season spent in the lowland rainforest has shown that in places, as many as 80 per cent of eggs laid never result in fledgling young, and that many of the young do not live to leave the nest. There is little doubt that the Black Butcherbird follows other birds around till they lead him unwittingly to their nest. When he discovers it he pounces and in one quick movement may take as many as two young at a time from the nest. Butcherbirds do not only attack the nests of small birds such as honeyeaters and flycatchers, but also pigeons and catbirds which are larger than themselves. Nor do they confine their predation to eggs and nestlings. Adult birds ferrying to and fro from their nest become weary and at times careless. Sometimes they are swooped upon by the butcherbird and killed instantly, but more often the victims are chased from tree to tree till they are too exhausted to resist attack. Under the perch used for dismembering prey by one pair of butcherbirds, the remains of two White-tailed Kingfishers and one Lesser Lewin Honeyeater were found, as well as those of snakes and lizards. More than once people have rescued exhausted birds from the relentless pursuit of Black Butcherbirds.

In the afternoon dark clouds build up around the distant mountain ranges and an occasional rumble is heard in the rainforest. Amongst the trees the stillness and humidity increase. The sun becomes hidden by the heavy turbulent clouds and the forest grows dark. The birds are silent and sit tightly on their nests. A soft breeze springs up followed by a distant roar that is more constant than the now deafening thunder overhead— the sound of the approaching rain and gale. The thunderstorm breaks overhead. The wind and rain rip and tear at the upper trees. Whole branches are snapped off and crash to the ground. Vines and twigs are whipped about.

As suddenly as it began the storm moves on and all is quiet. The late afternoon sun slants its last rays through the wet leaves. Birds shake the water droplets from their feathers and begin their evening chorus. Lizards lick water drops from the leaves. Some birds, which built high in the trees, such as the Wompoo Pigeon, have had their nests blown down. A honeyeater not far away still has its nest contents intact: it has a deep well-made structure that can withstand all but the very heaviest of storms. A Pied Flycatcher that had built higher than usual has had its nest overturned, but the well-grown young cling determinedly to the remains and will survive. Soon all is tranquil and peaceful again. Now the skinks hide under logs and stones, Rainforest Dragons flatten out on the tree trunks and goannas climb into hollow trees. Birds settle down on their nests or perch on a leafy twig. But still they are not safe. Brown Tree Snakes or White-tailed Rats will hunt them during the night.

But enough birds survive and rear young for another generation to carry on next year.

DAYTIME IN THE MONSOON FORESTS of Cape York Peninsula is a very different experience. The forests themselves are much less luxuriant with fewer vines and practically no epiphytes. Many of the flowering trees such as a *Eugenia* with pink blossoms or a sweet scented species of *Horsfieldia* are not seen in the rainforests south of Cooktown. In November, just before the season's first thunderstorms, insects are comparatively scarce, but here too many kinds are different from those encountered further south.

But the differences are really driven home when one considers the numerous kinds of birds. A visitor to these monsoon forests will recognise some old friends from the south such as the Spectacled Flycatcher, the White-tailed Kingfisher, the Wompoo Pigeon and other pigeons. Yet the whole atmosphere created by the abundance of the birds makes one feel almost in another country. Part of this lies in the fact that the undertone of sounds is not the cooing of pigeons but the much less gentle, often raucous babble of parrots and cockatoos.

The pale-eyed Red-cheeked Parrots scream from the tree tops; the large Eclectus Parrots cry harshly as they fly over. Another call of these Eclectus, the male of which is green with trimmings of red and blue, the female bright red and blue, is a metallic 'clang'. White Cockatoos, though found throughout Australia, seem particularly numerous and noisy. Birds in flocks of twenty to thirty yell at each other, crests erect, in unbelievably loud voices. The black Palm Cockatoo adds his soft whistle to this chorus. Not all the parrots are large; one of the smallest and most attractive of them flies in small groups amongst the trees. These are the Fig Parrots. The subspecies, *Opopsitta diophthalma marshalli*, living in these monsoon forests is brilliant green, the male with a bright red face while the female's is a pale blue. They are much more common, or perhaps more readily observed than the subspecies *Opopsitta diophthalma macleayana*, from the Townsville-Cooktown area. Favourite food of these five-inch birds is unripe figs which ooze a sticky white sap as they are bitten into. Now and again the parrots must pause to wipe their beaks clean.

Other new birds that the visitor might encounter are the Yellow-billed Kingfisher, the Manucode, the Magnificent Rifle Bird, the Blue-breasted Pitta, the Pearly Flycatcher, and a few others.

Some birds can be recognised as being very similar to those seen in the more luxuriant rainforest but on close examination there are differences in detail. A bird excitedly hopping over a tree trunk could at first be taken to be a Pied Flycatcher but lacks this bird's black band across the breast. It is in fact the Frill-necked Flycatcher. Another bird, clinging to the side of a tree, looks like a Pale Yellow Robin from the southern lowlands except for its clownish white face, and it turns out to be the White-faced Robin which in spite of its appearance retains its robin-like gravity.

The birds and many of the other animals which in Australia are restricted to the monsoon forests of Cape York Peninsula also occur in New Guinea. It is this New Guinea element of the wildlife that makes the area appear exotic to the visitor accustomed to the Australian bush. Yet there are enough species, purely Australian in distribution, to make him feel at home.

The Banded Gecko always carries its white tail elegantly arched over its back. It is ten inches long and one of the largest of our geckoes

5 On the Edge of Tropical Rainforest

WHEREVER TWO KINDS of habitat meet, a world exists that has some elements of each and as a consequence has a greater variety of species than either habitat has by itself. This variety is further enriched by plants and animals which specialise and live only on these border areas (called eco- tones by ecologists). But for the naturalist the rainforest edge is even more rewarding than other ecotones for here many animals, particularly birds and insects which usually skim and flutter out of sight over the forest's canopy, come down to lower levels and are more readily observed.

The precise make-up of species on the edge of the rainforest depends on which kind of habitat it adjoins; whether it is a eucalypt, paperbark or mangrove forest—a river, beach or lake, or perhaps an artificial clearing such as a road or a farm. The rainforest component along the ecotone is much the same anywhere and varies substantially only between the up- lands and the lowlands. Whether a White-throated Honeyeater comes to drink from the flowers of a rainforest vine or a Red-backed Sea-eagle roosts in a giant rainforest tree depends on whether eucalypt woodland or mangroves adjoin the rainforest.

This chapter deals only with the rainforest and specialist species of the ecotone.

The edge of the rainforest is a lively, bright and sunny place. For even though the tropics have a great amount of rainfall it is mostly in showers with intermittent periods of hot sunshine. These are ideal conditions for rapid plant growth particularly of vines which grow prolifically, massing together into a sheer wall of vegetation. As a result of the hothouse con- ditions and the plentiful supply of lush plants, insects are more prolific here than in any other habitat and directly contribute much of the bright colours. Indirectly they contribute even more for they attract many birds. The Eastern Spinebill hovers around the foliage picking off insects to feed its young high in a tree. Flycatchers and wrens of many species flit through the undergrowth. But liveliest of the animals along the rain- forest edge is a specialist, the brilliant Yellow-breasted Sunbird.

The sunbird has a bill and tongue specially adapted to obtain nectar from flowers and is often seen hovering in front of them, dipping deep with its beak. The three-and-three-quarter-inch bird has a strongly curved beak about a quarter of its own length, which it uses equally deftly for prising small invertebrates from the undersides of leaves and out of flowers; in its search the bird swings upside down from the vegetation. Spiders are another favourite food and the bird, hovering in front of the web, neatly picks them out. Nest building is also accomplished with the multi-purpose beak. The nest is built by the female alone. She makes a long structure, sometimes as long as two feet, though usually only half this length. It is made of grasses, slivers of bark and the furry fibre of palms and other plants. These are suspended from a vine or twig with spider web. Spider's silk is also used to hold the whole structure together and later to attach bark flakes and dried acacia flowers to the outside. The nesting chamber is built in the lower half of the nest and is lined with soft feathers. The female often builds a rough hood over the entrance but when she sits on the nest, incubating the eggs, her long beak projects even beyond the awning.

While the female is busy building, incubating and rearing young, the male pugnaciously defends his territory from the intrusions of other sunbirds. Only very occasionally does he come to the nest to feed the young. He never incubates the eggs. Sunbirds which live only along the lowland rainforest edge, can be seen at all times during the day darting about after insects, swinging from leaves, hovering in front of spider webs or chasing each other. Their brilliant yellow undersides and the male's metallic blue throat flash amongst the foliage. The twittering songs and call notes are ever present.

Another song frequent along the rainforest edge comes from another specialist, the male Yellow Figbird. Figbirds live in small colonies of twenty to thirty birds which nest together in trees standing just outside the rainforest while they forage for figs, berries of the White Cedar and other fruit inside it. But they never penetrate far into the dark forest. At first light the male figbirds congregate in a dead or sparsely leafed tree and sing. Early in the nesting season the male's plumage is brilliant. His yellow breast shines in the light, his glossy black cap sparkles, while in the excitement of courtship and song the bare skin around his eyes glows a bright red. But as the season wears on, the bird loses some of his lustre, for unlike the sunbird, the male figbird takes his full share of the incubation of the eggs and the rearing of the young. The males work so hard at this that their feathers become frayed and often stained with the fruit they bring to the young; their eyepatches fade to a dull red, though they can still flare into brilliant colour at times of excitement.

In the apparent calm of the forest edge there seems to be peace in the warm sunshine. Insects buzz and flutter apparently in sheer contentment. But the reality is very different—no insect moves without some definite inflexible purpose, and there is unceasing warfare between them. The total picture of all this vast purposeful activity is one of interdependence in complex chains, each link affecting directly or indirectly all others. The chain is a balanced whole, but break one link and the whole structure may collapse or show serious aberrations that may result in an explosion of one species into pest proportions. The insect links in the chains are intricately bound up with the plants but the variety and extent of the inter-relationships are still imperfectly understood.

In this chapter we cannot look at all the groups involved but let us examine just one of them, the butterflies. Butterflies, probably the most colourful and romantic of insects, are very characteristic of the edge of the tropical rainforests where almost three-quarters of the Australian species can be seen. There are at least two reasons for their preference for this ecotone. Firstly the foodplants of the caterpillars are mostly vines, mistletoes and small ground plants which abound here. The Birdwing, Swordtail, Cruiser, Lacewing, Glasswing, Crows and many others have larvae which feed on species of vines most prolific along the rainforest edge. Many triangles, swallowtails, skippers and blues feed on shrubs and trees of the forest margin. Mistletoes parasitise trees in both rainforest and open woodland but are most prolific where the two meet, and constitute the food for caterpillars of the various species of jezabel.

The second reason for the variety of butterflies is the attraction of an introduced plant, *Lantana camara*, which has run wild and seems particularly suited to margins of rainforest. Lantana is originally a native of Central and South America but was introduced to Australia from Europe as a garden plant. Now it completely dominates the areas around rainforests in dense scrambling, prickly masses. These masses are nearly always covered with pink or red and yellow flowers and it is the flowers which attract the nectar loving butterflies.

Butterflies spend the night hanging from the undersides of leaves with their wings closed. At the morning's first touch of sunshine they crawl to the upperside of the leaves and spread their wings to absorb some of the early warmth. Dew is still on the foliage when they fly off to suck nectar from the lantana flowers.

Early morning at a lantana patch is a scene of dazzling colour. Skippers in flight too fast for the eye to follow dart from one flower to another, land momentarily and streak off again in a whirl of dark blue or green. Spotted Triangles black with spots of lime green on the upperside, and pale green and pink on their undersides, also have a fast erratic flight and hover in front of the flowers to suck nectar. Though these butterflies are brightly coloured and almost three inches across, their fast flight and colour pattern, like sundappled foliage, make them almost invisible. The orange and brown Cruiser too is quick on the wing but it drinks nectar more leisurely. He lands and, with wings spread, methodically probes each flower in the cluster with his long tongue. The spectacular Red Lacewing feeds in the same manner but usually on the highest flowers and when finished with one cluster sails high into the air and lands on another at the opposite end of the lantana patch. The lacewing can take on many different colours as it rests, wings spread, in the brilliant sun. Depending on the direction of the light the wings may appear a delicate rose pink or intense scarlet. The border round the red may appear black or a deep velvet blue. Underneath, the wings are a mottled brown. When the butterfly closes its wings it resembles a dead shrivelled leaf and becomes difficult to see.

Most common of the butterflies are the various species of jezabels, *Delias*. The uppersides of their wings are white and as they flutter amongst leaves and flowers they appear as white flakes drifting on the breeze. But the undersides of their wings have various patterns of red and yellow, or red, yellow and black. Jezabels have a slow flight and settle on the flowers with folded wings, displaying their vivid under-patterns.

The pink lantana flowers attract butterflies from some distance and now and again patches of brilliant blue swoop down from the dark green tree tops. These are the Ulysses large butterflies with a wingspan of four to five inches. Their uppersides are an iridescent blue which changes in intensity with the direction of the light. The undersides are black with touches of brown. Each hindwing terminates in a black, spatulate tail and is scalloped with a fine white line. Lantana flowers grow on only a thin stalk which cannot support the added weight of a Ulysses Butterfly drinking nectar. So when the butterfly comes to a flower cluster it lightly touches down with its long black legs and keeps its front wings beating to stay in position. The beating wings flash black then blue in the sun as the butterfly probes flower after flower with his inches long tongue. When not feeding the tongue is tightly coiled like a watch spring.

As the butterflies flutter and dart amongst the lantana bushes with little attempt at concealment they are remarkably immune from the attacks of insect hunting birds. There are several reasons for this, one of which we shall mention later on but it may be the butterflies' fast zig-zag flight, or perhaps that their scale covered wings are unappetising. They are not free from the predation of spiders. The smaller butterflies are caught by even smaller jumping and crab spiders lying in ambush amongst leaves and flowers. But the largest of the butterflies are snared by spiders, the kinds that spin orb-nets between the shrubs and trees. The habit of the butterflies to fly up and away after a visit to a flower and come steeply down again further on, instead of moving from flower to flower through the bushes may be an action to avoid the snares of these spiders. It is not always successful.

Largest of the orb-weavers is *Nephila maculata* which builds webs of tough, golden silk. The grey-bodied spider sits in the middle of her web, her long black legs with yellow dots on the joints spread wide, as much as seven inches at the widest part. Occasionally even the large and strong Ulysses flies into the huge web. As soon as the spider notices the first touch of the butterfly she rushes to the disturbed web, grabs the insect between her golden-orange palps and gives it a quick bite, injecting a poison at the same time. Then she spins more silk around her prey till all movement ceases. The spider's legs and body have become covered with pinpricks of blue colour, scales that have rubbed off the wings of the struggling Ulysses. The spider feeds ferociously, the insect's tough wing-bases crackle under the onslaught of the spider's fangs. In a few hours the meal is over, the butterfly's wings are discarded and float to the ground.

Largest of all the Australian butterflies is the Cairns Birdwing. The female is eight inches across, the male one and a half inches less. They feed in a similar manner to the Ulysses. If the lantana grows close to the cater-pillars' food plant the birdwings sometimes fly around the flowers in great numbers. When this happens, as always when males and females of this species come together, a courtship dance takes place. Most of the dance is performed by the male while the female flops on her huge wings from flower to flower. He hovers only an inch or so above her and follows wherever she goes—his brilliant yellow-green and black wings and yellow body glint as he passes through a shaft of sunlight. From time to time he flies higher and sails down in front of her with wings closed till eventually she takes some notice of him. All thoughts of feeding are for-gotten and the two hover in the air almost touching. Males are more numerous than the females and one brown female may have as many as four or five males flapping and diving around her.

The nuptial dance complete, male and female land on some leaves and mating takes place. Subsequently the female takes little interest in the males though these still hover around in attendance. She leaves the lantana and flutters around the edge of the rainforest flying around and inspecting all kinds of leaves. She stops only when she finds the leaves of a particular kind of vine, a vine of the genus *Aristolochia*. On this plant and

A pair of Shining Starlings have begun to build their nest. So far it consists of only a few straws and vine tendrils wound around a bran

Scrambling masses of the introduced shrub *Lantana camara* grow along most rainforest borders and attract butterflies in a kaleidoscope of colour and beating wings.
ABOVE LEFT: Male Birdwing in flight
ABOVE RIGHT: The Ulysses Butterfly has a wing span of $4\frac{1}{2}$ inches

LEFT: A male Leafwing Butterfly sitting with wings folded shows his brilliant underwing pattern
BELOW: The Red Lacewing spreads its wings in the sunlight

no other she will lay her eggs. When she has found the right plant she inspects every leaf, flying all around and through the foliage. Eventually she lightly touches down on one with her long black legs and with wings still hovering she quickly bends her abdomen and deposits an egg on the underside of the leaf. It takes only an instant and without missing a wing-beat she moves on. As she moves amongst the thick foliage only an occasional yellow wingspot, or the bright red patch on her thorax, is seen moving amongst the leaves.

The birdwing's egg when first laid is pale yellow but gradually darkens as the larva develops inside. The black larva emerges after about a week by eating its way out of the egg shell. It eats the entire shell before it begins to eat the leaves. In a matter of only three days the caterpillar has eaten so much that is has outgrown its skin—which stretches but does not grow with it. After a rest period the skin splits and the caterpillar emerges in a new, larger one. During the next eleven days the larva changes its skin three more times, by then it has become a large caterpillar about three inches long and a chocolate brown in colour and velvet in texture. Its head is shiny and darker brown with a white V in the front. There are four rows of dark brown soft spines along its body with a flash of orange towards each tip. When it has changed its skin for the fourth time the caterpillar continues to eat and grow for another five days. At the end of this period the caterpillar departs from its food plant and settles on the leaf or stem of another plant, any kind with leaves large and strong enough to support it.

During the next day it covers most of the chosen leaf, its stalk and the place where this leaf joins the stem with strands of black silk. It spins a thick pad towards the tip of the leaf then turns around and hooks the tip of its body into the silken pad. Next it spins a girdle, made up of many strands, around the middle of its body. Leaning back on this girdle and attached to the silken pad the caterpillar is now ready to pupate. By attaching its supporting leaf to the stem an extra precaution has been taken. Even if the leaf dies it will now not fall off. The caterpillar rests, its skin becomes shrivelled. After about twenty-four hours a remarkable change takes place—the caterpillar's brown skin splits and a green, soft pupa emerges. The larval skin splits along the entire back and the pupa wriggles out. After a short time the old skin is just a crumpled bit of tissue around the tip of the new pupa's abdomen. Supported only by the girdle the pupa now lifts itself completely out of the old larval skin and embeds its tip, which is studded with myriads of tiny hooks, into the previously spun silken pad. A few more twists of the pupa and the old larval skin falls to the ground; the hooks at the tip of the old skin are no longer driven into the silk by the caterpillar's weight and slip out. It is very important to get rid of the old skin, if the pupa does not it may become misshapen and eventually die. At this critical stage, when it has just emerged from the caterpillar, the pupa is very soft and vulnerable, a slight bump may kill it. The next day the pupa has hardened into a glossy wax textured object. It is pale brown with patches of bright yellow, broken up by black dots and lines on its back. In the front some parts of the adult butterfly are already faintly visible. The wings are neatly folded forward, the legs, antennae and proboscis tightly packed between them.

The birdwing remains in the pupal stage for three to four weeks. Apart from a vigorous wriggle when touched, the pupa never moves, but this external immobility does not mean it is in a resting stage. Inside the pupa irreversible changes and rearrangements of tremendous complication are taking place. What is in fact happening is that a brown, leaf-eating wormlike creature is changing into a green, yellow and black nectar-feeding, winged insect. Just how this takes place is not completely clear. To date it is known that all the complex changes are controlled by hormones. The caterpillar has within it two growth patterns, the first of which determines its course towards development as a mature caterpillar. At this period the second pattern is already present in the form of dormant 'buds' that will develop later during the pupal stage. The second pattern is kept constantly in check by hormones during larval stage. For instance, wings are present in the caterpillar as buds, but only in the pupal stage do they develop when they expand 60 times in area. So within the pupa tissues are rearranged to form new organisms; legs are changed from stumpy claws to long black thread-like structures, mouth-parts are changed from leaf-chewing jaws to a nectar sucking tube, the muscular system is transformed and wings, reproductive organs and antennae develop. In all these arrangements, directed by hormones, pupal cells develop and grow into new organs by feeding on the dying larval cells.

Towards the end of these complex rearrangements the butterfly is clearly visible within the pupa, even its colour can be seen. The waxy pupal skin now turns milky. Then with an audible crack the pupa breaks open. First the butterfly's antennae appear, then the legs reach for a grip and the butterfly walks out and hangs down from a branch or leaf. The wings are still mere stumps but the butterfly's whole body pulsates as it pumps fluid from its body into them, and in about ten minutes the wings have expanded to their full size. They are still limp and soft. During the next two hours they dry further and final perfections take place. When the butterfly first emerged the proboscis was straight and in two halves. These two halves are now hooked together to form a hollow tube and it is coiled. On a warm morning the butterfly flies off about two hours after emerging from the pupa. Flight is expert from the very first. The birdwing may live for several months.

The adult butterflies have relatively few predators. As larvae, however, they have many enemies. Some of these are birds. Against these the caterpillars have elaborate defences. The birdwing and related species can suddenly eject a brightly coloured, strong smelling, Y shaped prong from behind their heads. Other defences are behavioural. The caterpillars feed at night when they are difficult for birds to find. Another defence is camouflage, or they may be covered by toxic hairs. Many caterpillars, including those of the birdwing, feed on poisonous plants and they are then unpalatable to birds both as caterpillars and later as butterflies.

If birds and mammals were the only predators butterflies would soon multiply so rapidly that their caterpillars would devour all the available food in a short time. The butterflies' main enemies are other insects. Like most insects living on plants they have many other species living at their expense as predators and parasites. It is largely as the result of this constant and relentless struggle that an equilibrium between plants and insects exists. The plant's own defences seem of little effect, for even the most toxic plants are attacked. The White Nymph, a butterfly, has larvae which feed only on leaves of the very toxic Stinging Trees.

Many kinds of insect predators attack caterpillars; mud daubing wasps carry them off as food for their larvae. Other wasps and also bugs suck their body juices from them. But the parasites are the most devastating. There is a tremendous variety of them and they attack the eggs, caterpillars or pupae in a number of ways. The vast majority of parasites are Ichneumonid and Braconid wasps and Tachinid flies.

Caterpillars of moths and butterflies with perfect camouflage, a covering of toxic hairs or other elaborate defences against predatory birds are completely helpless against the devastating attacks of insect parasites. It seems fitting therefore that the main check on these parasites are other insects—Chalcid wasps. Some species parasitise the larvae of Ichneumonid wasps and Tachinid flies, to which they are attracted by the dead caterpillars.

The wonder is not that the Lepidoptera do not strip all vegetation bare, it is rather that they survive to maturity. But there are no excesses in nature—plant toxicity, voracious caterpillars, insectivorous birds, parasites and parasites on parasites and many other factors work together to give a balance. Such balanced communities, be they rainforest, pond or grassland, are always the result of many different forces working together. Only man regularly upsets this balance.

There are over 10,000 different species of Lepidoptera described from the whole of Australia. Of these only 357 are butterflies; all the others are moths. Over the years a substantial amount of knowledge has been accumulated about the butterflies. With relatively few exceptions little is known about the moths, particularly about the species from the tropical northeast where they are most numerous. Their life histories, food preferences, and parasitic relations are, for the vast majority, unknown.

Moths are nocturnal and after dusk the rainforest margins abound with them. A large number are very small, less than a half inch across. Tiny as they are these moths have a startling variety of shapes and patterns most of which are directed towards camouflage. Some look like flakes of bark or have their wings and legs arranged to resemble thin twigs. Others have a heavy thorax with a chopped off appearance and resemble broken branches. Or they may have wings of a most delicate green colour and when flattened on young green bark become difficult to detect. Some of these Micro-lepidoptera do not seem to need camouflage and are patterned in bold bands or spots of brilliant yellows, oranges, reds and greens, possibly because bright colours are often warnings of unpalatability. Plume Moths are pure white with wings fringed with the most delicate and fragile hairs.

Moths flying in search of food or a mate are not nearly so free from the attacks of birds and mammals as the butterflies. Nightjars which during the day sleep motionless amongst the leaf litter of the forest margins stir themselves at dusk and on soft, silent wings catch moths and other flying insects. The greatest numbers of moths are caught by the insectivorous bats, many kinds of which hunt around the rainforest margins where there is less vegetation to dodge and there are more insects to be caught. The bats are very small, some have a body length of only two to three inches. During the day they rest in hollow trees or small caves. A few species hide under palm leaves.

Many flowers, those of the *Pittosporum* for instance, exude a perfume which intensifies at night and attracts moths that feed on their nectar. Not only moths and other insects, but a bat, very different from the quick manoeuvring insect-hunting species, is also attracted. This is the Tube-nosed Bat, *Nyctimene*. It is much larger than the insect eaters and has broader wings. It hovers in front of flowers and buries its face in them licking the nectar. The bat may land if the flowers are clustered close together and clamber all over them visiting one after another in rapid succession.

Day or night the edge of the rainforest, where two elements meet, is seething with life.

6 Subtropical Rainforest — February

ONE DAY in late February, a palm swamp in a low-lying part of the forest is the focal point of a steady procession of dark shapes flying in from all directions. Some approach low over the treetops with strong measured wing beats. Others dive down to the palm cove from a considerable height with their black, leathery wings flapping like sails in a storm. The Grey-headed Flying Foxes or Fruit Bats are mostly silent as they return to their daytime camp in the pre-dawn twilight. An occasional squeal to avert a mid-air collision is the only sound.

The large bats, with an average wing-span of about four feet, fly to their own particular territory within the communal camp. The territory may be staked out along a branch of an emergent forest tree or along a palm frond. Inside the camp the volume of sound increases as more and more bats return. The males in particular are vigorous in their defence of the territory, at dawn even more so than at other times of the day.

As the male lands he utters his territory cry and, while hanging upside down by his feet, flaps his partly opened wings over his chest. Every bat that lands near him is challenged aggressively and as the colony is large, containing perhaps 10,000 bats, each male is very active and very vocal. He rushes towards every newcomer and initially sniffs him or her to establish identity. Males which have territories close by are threatened but not immediately attacked as they are allowed to cross the territories of others to get to their own. Strange males are attacked immediately. To the accompaniment of aggressive shrieks the territory owner rushes the stranger and lashes out with the sharply hooked claw on his thumbs. But flying fox fights are ritualistic, they look and sound ferocious but always stop short of actual physical combat. The intruders invariably fly off and so end the fight.

The only flying foxes that a male will allow in his territory are his mate and her young, born the previous October. However the male's general aggression eventually drives the young away to join the pack of others his age in the centre of the camp. Neighbours, strangers, mate and mate's young are all identified by scent—the peculiar flying fox odour that each individual secretes through glands on the shoulders.

Activity has settled down to its daily routine by sun-up, when most of the bats have arrived. At this time of the year, between late January and early April, the camp is occupied on a definite and recognisable social structure. Scattered around the perimeter are the guards. These are predominantly males with a small number of females intermingled among them. The guards have no territories and they rest both high and low in the trees. The non-territorial bats form the camp's early warning system. As soon as predators, such as Carpet Pythons and Lace Monitors are spotted the guards give their high-pitched and penetrating alarm calls. Instantly all squabbling near the disturbance ceases and the flying foxes, gently swaying from side to side, concentrate their senses—particularly their eyes and ever active ears—upon the suspicious noise or movements. If the threat is immediate the whole section of the camp takes wing and the bats circle round till the danger has passed.

Within this perimeter of guards are the well established and evenly spaced territories—some consisting of a family of male, female and young, others of just a male and female, and others again may consist of a group of one male with two or more females. Mating will take place in these territories in March. Both male and female know and defend the territory.

At the centre of the camp there are the packs of young; the juveniles all hang close together, not spaced out in territories. A few adults, mostly males, are mixed with these young, and play a definite role. A large part of the youngsters' time in the pack is taken up with mock fighting. Occasionally this play transgresses the limits of safety, for the flying fox's claws and large canine teeth are dangerous weapons. Whenever fights become too serious, the adult males intervene and quickly separate the over-enthusiastic youths. There is some evidence which suggests that while in these juvenile packs and under the guidance of mature males, the new generation learns the laws that govern Fruit Bat society.

Flying fox camps are not structured along these lines all the year round. In fact in about six weeks' time, after mating has taken place, the summer camp will be vacated altogether. The bats then scatter to winter camps where the males and females occupy separate sections of the camp. The number of flying foxes in a winter camp and the actual location of the camp itself varies according to the available food supply which, for the Grey-headed Flying Fox, is predominantly eucalypt blossom. In late September the flying foxes return in increasing numbers to their summer camps—these camps are nearly always in the same locality and some have been known to be occupied for more than eighty years.

At first the sexes are segregated in the summer camps too. Soon after arrival, in early October, the young are born. For the first three weeks of their lives they are carried by their mothers. When three weeks old the young are left in the camp at night while their mothers fly out to forage. The young cannot fly until they are three months old. They are fully mature at eight months.

The sexes remain segregated in the summer camp till late December when mates are selected and the territories established.

To return to the particular February day. Dawn comes with brilliant sunshine dispelling a few wisps of mist from the valleys. The flying foxes settle down and apart from a few fights they rest intermittently throughout the day. A few hours are spent grooming. The soft leathery wings in particular receive meticulous care to keep them supple and well oiled. When the camp becomes hot in the late summer sun, the flying foxes fan themselves with their wings. Should a cloud pass over the sun, a breeze spring up, or perhaps one of the frequent showers sweep through the camp—the flying foxes wrap their waterproof wings tightly around their bodies, tuck one leg and the head in, and sleep. Throughout the day the male intermittently marks his territory by rubbing the branch with his shoulder glands, and pays attention to the female.

The constant noise of the bat camp drowns out the other sounds, such as the dawn chorus of birds, in its immediate vicinity. Travel only a little distance away from the turmoil of the camp and the bats provide a mere background noise with only an occasional extra loud shriek being distinguishable. At this distance the camp is completely ignored by the other inhabitants of the forest. Of these, the birds are most readily observed, but even so most are heard long before they are seen. The morning chorus of the subtropical rainforest has strange sounds, those of catbirds, whipbirds and pigeons as heard in the tropical forests.

It is possible to hear all these calls without even glimpsing the birds that make them. But remain motionless and other birds, those living in the undergrowth and those fossicking amongst the forest litter, will lose their fear and come to within a few yards, many of them are found only in the sub-tropics.

A pair of Spine-tailed Logrunners slowly make their way across the litter-strewn ground. They pause frequently and with sideways swipes of their strong legs dig down amongst the dead leaves and twigs. After every few strokes the birds lean back and prop on their strong tails to survey the ground they have uncovered. Then quickly they eat the small litter animals, the crustaceans, worms, snails and insects before these can crawl back under the leaves. So enthusiastic are the eight-inch birds in their digging and raking, that their mottled brown shapes are at times

completely hidden by the leaves they toss up. Autumn is the main breeding season of the logrunners and already pairs have formed. At the
moment courtship is still in progress. Every now and again the male,
uttering soft reassuring calls, hops to the female; she daintily accepts the
food offered. This action reinforces the pair bond already established.

As with Fruit Bats, it is interesting to look back to an earlier time of the
year. Take, for instance, the activities of birds on a remote slope on the
Lamington Plateau in southern Queensland during an early morning in
September when it is possible to hear one of the most gripping of all
bird songs.

This exceptional song is that of a small red-brown bird only six and a
half inches long, the Rufous Scrub Bird. It is a bird of the undergrowth
and the densest parts seem to be preferred. Here he runs like a mouse over
the ground, squirming under logs and leaves and even going inside
hollows to seek out the woodlice and insects he eats. Because of his
colour, speed and preference for dense undergrowth, the scrub bird is
rarely seen—but frequently he is heard, and to hear a scrub bird is infinitely more exciting than to see one. Because of the dense vegetation of
his home and his habit of hiding it is possible to be quite close when the
Rufous Scrub Bird is first heard. Should this be the case, the effect can
by shattering.

Calls of 'cheep–cheep–cheep' in tones of extreme clarity and volume
suddenly erupt from the bushes, so loud that at close quarters it is painful
to the ear. After these first notes the bird may go into his full song, a
continuous burst in which he combines his own particular notes with
imitations of others. His mimicry of the Yellow Robin and the Spine-
tailed Logrunner's 'be-kweek-kweek, kweek, kweek' are exceptional,
even rivalling those of the master of all mimics and songsters, the Lyrebird. But the quality of the scrub bird's song which is perhaps the most
astonishing of all, which is entirely his own, is his ventriloquism. The
ventriloquial notes are high pitched and drawn out and it is virtually
impossible to pinpoint the bird when it utters these calls. On one occasion
four people, all within ten yards of where the bird must have been, could
not see it. The ventriloquial calls seemed to come first from in front of
the observers, then from behind them. Just as they thought they had
pinpointed the songster, the call came from another direction. But the
bird never moved, for if it had it would have been seen. So here was a
six-and-a-half-inch bird calling from a thick patch of ground ferns—and
four people only yards away were confusedly walking in circles without
finding him.

The Rufous Scrub Bird is not the only extraordinary songster of these misty upland forests. The Albert Lyrebird—a different species from the Superb Lyrebird of the sclerophyll forests to the south—also sings, displays and nests during winter and early spring. Several Lyrebirds sing along the lower slopes below the scrub bird's territory. Their voices ring through these rugged valleys, with a song very much like that of the Superb, containing the same balance of clear lyrebird notes and imitations of others, Whipbirds, Yellow Robins and Crimson Rosellas. The Albert Lyrebird is even more elusive than the Superb. He is about the same size as the Superb, but more rufous in colour with a tail only slightly less splendid in size, structure and shimmering colour.

Apart from the sounds that delight the ear issuing from birds that remain largely hidden, there are colourful species that delight the eye. While standing entranced listening to the scrub bird chorus, a brilliant Yellow Robin perches only a few feet away. A Buff-breasted Pitta hops across a clear space between tall trees—a flash of green, brown and red. In the foliage overhead a black and gold Regent Bowerbird selects yellow and brown fruits as playthings to decorate his bower.

In late February, scrub birds and lyrebirds rarely sing, bowerbirds rarely visit their bowers. As the sun rises, it becomes warm. The damp of the season's rain combines with the warmth to create an ideal atmosphere for toadstools, mushrooms, and other fruiting bodies of innumerable fungi. Throughout the year the fungi's white threadlike mycelia were at work, decaying wood, leaves and other dead plant life. Now these hidden networks have thrown up their endless variety of fruiting bodies which carry the spores that will eventually establish the fungi anew in other parts of the forest.

Fungi like white lace festoon a dead stump; a fallen log is covered with little white umbrellas; bright orange coral-like growths erupt from the ground litter; a large leaf, dead and shrivelled on the ground, has a new life as the scarlet caps on hairlike black stems of a Horse-hair Fungus grow from it. Round fungi adorn a fallen branch with what appear to be bright orange buttons. A huge log is covered with white fleshy Luminous Fungi.

A few of the fungi are poisonous to animals but others are a valuable food source. A weevil attacks a white bracket fungus on a rotten tree stump. A shiny black skink, almost two feet long—the Land Mullet—methodically eats all the tiny white umbrellas from another log. Few of the older fungi are intact; they have been chewed by insects, snails, reptiles, mammals or other organisms.

The heavy rains of summer have also activated several species of frogs which live in the same high-altitude beech forests as the scrub birds. Two of these, unlike the majority of frogs, do not need to lay their eggs in water for the tadpoles to develop to maturity. Both are small. *Kyarranus loveridgei* measures just over an inch in length. With the first onset of rain the males begin to call from small burrows in the rain-sodden soil of a mountain slope. In this burrow the female lays her eggs. The large eggs contain enough food to carry the frog larvae through the tadpole stage and when the eggs hatch, small frogs emerge, not tadpoles as is the case with the vast majority of frogs.

The other species, *Crinia darlingtoni*, is even smaller, between a half and three-quarters of an inch in length. The males have been calling from under rocks, logs and other debris of the forest since spring. With their sharp and rapid 'eh–eh–eh–eh–eh–eh' sounds they attract the females. Just how these small frogs breed has not definitely been established, but it is known that somehow all the eggs laid by the female are transferred to brood pouches in the male's flanks. Again the eggs are large and the young appear to go through their metamorphosis while inside the egg and emerge from the brood pouches as small frogs.

A storm which has been building up since midday finally breaks in late afternoon. All activity comes to a halt. Insects crawl under leaves, birds hide and are silent, snakes and lizards crawl under logs and into holes. The only sounds are those made by the thunder, the beating of heavy drops on vegetation and the wind lashing the outer branches.

Just as suddenly as they began, the rain, the thunder, lightning and the violent winds stop. The sky clears in time for the last rays of the setting sun to make the drops of rain sparkle on the leaf tips. It is an invigorating time of the day, cooler now, and the birds sing enthusiastically till darkness falls.

The flying foxes, after grooming and drying themselves, fly out in long columns to their feeding grounds.

Crinia darlingtoni

7 Eucalypt Forests

EUCALYPT FORESTS DELIGHT and stir the senses. Never more so than on a crisp autumn day when the air is clear, the sun warm and bright. The finest details of plants and animals are cleanly outlined and colours glow. A skink basking on a tree trunk shines a metallic bronze. A Rufous Whistler's warm colours contrast with the grey-green of the eucalypt leaves; the bird's song carries far through the forest. A Black-tailed Wallaby pauses in a shaft of sunlight slanting through the trees, its dark red-brown fur sparkling in the sunlight. Textures are varied. Soft fern fronds brush against tough and prickly leaved shrubs with woody, knobbly fruits. The eucalypts may have trunks dark in colour, harsh and rough in texture while not far away another kind has a pale trunk, smooth and shiny on which the lightest touch will leave a mark. On the ground woody seed capsules, the gum nuts, and brittle fallen branches rest on soft, green mosses. The whole forest is pervaded with the odours of eucalyptus oils. In places a burst of wildflowers adds a splash of yellow, red or purple and scents of unusual sweetness. The scents, sounds and textures are details. Dominating all these are the tall straight forms of the eucalypts themselves. The eucalypts more than anything establish the scene as uniquely Australian.

TREES OF THE genus *Eucalyptus*, of which about 600 species and varieties are recognised, are virtually confined to Australia. Only six species are found outside the continent and only one of these does not occur in Australia at all. The other five are common to Australia and New Guinea. The single non-Australian species, *Eucalyptus deglupta*, has spread from New Guinea into Indonesia and the Philippines.

Within Australia itself the distribution of the eucalypts is also limited. No more than 25 species occur in the arid three-quarters of the continent and these only along watercourses and other favoured habitats. The vast majority of species occurs in the forests and woodlands of the higher rainfall areas; the norther tropics, the southwest corner, Tasmania and the east coast.

Woodlands and forests are quite distinct. Woodlands are defined as plant communities dominated by trees whose bole length is less than the depth of the crown. The trees are widely spaced and have rounded crowns which do not interlock. The ground cover is either grass or shrubs or a combination of both.

Forest communities on the other hand are dominated by closely spaced, tall trees whose bole length is greater than the depth of the crown. The extreme of this can be seen in the Mountain Ash forests of Victoria and Tasmania where straight trunks 250 feet or more in height are topped by small tufts of crowns 60 feet in depth. Other forest characteristics are flat-topped crowns which form a more or less closed canopy. Eucalypt *forests* therefore occur on a relatively small part of Australia. They are restricted to areas of 25 or more inches of rainfall in temperate and subtropical climates. Where rainfall exceeds 50 inches average which is evenly distributed over the year, rainforest occurs on suitable soils and eucalypts are completely excluded. In most of the tropics eucalypts do not grow as forests, but as woodlands for there is a prolonged dry season which limits the trees' development. The major area of eucalypt forests is along the Great Divide and coastal plains from southern Queensland to Victoria and in Tasmania. Less extensive areas of forests occur along Queensland's coast and the southwest corner of the continent, but these lack the species diversity and complexity of the forests of the southeast. This chapter is concerned only with forests.

The reactions of eucalypts to such forces as climate, soil and topography are infinitely subtle. Variations in rainfall, temperature, aspect, and particularly soil, will bring a change in the species composition of the forests. Before these forests can be understood it is first necessary to examine the eucalypt's intrinsic, that is genetic, characteristics and to be able to recognise the main groups—to tell a bloodwood from a blackbutt and a peppermint from a stringybark. Only then will it be possible to appreciate the patterns of forest trees and forest ecology.

It has been stressed that forest eucalypts are the essence of southeastern Australia. This feeling of Australian-ness is generated most strongly by the eucalypts' genetic makeup which determines their shape, their development, their flowers and fruits, their distinctive scent, the unmistakable and unique way in which they grow.

There are four ways in which eucalypts can produce new growth in the form of leafy shoots. The primary means by which these shoots are developed is from *naked buds*, and it is this method which gives a eucalypt almost unlimited growth potential. The other three are reserves; should the growing tip be destroyed in some way, these reserves give the trees their extraordinary hardiness and persistence in the face of adversity.

Poor soil, bushfires, defoliation by insects, trunks broken by storms— none of these can keep the eucalypts down.

As a eucalypt leaf unfolds from the growing tip a small bud on a thin stalk is present in its axil. This is the naked bud and it is present in the axil of every leaf that unfolds in the life of the tree. Each naked bud has the potential of immediate and rapid development into a new shoot producing a leaf at one to two-inch intervals on its growing stems. But not all these naked buds develop simultaneously. Only those near the tips of the major branches of the tree grow, producing the new shoots. The others further down the stem are held in check by hormones for as long as the tip continues to extend. When this tip dies or is eaten by an insect this inhibiting factor is removed and the naked buds further down the stem commence their growth and take over the role of leading shoot.

In this way new leaves are constantly produced until growth conditions are checked through cold, drought, or the need for a resting stage by the tree. Theoretically there is no limit to the number of leaves that can be produced by the growing tip of a eucalypt. But this potential is seldom, if ever, realised. Insect attack, which is continuous and severe, is, in Australia, the main limiting factor to the eucalypts' rapid development. Eucalypts introduced into other countries from Australia are not subject to these attacks since the oil in the leaves of the trees protects them. Growth of eucalypts in these countries is far more rapid. Long festoons of leaves, each perfect in every detail trail down from the branches. The profile of the tree may be completely different from its characteristic shape in its native country. This difference can be so great that botanists familiar with Australian grown species cannot recognise the same kind grown in South Africa or California. Insects determine the shape and comparatively slow growth rate of Australia's native eucalypts. A slower growth rate, however, is to the tree's ultimate advantage for its wood will be more durable and less brittle, and damage from high winds will be less of a threat. But in spite of setbacks, eucalypts in Australia can grow at a tremendous rate. Rose Gums, *Eucalyptus grandis*, planted near Coffs Harbour in New South Wales grew to a height of 100 feet in seven years.

The significance of the development of naked buds can be gauged when eucalypts are compared with elms, beeches, oaks and other forest trees from the temperate zones of the northern hemisphere. Eucalypts, through the growth from naked buds, can develop several new orders of branches in weeks. Oaks and elms can develop only one order of branching in a year. The buds (which are covered with protective scales) in the leaf axils of northern hemisphere trees will not unfold till the year after that in which the mother leaf unfolded.

Naked buds of eucalypts growing wild in their native country develop unchecked for only a few weeks at the beginning of the growing season. Then the insects begin their work. The naked buds may be eaten by stick insects, stung by gall wasps, sucked dry by lerps, tunnelled into by moth larvae. Once this attack has begun it usually continues in at least some branches for the rest of the season. The destruction of the growing tips and naked buds stops the hormone supply from them and this releases the first line of defence; development of leafy shoots from *accessory buds*.

As soon as the naked buds and growing tips are destroyed by any agency at all, new buds, accessory buds, arise in the leaf axils and develop rapidly into new shoots. These will grow as fast as the shoots from naked buds they replace and the check in growth due to the destruction of the original shoots is not severe, only a momentary pause. The bud-producing tissue which persists after the naked buds drop off and from which the accessory buds arise in the eucalypts' leaf axils is also resistant to drought and frost, both of which destroy the naked buds. Accessory buds give the eucalypts great durability in the face of minor setbacks.

But eucalypts will recover even from such major disasters as complete defoliation by fire or insects or a trunk snapped off during a storm. The tree recovers by producing shoots from dormant buds on the trunk and main branches or from the lignotuber.

The tissue that produces the accessory buds remains as a potential producer of new leafy shoots long after the stem leaves have fallen. As the shoot grows in diameter to form a tree's trunk or a large woody branch the bud-producing tissue keeps pace in growth, growing radially outwards from the centre of the stem. So at all times there are dormant buds just under the bark of the trunk and main branches of eucalypts. There is one bud for every leaf that once grew on the stem or branch. A tree 70 feet high would have roughly 7,000 of these buds, which, like the others, do not develop because of the actions of an inhibiting hormone produced by the growing tips. Just how effective a reserve these dormant buds are can be seen most dramatically after fire.

Immediately after the fire the scene is one of utter desolation. The undergrowth has completely disappeared, the ground is covered with ash. The eucalypts have fire-blackened trunks and have lost their leaves and fine twigs. The first thought that comes to mind is—how will anything grow here ever again? But provided the weather is not too cold and there is sufficient soil moisture available, partial recovery is rapid and dramatic. Within weeks of the fire new tender shoots, growing from the dormant buds, push their way through the bark—fragile signs of life against the dead, black outer bark. Numerous new shoots, called *epicormic shoots*, develop quickly from each dormant bud. The number of buds that develop depends on the severity of the disaster. After an explosive bushfire the whole trunk and the major branches will be covered with new growth. As the tree recovers after fire the epicormics in the crown eventually exert dominance and those of the trunk die and fall off. All that remains in later years may be some knobs on the trunk. The epicormic knobs, which in due course are covered by the tree's bark, were originally formed by the fusion of the bases of the numerous shoots arising from the dormant buds. These knobs on the trunks of trees are a characteristic feature of many eucalypt forests.

Recovery through the development of dormant buds does not exhaust the eucalypt's ability to recover from disaster. Should the whole crown and trunk of a tree be destroyed either by an unusually severe fire or storm damage, new shoots will appear from the *lignotuber*, a large woody, bulbous structure at the base of the trunk. The lignotuber develops very early in the eucalypt's life; in some species within weeks of germination. They begin as swellings at the base of the first pair of leaves of the seedlings. As the plant matures the two swellings fuse and increase in size and fold down the stem and wrap around the upper parts of the roots. Eventually the lignotubers work themselves so far down into the soil that their greater proportion is buried and is safe from fire damage. As long as the tree is healthy no shoots develop on the lignotuber but as soon as the trunk is broken or severely damaged, numbers of shoots develop and grow rapidly. Shoots from lignotubers can develop into new healthy trunks. Initial growth from a lignotuber after destruction of the main stem is rapid for the lignotuber also stores plant food.

Naked, accessory and dormant buds are a feature that all eucalypts have in common, but not all species develop lignotubers. The most conspicuous group without lignotubers is the ash group including the Mountain Ash, *Eucalyptus regnans* and Alpine Ash, *E. delegatensis*. Most but not all the species without lignotubers grow in moist habitats. The group of trees with the most highly developed lignotubers are woodland, not forest species, the mallees. Their lignotubers are huge woody structures well known as 'mallee roots' and once a popular source of firewood.

With its inherent characters assuring great hardiness and persistence, it might be speculated that eucalypts are extremely long-lived. This is not the case however. Forest trees in southeastern Australia such as the Mountain Ash live to 200–400 years. A few eucalypts, those which have the most durable woods such as the Jarrah, *Eucalyptus marginata*, of Western Australia and the River Red Gum, *E. camaldulensis*, may live to 1,000 years. Some oaks live to 1,500 years and certain northern hemisphere conifers for up to 2,000 years so on a comparative basis eucalypts do not live to a particularly great age.

The reason for the comparatively short lifespan of most eucalypts is that their wood is less resistant to fungal and termite attack than the very long-lived trees. When the eucalypts have reached maturity, their annual increase in growth cannot keep pace with the rate of attack within the trunks, which become weak and eventually will collapse. Another factor that restricts the age of a eucalypt is the physical limit to which it can grow and the amount of wood its trunk can support. The eucalypt's habit of developing rapidly from naked and accessory buds means that each crop of new leaves results in considerable extension of the branches. Each year they become longer and are subject to wind damage. This in turn exposes the tree to more attacks by fungi and boring insects and hastens its eventual death.

The eucalypts are not completely at the mercy of fungi and insects, they have their defences. As soon as the wood directly behind the bark is injured through any agency at all be it fire, borers or through the breaking of a branch, the injured area is flooded with an orange liquid called *kino*. On exposure to air this liquid hardens to a brittle, deep-red mass and seals the wound off from the air. No fungus or insects can now enter to decay or to tunnel through the wood. Some eucalypts produce these gum veins more readily than others and the flow of kino also varies. Bloodwoods are probably the most susceptible and many trees can be seen with the deep-red kino, like bloodstains, on their bark. Kino performs the same function as the resins in conifers, but is of a different chemical substance. It contains tannins and sugars which are attractive to certain animals. Ants will carry the kino of certain eucalypts to their nests and the Fluffy Glider, *Petaurus australis*, will lick the kino for hours. The gliders bite grooves in the trunks of bloodwoods, manna gums and other eucalypts to stimulate the formation of gum veins. They actively tap the kino as a food source.

The various kinds of leaf buds, the lignotubers and to a certain extent gum veins explain the eucalypts' extraordinary powers of growth and persistence in adverse conditions. Other features account for the trees' equally distinctive appearance. Nearly all 600 kinds of eucalypts and the very closely related angophoras are instantly recognisable and quite different from all other trees.

Characteristically, mature forest eucalypts have a straight clean bole

ABOVE: A Musk Lorikeet gathers pollen and nectar from the flowers of a Tasmanian Black Peppermint
LEFT: Buds and leaves of the Ironbark. Long pendulous leaves are typical of eucalypts
BELOW: Growing tip of a eucalypt showing naked buds in the leaf axils. These leaves will turn green as they mature

for half the total tree height or more (in the case of the Mountain Ash it may be three-quarters). The branches of all orders make an acute angle, mostly sharply acute, with their parent branch or with the trunk. An exception is the Tallowwood, *Eucalyptus microcorys*, which often has branches at right angles to the trunk. The most characteristic shape is derived from the fact that even the small branches are clean in outline and carry their leaves in tufts at their tips. If the twigs are very vigorous in development the leaves will be organised in long, drooping festoons.

The development of the clean outline of the eucalypt trunks, which is one of its most distinctive features, is possible because, as the tree grows, the lower, dead branches are shed in a very efficient way. More efficient than in most trees where the process is extremely slow. If this was the case with the fast growing eucalypts it would cause serious problems in the growth of their trunks.

This branch-shed mechanism works efficiently for branches up to one inch in diameter whether they are on the tree's trunk or on its main limbs. If a large branch dies the mechanism cannot always cope with it efficiently. The dead branch remains attached for years, even decades, and is slowly decayed. The decay moves along the branch to the heart-wood of the tree or the living part of the branch. Eventually the dead branch crashes down and the tree's bark covers the break. But it is too late to stop the decay which was also beyond the scope of the protection from kino. The result is a hollow branch or spout or even a large cavity in the trunk itself. Hollows of these kinds, evidence of failed branch-shed mechanism, are as characteristic of the eucalypt as the smooth boles, evidence of its success. The tree hollows play a very important part in the diversity of the forest's wildlife for they are roosting and nesting places for many animals.

The crowns of eucalypts do not closely interlock giving eucalypt forests a more open structure than rainforests. In good quality eucalypt forest for instance the light value at ground level is one-twentieth to one-fortieth that of full sunlight while in rainforest which has a completely closed canopy light value is as low as one-hundredth that of full sunlight.

The higher light levels in eucalypt forests are largely the result of the growth habits of the leaves. The dispersed crown, the result of long distances between individual leaves and their drooping habit, allows greater penetration of light. The trees of the world that cast good shade such as oaks have their leaves in rosettes which allows concentration of five or more leaves on one inch of stem, and the leaves usually lie in a horizontal plane. Eucalypts on the other hand have to push their leaves

ennett's Wallabies usually rest inside the forest
uring the day, grazing at the edge at dusk and dawn and at night. The
rs of this wallaby's large pouch-young are just visible above the grass

ever outwards and upwards and five leaves may take as much as ten inches of stem. This combined with the vertical orientation of the leaves gives a very open crown.

Leaves are one of the main factors in determining the shape and characteristic appearance of the eucalypts.

Eucalypt leaves are of a surprising similarity, most but by no means all, are long, narrow, sickle-shaped, tapering leaves that because of a twist in their stalk droop in situations of high light level. The trees are evergreen. In the forests of southeastern Australia there are no deciduous species and only a few occur in other parts of the continent in areas of severe seasonal drought.

The colour of the leaves varies. In some species it is a brilliant green, in others such as the Silver-leafed Ironbark, *Eucalyptus melanophloia*, it is a bluey-grey. New growing tips and their stems are often brilliant red. But most forest species have dark green mature leaves which are tough and leathery. New shoots stand out a paler yellow-green, soft and delicate ag inst the drabness of older leaves. A most important feature of the leaves, and one of the highly characteristic features of the whole genus, is the presence of oil glands also present, to a lesser degree, in the flower buds and leaf stalks. The volatile oils give the eucalypts their unique scent. Some eucalypts are so rich in oil that these can be extracted from the leaves. Most eucalypt oils, of which there are several kinds, are used for medicinal purposes but some are of importance in industrial processes.

Flowers and fruits of the eucalypts, like the leaves, have a certain similarity though within their basic design there is an intriguing variation in shape, arrangement and colour.

The eucalypt's flowers develop in clusters in the leaf axils or on the end of leafy twigs. The number of flowers in a cluster, called an *umbel*, varies tremendously. Most common numbers are three, five and seven but some species, like peppermints, for instance, have as many as thirty flowers to an umbel. Solitary flowers are rare but do occur, as in the Southern Blue Gum, *Eucalyptus globulus*, for example. Flowers developing in the leaf axils are frequently obscured by the leaves of the developing shoots. The most showy of the flowering eucalypts are those in which several umbels combine into large rounded bunches of flowers on the end of the leafy shoot. Bloodwoods are the most spectacular of this kind. Some trees such as the Pink Bloodwood, *Eucalyptus intermedia*, may have bunches of flowers eight to twelve inches across which make the branches droop with their weight.

When the bud of a eucalypt flower is examined closely it can be seen that it is divided into two parts by a well defined line. As the flower opens the top portion is pushed off and falls to the ground. This is the cap or *operculum* and is made up of the flower petals and sepals fused together. It is this character that gave the eucalypts their name. The word *Eucalyptus* is of Greek derivation and means well covered.

The lower part of the bud is called the *receptacle* and contains all the floral parts. As the cap falls off it exposes the flower *stamens*, neatly arranged in a series of thin stalks around the rim of the receptacle. Each stamen, the male part of the flower, is tipped with two pollen sacs. The *stigma*, the female part of the flower, rises from the centre of the receptacle; the cup-shaped area between stamens and stigma is filled with nectar. The honey-flow in eucalypt flowers is copious and plays an important part in the forest ecology. Such diverse kinds of animals as moths, ants and numerous other insects, parrots, honeyeaters, gliders and flying foxes depend on nectar and also pollen for at least part of their diet. A flowering eucalypt is invariably a focal point for animal life and without the profuse blossoming of nectar-rich flowers the animal populations in eucalypt forests would be much poorer in variety.

The animals are, of course, of importance to the eucalypts for they carry out the vital task of cross-pollination. Wind pollination is of no great significance in the fertilisation of the eucalypts; insects and birds are the main agents. Bats, gliders and possums play a minor role in this respect. Cross-pollination is vital to eucalypts as it maintains their genetic vitality and also produces hybrids which eventually may lead to new varieties. These new varieties and hybrids often make better use of a given set of environmental conditions than either of their parent species.

Cross-pollination is not essential to all the eucalypts. In some species which have been studied, it was found that the flower was already fertilised when the cap fell off. These species can produce viable seed without the benefit of outside pollinators of any kind.

Eucalypt flowers do not vary within the arrangements discussed. They are flowers without petals and sepals, as these fall off in the form of the operculum. The colour of the flowers is determined by the stamens and in forest species this is nearly always cream-coloured or white with an occasional pink-flowered species. The really colourful flowers of eucalypts, brilliant orange, scarlet, yellow or deep red are on smaller woodland trees. The arrangement of the flowers may be the same but there is a great variety in the shape of the caps and the receptacles. The caps may be smooth, ribbed or fluted, rounded, flat-topped or acutely pointed, large or small. The receptacles show even greater variation, particularly once they have shed the stamens and have developed into the woody fruits, the gum nuts.

As with the operculum there is a variety of attractive shapes amongst the gum nuts. In fact there is so much variety that the fruit shape is a useful character in the identification of eucalypts. The only limitation of the fruits is that they are always woody, always enclose a capsule containing the seeds and that these capsules are sealed by a varying number and arrangement of valves. The fruits are generally small and rounded; very few exceed one inch in length. But apart from that their shape may be spherical or pointed; the valves may project above the fruit's rim or be sunken below it; the surface may be smooth, knobbly or ridged; it may be wider at the bottom than at the top or with a narrow base and a wide top. There are nearly always some fruits on a mature tree for eucalypts have a high fertility rate and a tree is at times laden with several generations of gum nuts.

The last of the eucalypts' distinctive characters is the bark. Unlike the trees' flowers and fruits there is no basic limitation to bark type. There are all manner of colours and textures and they are the single most important character to give variety in the appearance of the forests.

If the barks were as limited in their appearance as the leaves or flowers, eucalypt forests would be very monotonous places to travel through. But luckily this is not the case and the changeability of the forests as a result of their varying bark types is one of their most attractive features.

Best known of the barks are the smooth types, the gums. A large number of eucalypts have this type of bark and there is usually at least one of them in any particular forest. Each year the smooth-textured trees shed the outer layer of their bark. On the east coast this usually takes place at the height of summer and as the old bark peels away in large sheets or in ribbons trailing down in long strips the new bark lies exposed in startling varieties of colours. The delicacy and lightness of the smooth trunks of the gums only emphasises the heaviness of some of the other types; the thick, black and furrowed surfaces of the ironbark; layered grey or brown surfaces of the stringybark trunks; the dark brown scaly bark of the Tallowwood. Bark, as we shall see later, is a very useful criterion in classifying the eucalypts into groups. But for the tree the bark is neither decoration nor a guide to its identity. It is an essential protection for its tender growing wood. Bark protects the wood from drying out, from damage by fire, and from the ever present threat of fungal and insect attack. Any break in the bark causes the living wood of the tree to dry out and leaves it open to attack. Extensive bark damage causes serious loss of growth to a tree.

Eucalypt bark is thick and its most remarkable feature is its great insulating quality. It is so efficient that even during a very hot summer bushfire the inner bark and sapwood do not experience excessively high temperatures. The outer bark may be charred and all the leaves burnt or killed but because of the bark's protection the tree can recover. Just how effective the protection of bark is, was shown in an experiment on a Spotted Gum, *Eucalyptus maculata*. A blowtorch flame, which melted an aluminium tag on the bark surface in six seconds, was directed at the tree's half-inch bark for eight minutes. The damage to the wood behind the bark was negligible.

The inherent characters of the eucalypts discussed so far are so flexible and vigorous that one or more species of the genus have developed for almost every habitat except the excessively dry and excessively wet. All other conditions have produced at least one eucalypt. The result is a very large number of species. Before examining how all these pieces form a pattern, though this is as yet only imperfectly understood, it is useful to try to find a way through the maze of eucalypts. The genus is so complex that it is beyond any one person to be able to recognise instantly all the species. However, much confusion can be avoided and the forest eucalypts be better understood by classifying them into a number of groups.

Classifying the eucalypts is an extremely difficult task and no wholly satisfactory method of identifying all the species exists. The major difficulty is the large number of species involved and this is compounded by the great variability of certain types and a widespread geographic distribution of others. Another great difficulty is that no *single* character has yet been discovered on which eucalypts can be readily separated. Classification systems based on the characteristics of the bark, operculum, fruits, venation of the leaves, chemical nature of the kino, cross-section of the leaf-stalk, cotyledons, juvenile leaves, type of oil in the leaves and the shape of the anthers have all been proposed by botanists since the first eucalypt was described in 1789. Out of these various systems two have arisen which are currently in use, each system being used for a different purpose. Firstly there is the scientific, or taxonomic, classification used by scientists; this is based on a single feature, the physical characters, mostly shape, of the anthers. These are the pollen-bearing organs that tip the stamens of the eucalypt flowers. This system's purpose is to classify the eucalypts in a way that shows natural groupings and relationships. The second system is not based on one character but on several and its purpose is to identify eucalypts in the field. The characters used are bark, fruit, operculum—which is present only in the bud, and sometimes leaf venation. This second system is, of course, necessary for field work as anthers are extremely small, sometimes almost microscopic, and present only when the tree flowers which is for short periods in its life. In trying to identify the eucalypts in the field, bark characters are mostly used to divide them into groups such as the gums, stringybarks, ironbarks, bloodwoods and so on. Then the arrangement, shape and ornamentation of the fruit and buds are used to refine the system and most forest species can be identified this way. Both systems perform an essential function but neither is completely workable.

It is beyond the scope or intention of this book to be a guide to all the eucalypts. However a brief discussion of the main groups of forest species based on bark characters may be useful. There are a few anomalies in the system and son e well known eucalypts do not fit this pattern—but it is a beginning.

Gums form not only the largest but also the best known group. Their name, which is sometimes used for all eucalypts collectively, refers to the trees' often copious flow of kino. Gum bark is smooth and often has a dull glow. There are several divisions within the gum group. Blue Gums, so called because of the blue-grey blotching of the bark of some species, form a natural group. The trees, of which the Southern Blue Gum, *Eucalyptus globulus*, is the best known, usually grow on fertile soils of fairly high rainfall. Their clean trunks are a feature of many forests of southern Victoria and Tasmania. Another group of gums, with very similar bark, are called Red Gums, but the name refers to the colour of the timber, not the bark. Some of the trees of this group have the widest geographic distribution of all the eucalypts. The Forest Red Gum, *Eucalyptus tereticornis*, ranges north from Victoria along the entire east coast and is also found in New Guinea. The River Red Gum, *Eucalyptus camaldulensis*, is found throughout inland Australia. As the name suggests, grey smooth bark typifies the Grey Gum assemblage of species. One Grey Gum, *Eucalyptus propinqua*, has particularly colourful new bark which adds splashes of orange to the coastal forests of southern Queensland and New South Wales in summer. On the more fertile soils of this same area grow two of the most imposing gums of another group— Flooded Gums, so called because the gullies in which they grow are often flooded. These are the Rose Gum, *Eucalyptus grandis*, and the Sydney Blue Gum, *E. saligna*. They are tall trees growing in forests with a heavy undergrowth, often of rainforest species and their clean, often pure white, trunks rising sheer out of the tangle of undergrowth are one of the finest sights in the Australian forests.

Another group which impresses with size and straightness is the ash group which includes smooth- and rough-barked species. Amongst these are the tallest eucalypts, and one of them, the Mountain Ash,

Eucalyptus regnans, is the tallest tree in Australia and the second tallest in the world. They occur in Victoria and Tasmania. The trees in a good stand are spaced closely together and are over 250 feet tall; the tallest may be 320 feet high. Their slender trunks with rough bark only at the base are smooth and straight; last year's bark may hang down in long ribbons. Over 200 feet of the tree's height is without branches. All else in the forest is dwarfed. Another ash, the Messmate Stringybark, *Eucalyptus obliqua*, grows almost as tall as the Mountain Ash and often in association with it. Its trunk is rough barked, but the branches are smooth. Other ashes are the Alpine Ash, *Eucalyptus delegatensis*, the Brown Barrel, *E. fastigata*, and the Silvertop Ash, *E. sieberi*. All are important forest trees and all are straight and tall, with rough bark on the trunk and smooth on the branches. The name ash is applied because the white timber resembles that of the northern hemisphere tree of the same name.

Of all the eucalypts, one group has a greater supply of kino than the others. The dark red substance drips from even superficial bark damage and appears like bloodstains on the trunk. This group of species is appropriately known as the bloodwoods. Their bark is fibrous, soft and tessellated, like a crocodile's skin, and usually pale brown or grey in colour. Some have yellow bark like the Yellow Jacket, *Eucalyptus eximia*. The first eucalypt collected from Australia, by Banks and Solander in 1770, was a bloodwood—the Red Bloodwood, *Eucalyptus gummifera*, a typical forest species of the east coast.

Stringybarks form a well-defined group whose main feature is soft, thick, fibrous bark. This bark is persistent along the whole trunk and on all branches. On mature trees it forms a rather loose, interwoven structure composed of long strips. These strips are easily pulled off in long strands and are wonderfully soft in texture. It is ideal material for ringtail possums to line their nests with and at night in a stringybark forest nest-building possums are sometimes seen carrying bundles of the bark coiled in their tails. Other eucalypts have bark of a similar nature, though usually not as thick and spongy nor made up of so many interwoven strands as the typical stringybarks. Characters of the juvenile leaves, fruits and buds will confirm the identification of stringybarks if bark structure leaves the issue in doubt.

The bark of the peppermints is similar in structure to that of the stringybarks, but the strips are much finer and are much more tightly interleaved. The two could not really be confused. Also peppermints shed the bark on the upper part of the trunk and on the smaller branches. Peppermints derive their name from the scent of the oil in their leaves. This group of species has a very high oil content and forms the basis for the eucalyptus oil industry. The Broadleaved Peppermint, *Eucalyptus dives*, and a few other species usually occur in association with other eucalypts mostly ashes and stringybarks and add a distinctive character to the forest by their drooping foliage and the refreshing scent of their leaves.

Originally the box group of eucalypts was named after the unrelated European Box as its timbers have the same hardness and a similar interlocking grain. But this origin has been lost sight of and 'box' now refers to a particular type of bark—tight scaly or flakey on the butt or 'stocking' of the tree and with a gum-barked top. Boxes are mostly woodland eucalypts and one of them, the Yellow Box, *Eucalyptus melliodora*, is an important woodland tree on the tablelands areas of New South Wales. The honey derived from this tree is of a particularly fine quality.

Ironbarks have the heaviest bark of all the eucalypts. The bark is thick, dull charcoal grey, deeply furrowed and hard. It is impregnated with kino which on exposure to the air hardens to a rock-like substance. Ironbarks are as tough as their appearance indicates. They can withstand great hardships in their environment such as prolonged drought and poor, stony soil. 'Hungry ironbark ridges' is a term in common usage and indicates a harsh environment. However, not all ironbarks grow under these conditions; some grow on fertile, high rainfall areas of the coast where they grow into tall, straight trees. Under more difficult conditions they will grow as woodland trees with short trunks, often leaning or twisted.

Another group of trees, known as apples, is very closely related to the eucalypts and could even be regarded as a subdivision of the genus. This is the genus *Angophora* made up of eight species found only in eastern Australia south of Rockhampton in Queensland, but not in Tasmania. Angophoras or apples have the same growth habits as the eucalypts; their main differences are that their flowers have petals, and no operculum, and that the fruits are less woody and more papery in structure. To the untrained eye it is almost impossible to distinguish between eucalypts and angophoras. The best known angophora is probably the Smooth-barked Apple or Rusty Gum, *Angophora costata*, which has pink, smooth gum bark. It is a common tree native to the Sydney area, and the first timber used in the new colony of New South Wales in 1788 was of *Angophora costata*.

These are the main groups of eucalypts based on bark types alone. On the whole, they closely parallel the natural groupings based on the classification of anthers, buds and fruits. But there are exceptions. There is the Spotted Gum, *Eucalyptus maculata*, which has gum bark but is really a bloodwood as the flowering type and profuseness of kino and gum veins indicates. But exceptions like these are few.

The division into a number of groups based on bark types accounts for most forest eucalypts, but a few other well known species do not readily fit into this scheme. Some of these are important trees of the east coast and their names are in everyday use.

Tallowwood, *Eucalyptus microcorys*, is a large forest tree of the Queensland New South Wales border regions that grows to 150 feet in height. Its name is derived from its yellowish-brown, shiny, greasy timber.

Scribbly Gums, *Eucalyptus racemosa* and *E. haemastoma*, are common on coastal areas of low fertility such as the wallum in southeast Queensland and the Sydney sandstone area of New South Wales. They have white gum bark which is covered by squiggles and scribbles, like hieroglyphics, which are the tracks left by a bark-boring moth larva. Scribbly Gums are closely related to the ashes.

Another group of gum-barked species comprises the four different snow gums of the alpine country of the southern tablelands and Tasmania.

The Blackbutt, *Eucalyptus pilularis*, has the lower part of its trunk covered with persistent peppermint-type bark. This part is often blackened by bushfires. The upper part of the trunk and main branches are gum-barked. Blackbutt is one of the major forest trees of southern Queensland and coastal New South Wales and occurs over large tracts of land often in pure stands. It is extremely vigorous in growth and grows up to 200 feet tall in favourable sites.

Several trees are called Ribbon Gum, a name which refers to their habit of shedding bark in long, thin strips which may hang in the trees for many months. Ribbon Gums are alternate names for at least two species, the Mountain Ash, *Eucalyptus regnans*, and the Manna Gum, *E. viminalis*. The Manna Gum is an important gum-barked forest species of the east coast, including Tasmania, where it grows to its greatest size— almost 200 feet tall. The word 'manna' refers to the exudation of sugars known by that name, from the tree's bark and leaves. This substance collects around the base of the trees in small white globules and certainly is manna for the ants and other insects which gather it as food.

Some eucalypts are called mahoganies, a term which refers to their dark wood. They are not a closely related group of species; the White Mahogany, *Eucalyptus acmenioides*, for example is a true stringybark, while the Southern Mahogany, *E. botryoides*, is in the Eastern Blue Gum group, even though it is rough-barked.

By examining their growth habits and classification, it has been possible to gain some understanding of forest eucalypts as dynamic, hardy trees. This understanding, however limited it might be, is also a starting point for exploring the forests, not in terms of eucalypts as individual species, but as living, self-perpetuating and ever-changing assemblages of living organisms; assemblages dominated by the eucalypts but which also include many other plants and the animal life. All elements are closely linked together. The best way to begin this exploration is to place the trees in their natural, living context and to observe their response to such environmental forces as climate, soil, topography, fire and animal life.

These responses are very sensitive. Changes in soil, shelter or exposure of the site, and rainfall, will bring changes in the species of eucalypts making up the forest. These forests are sometimes made up of a single species, but more commonly two or three kinds of tree grow as co-dominants. It has been found that when more than one species occupies a certain site, the trees grow better in association than any one of them singly. Forests consisting of a number of co-dominant eucalypts make maximum use of the site's available nutrients and soil moisture. On most sites a single-species forest would not make the most efficient use of the resources.

With each change in aspect, whether the site is exposed or sheltered, on a slope or on a coastal flat, change in soil or change in rainfall, there is a change in the species of eucalypts in the forests. So the large tracts of forests of the east coast are in reality mosaics of forest types, each made up of a different group of species. Some of the major types, named after the dominant trees, are Blackbutt, Grey Gum—Ironbark, Tallowwood—Blue Gum, Stringybark—Silvertop Ash, Messmate—Brown Barrel and so on. In total, some hundreds of species of eucalypts are involved. This is complex enough, but in many sites further complications of the forest patterns are introduced by the presence of rainforest and rainforest plants as an understorey to eucalypts.

As an example of forest patterns consider the changes that take place in forest composition when walking up a mountain slope in southern Tasmania. In the gullies and on sheltered slopes with good soils, grow tall, clean-trunked Mountain Ash with an understorey of rainforest species. In places sheltered from fire there is rainforest. With changes in soil, the Mountain Ash may have Manna Gum or Messmate Stringybark, *Eucalyptus obliqua*, growing in association with it. Higher up on the mountain slopes are stands of Alpine Ash, *E. delegatensis*, tall, straight trees with fibrous bark on the trunk but smooth-barked branches. With further changes in altitude and soil and a more exposed aspect, Tasmanian Yellow Gum, *E. johnstoni*, the Urn Gum, *E. urnigera*, and a peppermint, *E. tasmanica*, may be present in increasing numbers. They add more colour—smooth yellow-green trunks in the case of *E. johnstoni*—and diversity to the forest. Higher altitude means trees with shorter trunks, until eventually most give way to shrubs. Only the Tasmanian Snow Gum, *E. coccifera*, grows on the exposed mountain slope. In an area of similar climate and altitude change in northern Europe for example, the forest type would not change to such a degree.

In spite of the complexity of forest patterns, it is possible to distinguish readily two basic types, based on the kinds of undergrowth they have. One type of forest, called *wet sclerophyll*, has an understorey of small trees, shrubs and herbs which have soft leaves—many of them rainforest species. This type of forest is associated with the higher rainfall areas and better soils. Mountain Ash trunks rising sheer out of a dark green understorey of tree ferns, wattles, Sassafras and Antarctic Beeches is typical wet sclerophyll forest of Victoria and Tasmania. This type of forest in the Queensland-New South Wales border regions usually has a canopy made up of Rose Gum or Sydney Blue Gum crowns and with an understorey of a great variety of wattles, palms, pittosporums and other rainforest species.

Lower rainfall and lower fertility give rise to the second type of forest, predictably called *dry sclerophyll*. Its understorey is of smaller trees and shrubs, which have hard or even prickly leaves, herbs and grasses.

The word sclerophyll means hard-leaved and Australia's hardwood forests are the largest sclerophyll forests in the world. Dry sclerophyll forests are by far the most extensive.

Another major ecological force, one that in Australia is as much part of the climate as rainfall, is fire. All the coastal forests and heaths, with the exception of rainforests, are swept by fire at irregular intervals. Only the most severe fires leave permanent scars and these scars can be found in every eucalypt forest.

One of the most striking qualities of eucalypt forests is their resistance to fire and also their amazing powers of recovery. Eucalypts constitute the most fire-resistant group of trees in the world; of all its almost 600 different kinds, fewer than 20 would be killed outright by high intensity bushfires. The others are able to survive because of the tremendous insulating qualities of the bark and the low levels of inflammability of the wood. Their ability to develop new shoots from dormant buds, which are protected by the bark, and from lignotubers which are protected by the soil, make it possible for the eucalypts to recover after severe fires have swept through the forest. Most undergrowth plants, except rainforest species, also quickly regenerate either from seed or from rootstock. The result is that after fire the eucalypt forest will in time recover and its component species will be exactly the same as before the fire. This is in strong contrast to the northern hemisphere forests which are virtually destroyed by an intense fire.

The vigour and power of quick regeneration after devastation by fire is one of the eucalypt forest's most impressive qualities. However, this power is not unlimited. Even though fire has been part of the Australian climate long before man—including Aboriginal man—arrived on the scene, it was less frequent, and frequency of fire as well as intensity of fire determines the damage done to a forest. If eucalypts are defoliated by fire two or three times in quick succession, they die.

Low intensity fires occurring at intervals of no less than four or five years have little or no effect on the trees, and the undergrowth recovers its original make-up quickly. But if fires are more frequent and more severe, changes take place. The soil becomes poorer because ash washed away in rain depletes the soil of plant nutrient. The shrub layer, including regenerating forest trees, is soon completely destroyed and is not re- placed. Even the grass species change from the succulent and nutritious species to the rank, unpalatable blady grass. Since European man has settled Australia he has been in the habit of annually burning the more open forests either deliberately or through carelessness. The result is that once diverse forest types, with a great variety of flowering shrubs in the undergrowth, have become monotonous tracts of fire-blackened trunks rising out of a short cover of blady grass and bracken fern. Erosion also creeps in, scouring creeks once overgrown with shrubs and grasses. In this way, the diversity inherent in the landscape has been destroyed.

On the other hand, if no fire occurred, species diversity would also be lost, for a few vigorous eucalypts and undergrowth plants would over- whelm the remainder. In some eucalypt forests the eucalypts would die if periodic, low intensity fires did not keep the wattles, brush boxes and other undergrowth shrubs and trees in check. The balance between fire and forest is a delicate one—too much too often will kill the trees and create permanent undesirable changes. With no fire at all the forest would lose diversity. The delicate balance is further indicated by the unusually large number of factors that can influence fire intensity.

Slope is important, for fire can travel four times as fast up a steep slope than along level ground. The moisture of the ground litter, the leaves, twigs and branches, is one of the most important factors and one that can change hourly. Air temperature and wind velocity also affect the in- tensity of the fire as does moisture in the air. All factors are subject to rapid change. Seasonal conditions also play a part. Hot dry days are not so dangerous with respect to bushfires after a wet winter and spring than if they occurred in a dry year. In the 1964–65 summer, for example, the regular summer rains failed in Queensland and New South Wales. This failure succeeded an unusually dry winter and spring, and the two created explosive conditions for bushfires. Many severe fires did indeed occur that summer. If a dry summer had succeeded a normal winter and spring, conditions would not have been quite so dangerous as the undergrowth would have retained some moisture. Severe bushfires are comparatively rare in these parts, an area of summer rains.

Other factors which influence the severity of a fire are whether it is sunny or overcast, the stability of the atmosphere, i.e. whether sudden changes of wind may occur. A condition less subject to change is the inflammability of the undergrowth. Dry sclerophyll forest with its woody, dry-leaved shrubs, is subject to more severe and frequent fires than the less inflammable, generally more moist, wet sclerophyll forest.

In the southern parts of eastern Australia, the factors outlined above combine to produce explosive conditions for bushfires at least once in every 20 years and sometimes more often. If fire breaks out during these days, perhaps only two or three in the season, the most severe fire imaginable rages through the forests.

Three things characteristic of eucalypt forests increase the fire hazards created by these weather conditions. The first is the fact that eucalypts produce more dead woody material than any other tree. The logs, twigs, branches, and gum nuts, accumulate in loose piles on the forest floor and, together with the dead leaves, are highly inflammable fuels and occur in greater quantities than in most forests. Secondly, the eucalypts' leaves are full of a volatile inflammable oil that, in a running crown fire, literally explodes. The running crown fires are spread far in advance of the main front by the third factor called spotting; a factor unique to eucalypt forest fires. This is created by the trees' bark. The barks of Ribbon Gums and stringybarks catch alight and the strong updraughts created by the fire whip strips of burning bark high into the air where they are swept along by the wind. These burning pieces of bark can start spot fires five to six miles in front of the main fire, in extreme conditions even twelve to fifteen miles. It must be remembered that one small glowing ember can start these catastrophic fires if the weather conditions are right.

Conditions for explosive running crown fires can develop in a few hours in the ever changeable weather of southeastern Australia. These are areas of cool, wet winters and generally dry summers with very hot periods in January and February. These hot periods are the danger times, particularly if they follow seasons of below average rainfall, when the eucalypt forests are tinder dry.

Any dry summer's day is a day of fire danger in the southeast corner of Australia. One day in a hot spell may be explosive. This day may begin like any other, cool in the early morning with a little dew. The first signs of danger occur shortly after this dew has dried. The temperature rises rapidly and may be 38°C (100°F) before 10 a.m. A dry, gusty wind springs up; the sky is cloudless; the air is dry. Then suddenly the scale is tipped from dangerous to disastrous when a strong, hot, dry wind comes roaring from the north.

The fire can start in a number of ways—a match or cigarette butt thrown from a car window, someone burning off garden rubbish, a smouldering fire no one has bothered to put out during earlier, cooler days. When the heat and dryness become effective the fire blazes hotly through the undergrowth, but with the assistance of the wind it soon races up the tree trunks and explodes in the crowns and then roars along with indescribable noise. Bark flakes and strips create spot fires ahead of the main front. Within hours a whole range of hills is engulfed in flames destroying everything before them. It is impossible to put the fire out, only a wind change or cooler, wet weather will check it.

After the fire nothing visible is alive, everything is charred, a white ash covers the ground. All the undergrowth plants and litter have burnt away. A huge log still smoulders.

Not a leaf is left on the eucalypts. No animal can be heard. Countless birds, particularly the small undergrowth species, have been killed: nearly all the insects are wiped out. Yet beneath the ash and charred remains the forest is still alive. Burrowing animals from Wombats to ants have survived in their underground places. Possums deep in hollows also are still alive. With a return of cooler weather and a little rain the eucalypts will send out new shoots, seeds of wattles will germinate, other shrubs, grasses and ferns will send up new shoots from underground root stock. The revival may be too slow in coming for some of the surviving mammals which must find food soon to survive, but some will live.

The destruction has been immense, but in spite of a catastrophic setback the forest recovers in time.

These extremely severe bushfires pose acute dangers for man as well and some of the worst fires have claimed many lives and inflicted inestimable damage on forests, property and livestock. The worst fire day ever was 'black Friday'—Friday January 13th 1939 when 71 people lost their lives in southern Victoria. A more recent explosive fire occurred in Tasmania in February 1967 when over 50 people died in the fires. These

were the worst, but as early as February 1851, ten people died in bushfires in Victoria. Bushfires of this intensity are rare in the summer rainfall
areas of northern New South Wales and southern Queensland.

The worst fires will kill some of the trees. Most susceptible to this
destruction are the Mountain Ashes. In a way they destroy themselves
for the cause of their death is the accumulation of their own litter, particularly shed bark, around their bases. This litter burns slowly and is in
contact with the tree's bark with the result that the bark is exposed to a
long slow burn which even its great insulating ability cannot deal with.
The tree is in effect ringbarked. The skeletons of trees killed in this way
in the 1939 fires in southern Victoria still cover the hillsides, towering
over the new regenerating forest.

Since the 1939 fires it has been found that Victoria's regenerating ash
forest is the habitat of a particularly interesting marsupial, Leadbeater's
Possum. It was first recorded in these new forests in 1961. The find caused
a great deal of excitement for previously the little possum was known
from only five specimens, the last of which was collected 50 years
previously. Leadbeater's Possum was thought to be extinct. But since
that first find in 1961 these possums were found to be not uncommon in
the forests regenerating after the disastrous bushfires of 1939. Zoologists
now consider that Leadbeater's Possums need this kind of habitat and
will disappear from old, mature and over-mature forests. If this is so, it
can be said that the possums' long term survival depends on fire.

Fire plays an even more specialised role in the balance between rainforest and eucalypts. This point can best be illustrated by considering the
relations between the Mountain Ash and the temperate rainforests of
Victoria and Tasmania. In these States there are large tracts of forest
which in reality are rainforests with the eucalypts superimposed. The
perpetuation of this vegetation type depends entirely on fire.

Mountain Ash cannot regenerate under the dense cover of the rainforest trees, the Antarctic Beeches, Sassafras, tree ferns and blackwoods.
The reason they can survive in association with them is their tremendous
vigour, they outgrow the rainforest species, in fact the eucalypts which
are the same age as the rainforest trees tower high above them. If no fire
occurs during the eucalypt's life span of 300–400 years these trees will die
off and disappear as they cannot regenerate. Pure rainforests will be left.
But in Australia's climate this is an unlikely event. Fire will sweep
through the area eventually one explosive day after a series of dry
seasons. All the trees will probably be killed for the accumulation of
litter will make the fire too intense for even the eucalypts to survive.
Regeneration will be from seed. The fire will have prepared a perfect

seed bed and all tree species that were there before the fire will grow again. The eucalypts survive because their greater vigour allows them to gain enough height so that they will not be overshadowed by the rain-forest species. The cycle will renew itself. If the fires are less intense and more frequent the rainforest species will eventually die out and the understorey will become of the wet sclerophyll type.

A eucalypt tree produces a vast amount of seed during its lifetime—a River Red Gum for instance may produce 100–150 million seeds before it dies and is replaced by a single tree growing from a single seed. Huge quantities of seed are available in a virgin eucalypt forest at all times, but it is not needed until a gap forms or a fire prepares a seed bed, which may not be for hundreds of years. The excess seed does not go to waste, how-ever, for it is the food for many kinds of animals—particularly cockatoos, parrots and a small number of insects. Cockatoos can in fact systematically eat a forest's whole seed crop while ants may gather the fallen seeds on a similar scale.

So far only the plants of a eucalypt forest have been considered but all the animal life is inextricably tied to the plants; a large proportion to the eucalypts themselves. The animal life benefits either directly or indirectly from the eucalypts and other plants. The vegetarians live on the euca-lypts and other plants themselves, the leaves, flowers, bark, sap, roots and even on the wood. A whole host of insectivores and carnivores live on the vegetarians; this group keeps the plant eaters under control and stops them from overwhelming the trees. Like any ecosystem* the eucalypt forest is maintained by a sensitive system of checks and balances between growth and growth producing factors such as climate and soil, attacks on the growth by vegetarian animals, and the predation on these plant eaters.

In the forest as a whole there is a constant interchange of influence between trees and animals. But as far as the eucalypts are concerned one animal group has a far greater effect than all the others combined. It is largely a hidden force constantly gnawing at the trees, and working under cover or being well camouflaged. This force is ceaselessly at work and has as much influence on the appearance of trees and therefore the forests, as fire, soil or climate. This force is composed of countless millions of insects which live on all parts of the eucalypts and in all stages of their lives. The majority, such as termites, scale insects, lerps, galls and borers, are so well hidden or so small that they are rarely seen by humans. Others are much larger but they escape attention because of their camou-

* A system in which the inorganic and organic components of the environment are integrated to form a natural unit

Only at night are the tree climbing marsupials like this Common Ringtail active in the eucalypt forests. In the daytime they are hidden in nests or curled up in a tree hollow

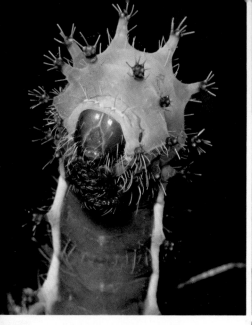

ABOVE: Disturbed while feeding, a caterpillar of the Emperor Gum Moth assumes a defensive attitude. The 4-inch caterpillars feed only on eucalypt leaves

ABOVE RIGHT: Male Dainty Tree Frog calling. His enormously distended throat acts as a resonator

RIGHT: The Male Emperor Gum Moth has a wingspan of up to six inches

BELOW: Thick-tailed Gecko. During the day this six-inch gecko hides under rocks in a hilly forest. It emerges at night to stalk insects among the ground litter

flage or because they live only in the topmost parts of the trees. Included in this group are the stick insects, scarab beetles, leaf beetles and sawflies, which are all known to have completely defoliated trees or even whole forests. After such an onslaught the forests look as though they have been ravaged by fire and indeed recover in the same way—by sending out epicormic shoots.

The forests as the result of the growth patterns inherent within the trees themselves, the soil qualities, the weather, fires, regeneration and animal influences, are ever changing and ever dynamic. In the end all influences balance out and produce the types of forests that now stand in southeastern Australia.

Raised on her hindlegs, a female Barred Bandicoot watches over her two young-at-heel. At this age, when they are too old to fit in the pouch, but still too young to be aware of the dangers of the forest, the youngsters are most vulnerable. This bandicoot's usual litter is three

8 Night in Eucalypt Forest

IT IS NOVEMBER, early summer, in a dry sclerophyll forest in Tasmania's northeast corner. With the first touch of coolness in the afternoon air a small group of Bennett's Wallabies rise lazily to their feet and hop from the cover of a patch of wattle trees. Slowly they make their way to an open, grassy space. But before they begin the night's grazing they sit upright at the clearing's edge. The last light streams through the forest from behind them and catches the long hairs of their thick pelts. They stand outlined in light as they clean their faces, scratch their chests, or just stand still, ears pricked, in the last relaxed moments of daylight.

Just before daylight melts away completely a sturdy animal, even blacker than the evening light, shuffles out from a hollow in a large fallen tree. At the entrance to his lair he raises his large, moist nose and in a series of loud snorts, like explosively exhaled breath, sniffs the air. He is not testing the air for danger—he has no natural enemies—but rather for any possible food, for the black animal is a scavenger, the Tasmanian Devil. When he leaves his lair in a slow shuffling gait it is possible to see his size and build. It is a male, with heavily built muscular shoulders and neck and an immense head with jaws so powerful that he can crunch easily through bone. His hindquarters are not so strong and taper off into a short black tail. He would weigh about 25 pounds and he stands 12 inches at the shoulder. His coat is glossy black relieved with crescent-shaped patches of white on the chest and rump. In some Devils these white patches are very small or may be absent altogether.

The Devil moves off in his shuffling lope to search the forest for anything edible. Being slow in his movements, depending on strength and persistence rather than speed, he will not be able to hunt any quick animals for himself—nor does he try. Possums and wallabies can easily outmanoeuvre him. At times a Devil, using stealth and cunning, may take a young inexperienced wallaby or possum. But normally he eats mostly carrion. He makes for a small stream which flows through the forest and with his ultra-sensitive nose detects some freshwater crayfish which he catches and eats. The crayfish are only appetisers for the Devil and he does not stay long at the stream, snorting and snuffling, guided by scent and aided by his wire-like sensory hairs on lips, cheeks and chin, he sets off to find more sustaining food. He moves on tireless legs. He is over a mile from his lair when he suddenly stops in his tracks. Nose raised to the sky he tests the air carefully; the unmistakable scent of a dead wallaby reaches his nostrils. Wallabies are abundant in the forest and in his mile's travel the Devil stampeded many in front of him, but he did not give chase. This is different; moving faster now he heads directly to the source of the scent. About 200 yards further on he finds the wallaby where it died earlier in the day. It succumbed to the combined effects of old age and a respiratory ailment.

The Devil is the first of his kind to find the wallaby and is still cautious. He trots up and down behind the bushes that hide the wallaby, and snorting and softly growling, circles several times. Soon he cannot contain himself any longer, breaks cover and begins his meal. Devils are among the most efficient eaters. In the case of this wallaby the Devil begins simply at any point, tail, leg, head and keeps crunching till he has had enough. That is, if he had this windfall to himself. But even though wallabies are extremely numerous, not many die on any one day and other Devils have picked up the scent. Before long, one, then two, other black shapes are seen approaching and run up and down behind the bushes. The new arrivals are greeted with snarling, growling and snorting. Circling ever closer, the other two Devils, one a female and smaller than the other two, also growling and snarling, eventually snatch at the food. A three-way tug-of-war ensues, but while pulling and growling the Devils keep on eating, crunching relentlessly. The meal, towards the end is frequently interrupted by savage fighting. Slow as they are, the Devils can inflict serious wounds on each other. Standing face to face they snarl and lash out with their huge canine teeth. These fights sound ferocious, growls and snarls occasionally rising in pitch to a scream, but tonight no damage is done. However, the newly arrived male is an old warrior and must have fought many more damaging duels. He has large scars on his head and neck, and slashes across his lips and nose have distorted his features.

The wallaby is soon demolished, only fluffs of fur and bone splinters remain. With a few parting growls, each of the Devils goes his own way. When out of each other's sight they stop, sit on their haunches and using both hands clean their faces thoroughly. On their own, the Devils are quite beautiful, their surly dispositions do not show. They are in sleek condition, the black glossy, the white spotless, their noses moist, their whiskers with a metallic shine.

Eventually, their stomachs full, the Devils return to their lairs, which may be as much as two miles away. They will retire to digest and if tomorrow is a sunny day, they may come out and bask in the sun.

While the Devils were feeding and fighting, a pale bushy-tailed animal flitted by several times. He, too, was attracted to the dead wallaby, but while the Devils were there he had no chance. But this slightly built marsupial is not really a scavenger—he is a hunter of consummate skill and infinite grace. He is inquisitive, where the Devil is suspicious and snarling; he is fast and has finesse, where the Devil is slow and ponderous. He is the spotted Quoll. Quolls, too, are common in these forests.

Not long after the Devil left his hollow log, the young Quoll emerged from his nest of grass hidden amongst the rocks of a hill slope. He was immediately alert, ears pricked, eyes wide, sensitive nose twitching. His every movement is quick and decisive. Before long he has set off into the forest. This Quoll is lightly built and does not yet have the hard muscles and greater toughness of the fully mature animals. However his total length of 30 inches, of which eleven inches is tail, is that of the full-grown animal. But he is still lighter in weight than the adult. The young Quoll has dense soft fur. On his upper side he is warm yellow-brown and underneath, including the underside of the tail, he is white. He has about sixty white spots sprinkled over his back, but none on his face or tail.

The young Quoll was born in early June, in the cold of winter. At birth he was just over an eighth of an inch in length and shared his mother's pouch with five brothers and sisters. He grew rapidly; within two days he was twice his size at birth and within a week had tripled his size. Even so he was still small, pink and helpless. Only his mouth and front paws were developed to any degree—his ears, tail and hind limbs were just tiny buds.

By the time the young were six weeks old they were quite conspicuous, their tails and bodies hanging from their mother's rudimentary pouch. At this age the spots on their backs also began to show faintly. By late August when two and a half months old, the young Quolls became detached from their mother's nipples for the first time and she now left them in the nest occasionally. As soon as she returned after a foraging trip the young would call out to her and she would scoop them under herself. But it is difficult for the mother to get away from them. All six cling to her whenever they can, hanging on to her fur tenaciously with claws and teeth.

From late August onwards, the young became increasingly adventurous and playful and wrestle, roll and generally play with each other outside the lair. Standing toe to toe, they box each other's ears, making mock attacks at each other's throats, or rushing in after a careful stalking.

By the end of October when about eight weeks old they no longer hang onto their mother and at four and a half months become entirely independent. Now, in late November, the young have drifted away and have found their own nests and own hunting grounds.

After emerging from his lair and skirting the quarrelling Devils, the Quoll lopes towards a more open part of the forest, a stony ridge where grass is sparse and short and no bracken ferns grow. Here he begins his hunt—always active, always alert. He covers the slope in his easy, fluid rhythmic jog, his nose close to the ground, ears pricked, bushy tail straight out behind. His nose is the first to detect prey—it leads him to a grass tussock. With rapid digg ng motions he has soon uncovered a beetle larva which is quickly eaten. No time to pause and on he lopes to where a branch fallen from a eucalypt lies on the ground. This is thoroughly investigated—the Quoll pokes his nose in here, digs a little there, but finds nothing of interest. On he goes. He is still young and somewhat inexperienced. He is easily frightened. A large Masked Owl, a female, lands in the branches overhead and the Quoll races off at great speed, as if his life depended on it, his tail straight up in the air. The owl is concentrating on something else. Like all wild animals, the young Quoll has soon forgotten his fright and continues as if nothing happened.

His ears pick up a faint rustling sound—he freezes, tense, pointed nose straining forward to get a scent, one front paw raised ready for immediate action. His nose soon confirms that he is on the trail of a small native mouse, gnawing and feeding not far from the shelter of a large flat rock. Slowly the Quoll stalks closer in the virtual darkness. But it is no too dark for his large sensitive eyes to spot the mouse. He positions himself to cut off the rodent's retreat to the shelving rock—bobs his head to gauge distance—sets himself like a spring.

The mouse never knew. A soft squeak and it was all over. The Quoll carries it off to a sheltered spot and there eats his small meal alone.

The Masked Owl watches the drama from her perch low in a eucalypt. But only from the corner of her eye; she is now leaning forward, her attention riveted on a Tasmanian Ringtail Possum gathering nesting material in a small paperbark tree. The sooty-grey possum is biting off small twigs and collecting them in a coil of his tail. He is so busy that he did not notice the owl landing silently in the eucalypt only 50 yards away. Rustling noises made by the possum are listened to intently by the owl, for she can strike accurately, guided solely by her hearing. Tonight this is not necessary, for a half moon has risen and shines from a cloudless sky. The owl watches for the possum to emerge from the cover of the paperbark to make her strike.

His tail clutching a thick roll of twigs for nest building, the ringtail climbs to the outside of the paperbark's crown and reaches out for the branches of a neighbouring eucalypt. This is what the owl has been watching for. She glides down from her perch, huge talons extended. In a whirl of soft feathers and dagger-like claws the possum is snatched in mid-stride. His load of twigs spills to the ground. The owl is a huge bird and her talons strike deep—killing the possum instantly. Hardly pausing in her flight she flies on to land in the crown of a tall eucalypt where she devours the ringtail. The whole episode took place in complete silence.

The carnivorous hunters, marsupials and bird, give tension and drama to night in the bush. The more peaceful vegetarians and insect eaters add liveliness, charm and a dash of the unexpected.

Most of the surprises come from the large Tasmanian Brushtail Possums. The brushtails, with their dense, long, soft and shiny fur, are everywhere. They race through the trees with a skill that has an element of audacity, even recklessness. They just do not seem to care if they crash down—it never seriously hurts them.

At this time of the year the mature females have well-grown young. As a result they are an odd mixture of extreme tolerance and aggressiveness; tolerance towards their young who can be very trying, and aggression towards other mature possums—particularly the importunate males. There are two colour forms of the possum. Most common is the silver-grey; the other is a rich deep chestnut that seems even glossier than the grey variety. Brown coloured possums are only slightly less numerous than the silver-grey ones. Mainland Common Brushtails are always silver-grey.

Shortly after sunset two possums emerge from their den in a large hollow in a dead eucalypt. For a moment they pause, their black bushy tails outlined against the still-bright sky. The larger possum then marks several broken branches near the hollow's entrance by rubbing it with scent from a gland on her chest. This marks the hollow as exclusively hers. The silver-grey adult, with her chestnut joey riding on her back, climbs down the tree head first and when about five feet from the ground, leaps down. The two then amble, flat-footed, toes turned out, towards a Black Peppermint with a dense crown, the young following his mother like a shadow. Rapidly they climb to the top and begin to feed on the green shoots. The tree is in flower, attracting many insects, and both flowers and their visitors are added food for the possums.

The young possum is irrepressible—he rushes all over the place. He lunges out at flying insects, hangs upside down from a clump of blossoms, dashes from branch to branch, rushes back to his mother. She, meanwhile, is feeding methodically but is never left in peace by the young for long. He grabs at the leaves she is eating, climbs over her back, playfully boxes her ears. All these indignities are tolerated, or more accurately ignored, without reprisals from the indulgent parent.

Brushtail possums abound in the forest and bark-scrabbling gallops indicate the arrival of more of the uninhibited marsupials. Adult possums are not very tolerant of each other at close quarters and soon screams, growls and explosive coughs from the crown of the peppermint testify to several encounters. Besides vocalising, the possums communicate with scent from glands on their chins, chests and beneath the tail. The glands at the base of the tail exude a strong musky odour. This gland plays an important part in establishing territory.

Through the system of scent and voice the possums in the peppermint keep their distance and no damage is done. It just sounds ferocious. But should any of the codes be transgressed, fights break out. These can be serious, for under the soft fur the possums have razor-sharp claws and ripping teeth and a temperament that allows free use of them. In fact, a mature Brushtail possum can be a more formidable adversary than a Quoll.

A dark, bulky shape walks along a narrow track. Underneath the peppermint it stops, squats down and scratches its chest with a strongly clawed hind foot and continues slowly on its way. The Wombat is unperturbed by any commotion of possums above him and walks on with his lumbering flat-footed gait. After a few minutes he stops and begins his browsing and grazing for the night. Grass is nipped off with the incisors and crunched between the large molars in the jaws of the animal's broad, strong head.

Strength, indomitable strength, is the impression the Wombat makes most vividly. He is a round, barrel-shaped animal without a visible tail and about three feet long. His fur is coarse, his muscular front feet are strongly clawed. Strong claws and legs are needed for digging the large burrows in which he spends the day.

Strong, perhaps plodding as the Wombat might at first appear, he can be quite fast in galloping over a fallen log or bulldozing his way through the undergrowth.

The Wombat, walking and grazing, eventually reaches one of the many open patches in the forest, a place where a huge eucalypt has crashed down. Frequent fires have prevented regrowth of the trees. In their place is an area of tussocky grass forming an ideal habitat for bandicoots.

Bandicoots are nervous, highly strung animals and the arrival of the dark Wombat snapping a twig underfoot has alerted them. One nearest the Wombat, with a sneeze-like squeak, jumps straight into the air with alarm and then makes off through the grass. The bandicoot, small, lightly built, fast and above all elegant, is the very antithesis of the lumbering Wombat that disturbed it.

A group of three Barred Bandicoots, a mother with two young close by her, are busy in the tussocky patch. At this time of the year Tasmania's bush abounds with young mammals. The two young bandicoots are still small, less than half the adult size and could easily nestle in a person's hand. Their pattern is more pronounced than their mother's and shows the bars across their rumps, though this is difficult to see clearly as the little ones are never still. They race through the grass. The mother's colours and build are more easily studied, for she is watchful over her vulnerable young. Sitting upright she sniffs the air in the Wombat's direction, raised on her hindlegs she exposes the white underside and the fineness of her limbs, and her long pointed muzzle. The pink nose twitches, as do the long slender ears. Her black button eyes glisten in the pale light. All is well. She resumes her hunt. With her long nose she snuffles and snorts amongst the fallen leaves and grass tussocks for slugs, snails, slaters, worms and insects. The young return to her from time to time—get between her feet, jump on top of her, snatch food from her mouth, then dash off again. Like all marsupials she tolerates it with an air of benign dignity.

Now she is on the trail of something interesting—she concentrates hard to pinpoint its exact location with her nose and not even the young can distract her. She has found the spot where the beetle larva, buried in the ground, is feeding on grass roots. She digs down with a rapid action of her sharp claws, pauses, inserts her nose, snorting briefly, then digs further. It is a large larva and wriggles vigorously when it is exposed. Highly strung, the bandicoot leaps high in the air with fright. She is back immediately, kills the larva with scratching movements of her claws and eats it before the young can take it from her.

Before continuing her search, she listens for possible danger. Something rustles on the slope and she sits upright, her nose twitching above the grass.

What drew the bandicoot's attention was a Bettong leaving the grassy patch. Hopping slowly, the pale grizzled brown rat-kangaroo makes his way along the slope. Every time his feet touch the ground he lets out a wheezing snort. Long after his little shape has disappeared amongst the tall ferns his 'snort, snort, snort' is faintly audible. His track, like a tunnel

A Koala rests between the trunk and stout epicormic shoots of a Manna Gum. Ribbons of bark trail from a well-developed epicormic knob.

ABOVE: Boobook Owl
TOP RIGHT: Leadbeater's Possum clinging to the drooping foliage of a Mountain Ash
BOTTOM RIGHT: Female Greater Glider with her young

This black form of the Eastern Quoll is much rarer than the usual
brown variety. Black and brown sometimes appear in the one litter

through grass, bracken and shrubs, seems to finish abruptly at the remains of a fallen eucalypt—but when he gets there the Bettong effortlessly leaps over the four-foot high obstacle—seeming to erupt from the green ferns—and continues on his way. His track will lead him back to his grass nest, carefully dug and placed against a big rock.

Low in a small, dead eucalypt on the sparser forest of the slope, is a small knot-hole. The entrance is only just over an inch in diameter and leads to a small chamber. This is neatly filled with a nest made of gum leaves. Eucalypt scent clings to the little nest. Its occupant, the tiny Tasmanian Pygmy Possum, has long since left to look for small insects amongst eucalypt leaves and behind bark. When he left his nest he climbed to the top of the dead sapling and from there to a eucalypt with smooth, white bark glistening in the moonlight. In that tree he finds all his food. The midget, his head and body combined barely three inches long, is inspecting the few loose strips and flakes of old bark still clinging to the new. He uncovers a few small insects which he quickly eats. The lightweight possum races over the new bark with great agility but without leaving the slightest mark on the smooth, waxy surface. This is because he runs over the tree on his soft pink cushions of toes. He does have claws on his toes but these are situated above the padded tips and are rarely used in climbing.

After crunchily and daintily dismembering a small insect pulled from behind a bark flake, the pygmy possum freezes momentarily then strains forward with ears, eyes and long sensitive whiskers. He sits on his haunches with hands clenched like fists. He is anchored by his pink tail; everything is ready to lunge out at an Emperor Gum Moth, a female looking for a place to lay eggs. The moth, larger than the possum, comes closer and closer, inspecting one eucalypt leaf after another. She is only inches from the possum. He darts forward, claws outstretched and grabs at the insect. He hits the moth and with his claws rips the insect's wings— but she flies too strongly and veers away into the darkness—leaving the tiny marsupial in a whirlwind of fluff from her furry body and wings.

Possums are fastidiously clean animals and he settles down on his hind legs to clean himself thoroughly. First his face and whiskers, which are washed with forward strokes of the hands, moistened by licking, then the rest of the insect's fluff is shaken off by scratching and further licking. Immediately after his cleaning session he leaves tiny wet footprints on the tree's bark as he sets out to continue his search.

The eucalypt forest at night has a wildlife rich in unrehearsed drama. Participants in the drama, both large and small, return to their respective resting places at the first hint of daylight and, except for an occasional

---

pair of Mouse Sminthopsis with the male on the right. Amongst the most delicately built of all the marsupials, they are none the less quite tough, killing centipedes and grasshoppers their own size

wallaby, they withdraw deep into the forest's hidden recesses. Here they rest, unseen and largely unsuspected by the noisier creatures of the day.

AN ABUNDANCE of marsupials in the peak of condition with rich pelts and a healthy alertness is the key feature of a night in undisturbed dry sclerophyll forest in Tasmania. Marsupials are numerous in the mainland forests also but they do not dominate the nightlife as much as they do in Tasmania. Other animal groups, bats, insects, spiders claim a greater share of the attention.

A good place to experience the nocturnal wildlife on the mainland is in a coastal forest somewhere near the New South Wales-Victoria border. Early autumn is an excellent time of the year. The heat of summer has passed; the nights are not yet cold.

THE FOREST, on undulating sandy terrain, is a dense mature stand of Silvertop Ash with here and there a sprinkling of Yellow Stringybarks and Red Bloodwoods. No bushfires have ravaged this forest in recent years and the understorey plants are as vigorous as the eucalypts. Tall shrubs and small trees—wattles, hakeas and occasional patches of Hill Banksia—rise out of thick grass intermingled with bracken ferns and short prickly bushes. A rich, virgin forest which has many ancient trees with hollows in their trunks and branches.

Twilight. One by one the day birds fall silent. A family of Blue Wrens twitter intimately to each other as they cuddle closely together on a branch. Soon they ruffle their feathers, tuck their heads under their wings and sleep. The last echoes of the Kookaburra's raucous laugh fade away with the last light from the forest. Day insects fold their wings and settle down under leaves, on bark or along grass stalks. The forest is in darkness, but for another hour the sky is still bright. The wind drops—for a moment there is complete silence.

A howl from the ridge top shatters the silence. A Dingo signals the beginning of the nightlife. He howls several times more and is answered by others so far away they are only just audible. But it is not a prolonged chorus tonight and soon the Dingo sets off on his hunt, trotting silently on cushioned feet along a forest track.

The Dingo's howl has made the wallabies uneasy and restless—a rustle of wind, a falling twig, makes them snap upright, ears and nose scanning the forest for danger. At any suspicious noise they dash off into the undergrowth, thumping their feet hard into the ground for the first few bounds as a warning to others.

The rest of the forest wakes. In the trees heads pop out of hollows and for some time their owners quietly look over their domain. Then suddenly there is action. A ringtail leaves her nest in the thick foliage and in a smooth-flowing, climbing action transfers from an undergrowth paperbark to a eucalypt and climbs into the crown. Sugar Gliders cavort with each other around their nest hole before, one by one, they glide down into the forest. In a Yellow Stringybark the Greater Glider is climbing to the topmost branches of his home tree. He is joined by his mate which slept in another hole in the same tree. They do not stay in the home tree for long but, bunching their feet under them, spring into space from the stringybark's topmost branch. Airborne, the gliders spread their legs and arms, putting their fists under their chins with elbows stretched out. The air catches under the furry gliding membrane and billows it taut. The gliders parachute gently down to the butt of a Silvertop Ash where they land with resounding 'clops' of claws on bark. Both animals gallop up to the top of the ash and take off again gliding another 80 yards or so. As they glide, their bushy 20-inch tails stream out behind acting as rudders as they weave amongst the trunks and branches. Greater Gliders are the largest of their kind. They are slender, loosely built animals and in spite of their size of just over three feet are surprisingly light in weight.

At almost the same time as the Greater Gliders speed to their feeding tree, the slightly smaller Yellow-bellied Glider leaves his home. Uttering his gurgling shriek as he floats gently down, he weaves in and out amongst the trees. He shows remarkable control through the air, at one stage making a curving 90° turn to land in a favourite tree. His gliding membrane extends from his ankle right to his fingers. And unlike the Greater Glider, where the membrane reached only from elbow to ankle, he spreads his hands wide. He does not tuck his fists under his chin. He lands at the base of a large eucalypt, climbs to the top, not quite as quickly and expertly as the Greater Glider, and resumes his way along his aerial route. It is a well marked route, its landing stations marked by patches of scuffed bark. The Yellow-bellied Glider's progress through the forests can be followed by sound—nearly every glide is accompanied by his wild call.

With darkness, a Tuan uncoils from his sleeping posture and is ready for action. Perhaps the quickest animal in the forest, he is off, moving through the trees with quickness and lightning reflexes. He pauses here and there, tapping the tree bark with his front feet or a gentle slapping of his black, bottlebrush tail. At one place the tapping is answered and soon two Tuans have joined forces.

High in his tree roost, a Long-eared Bat unfurls his ears, lifts his head and for a while quivers all over as he warms himself for the night's flight.

Using clawed feet and clawed thumbs on his wings, he crawls to the roost's entrance and squeezes out through the opening. Ears fully erect and longer than his head, he casts about him with beams of ultrasonic sound, then on broad leathery wings flies off, instantly merging with the darkness.

At the same time as the tree holes and nests are vacated and the Dingo trots along his forest track, there are stirrings of wakening life amongst the grass and small bushes. A Wombat is busily scratching and digging at his burrow entrance, sending a great arc of sand down the slope with every powerful stroke of his front feet.

Uttering a few squeaks, a Short-nosed Bandicoot explodes from his grass nest and skips daintily off. Graceful as the bandicoot is, he must take second place to the Mouse Sminthopsis which jumps lightly from his hollow log. Grey above and white underneath, the marsupial mouse is of the most elegant build. His legs are slim; large sensory whiskers flank a sensitive tapering muzzle; his eyes are round, dark and large; his ears finely sculptured and like his nose are never still. The marsupial is only a few inches long and soon disappears amongst the fallen leaves and ground plants.

The first sounds of the night transform the nocturnal birds. With large eyes wide open and an alive, alert posture, they change from unobtrusive bundles of feathers to live, vital animals. At the same time as he opens his large yellow eyes, the Boobook Owl sleeks his feathers and is ready for action.

The change in the Tawny Frogmouth is even more dramatic. With an intense stare of yellow eyes over thick horny beak, he no longer resembles a branch stub. He is perched, looking for prey in the lower levels of the forest where he is most interested in the activities of ground animals such as centipedes and large spiders.

Before the light has completely drained from the sky, the White-throated Nightjar springs from the ground on his small legs and is airborne on large pointed wings. His feathers are soft and flexible and his wingbeats, like those of all nightbirds, are soundless. His neat, hawk-like silhouette cleanly outlined against the sky, the nightjar wheels and turns around the tall eucalypts catching insects in his large beak.

Night life wakes in the smallest patches of ground and in the deepest corners of the forest. A green-coloured tree frog is distracted by a moth flying by and he relaxes his rigid, folded pose against the plant stem. Other frogs, hidden in the soil and litter, push their way out of the ground.

A Bandy-bandy snake, neat in alternate black and white bands, eases himself from under the log and slowly, sinuously pushing his smooth 15-inch body through the undergrowth, seeks out another termitarium to feed on the termite larvae, eggs and mature insects. Scorpions, which were flattened in cracks and hollows, now walk on the butts of trees and logs, pincers held high, tail with poisonous spine arched over the back. Centipedes rustle amongst the leaves but seldom show themselves for fear that an ever watchful frogmouth will pounce.

The cryptic moths shake off their disguises and flutter through the air, safe from the attacks of the day birds but not from bats which sweep down on them even in the darkest parts of the forest. Numerous spiders have left their silken retreats and are building traps and snares to catch the moths and other insects. At night, as during the day, the bush is alive.

Such is the awakening of the hunters and hunted of the night. A few hours after waking each is engrossed in his own speciality. Specialisation is directed towards three points—to obtain food, avoid predators and, at certain times of the year, find a mate. This nocturnal activity is perhaps best observed by revisiting the animals some hours after they have left their homes.

The ringtail sits hunched on the leafy branch of a small tea tree. With her hands she pulls other branches towards her and snips off the growing tips with sharp incisors.

A late flowering Red Bloodwood has attracted the family of Sugar Gliders. One by one the small grey gliders move unhesitatingly from one tree to another till they reach the bloodwood. They land low on the tree's brown bark and, sending down a fine shower of flakes, they gallop to the topmost branches. Sugar Gliders are amongst the more vocal marsupials and they communicate in a series of insistent 'chirring' sounds, quite angrily and aggressively, if they get in each other's way. But the tree is large, the gliders are small and soon they have dispersed to the outer branches. Flowers are clustered together in white, hemispherical bunches, large enough to support the added weight of a glider. The marsupials arrived at a gallop and in the same breathless speed, without pausing, bury their faces deep into the flower clumps and lick the nectar. However busy they may be with the flowers, their senses are receptive to other stimuli and their reactions are quick. Insects on the flowers are snatched up and eaten. Leaf-eating beetles lumbering by on buzzing wings are followed with intense interest. Only when they have taken the edge off their appetite do the gliders slow a little, clean their faces and comb their fur.

The Greater Glider, though alert, is not quite the whirlwind that the

Sugar Glider is. He also made his way to a Red Bloodwood, a different tree that has finished flowering and is now heavily laden with woody capsules. He prefers the highest branches of the tree's crown and there settles down to a meal of the tender new shoots of the eucalypt. Shortly afterwards another 'clop' on the bark and he is joined by his mate. The two settle down to a quiet, lengthy meal, pausing frequently to peer over the forest, on the alert for their main enemy, the Powerful Owl. As the half moonlight penetrates and brightens the sky the silhouettes of the two gliders stand out sharply—slender, furry shapes with long, bushy tails gently swinging in the breeze and round, fur-fringed ears twitching to catch the faintest suspicious noise. Both silhouettes seem black against the sky, but in reality they are of a very different colour. The male is the usual colour form—very dark, almost black, but with white fur on the underside. The female, however, is ghostly pale. Her head and under-parts are pure white and her back is also white but suffused with the palest smoky grey.

Red Bloodwoods occur only as pockets in the ash forest but these are focal points for the feeding gliders. On the flat below the gentle slope where the Greater Gliders are calmly feeding, a pair of Yellow-bellied Gliders landed earlier. They arrived from different directions, keeping in touch with each other by their characteristic gurgling shrieks. Eventually they converged on the same tree and shuffled up the trunk till they came to the first main branch. Head to head they concentrate here, licking furiously at the bark. The prize is the bloodwood's rich flow of kino oozing from one of the grooves which the gliders themselves have bitten deeply into the bark. Here at this bark wound the gliders stay, licking kino for about an hour and a half, lifting their heads only as they see the hunting Dingo trot past or a bat wheeling in close; their brown bodies are pressed close to the brown bark which highlights the dark stripe down their backs and the rich quality of the bushy tails.

A pair of marsupial hunters dash through trees and over the ground in a more open patch of the forest. These are the two Tuans that teamed up earlier in the night. Tuans are irrepressible, never still. Their tails reflect their every whim: now bristling like a bottlebrush, now hanging limp in a cascade of black silk. Any animal life of a size they can tackle is potential prey for Tuans; they can be ferocious and tenacious killers. But mostly they hunt insects and other invertebrates; sometimes they lick nectar from flowers. Tonight they do not need to hunt. They find their food. The day has been exceptionally warm and activated a Tiger Snake to hunt: he found a bush rat, struck at it but missed his mark, giving the mammal only a glancing bite. The rat sped away but was fatally wounded and eventually died out of reach of the snake. But the Tuans find the victim. Unlike most meat-eating marsupials they do not fall to immediately, but drag their prey away. The larger, male Tuan who found the rat, drags it backwards towards the nearest tree which he ascends tail first, the rat firmly held in his jaws. His mate joins him there and the two eat together.

After leaving his roost the Long-eared Bat cruised amongst the trunks and shrubs of the forest, wheeling round and through the crowns of the large trees. He flies at considerable speed in virtual darkness, catching his food on the wing and never as much as brushing a leaf. For both dodging obstacles and catching flying insects the bat navigates entirely by the sending and receiving of beams of ultrasonic sound. By this process of echo-location he can not only detect obstructions to his path but also determine whether the objects in front of him are edible or not. With his beams of sound the bat picks up the smallest insects, such as mosquitoes, closes in on them accurately and catches them in his mouth. For this he needs supreme flying skill as well as the efficient echo-location system. In fact the insectivorous bats have greater manoeuvrability and flexibility in flight than most birds. Small and fast, the little bats are amongst the marvels of the forest.

The animals of the forest floor and the birds continue the foraging and hunting just as they began it almost immediately on waking. The Dingo from the ridge top is now more than a mile from his lair and, joined by two of his kind, has singled out a wallaby for attack. They are now in relentless pursuit. The Wombat ambled only a quarter of a mile from his burrow and peacefully grazes in a small patch of grass. Scratching under small logs, and feeling under leaf litter with its dainty white hands, the Mouse Sminthopsis searches for insects and centipedes. Bandicoots alternately digging in a frenzy and skipping through the grass, gather their meals of burrowing insects and a few soft fruits of shrubs.

Shortly after dark the Boobook Owl caught a large bush rat and is now perched with the rodent clasped in his talons, pulling off the last pieces of meat and fur. He drops the tail and hindquarters to the ground. The frogmouth, too, is temporarily satisfied, he has eaten several large ground spiders and crickets, and perched low in a tree utters his soft monotonous 'oom-oom-oom' on and on. The nightjar rests temporarily after his first swooping and diving flights in pursuit of flying moths and beetles. Unlike the bat he has to rely entirely on his eyesight to catch the insects. No Australian bird is equipped for echo-location. The smaller, cold-blooded animals are busy. A tree-frog has just made a prodigious, accurately judged leap at a flying moth and caught it in his jaws. After landing he pushes the struggling insect into his mouth with his hands and swallows hard.

Having emerged from their silk-lined and silk-sealed shelters behind bark or between leaves, the spiders have readied themselves to trap prey in an astonishing variety of most ingenious ways.

Some of the spiders do not make many preparations. Huntsman Spiders, hidden behind a loose sheet of bark on a eucalypt, walk from their retreats and watch from the tree butts for insects below them.

There was no sign at all during the day of the large web which now spans the space between two bushes. In the middle of the large web sits its owner, a female Garden Spider. Each of her eight legs rests lightly on one of the orb's radiating lines of silk.

Not all spiders place their snaring webs between supporting leaves or branches. The Net-casting Spiders, for example, hold expanding nets between their front legs. One such spider, a female, *Dinopis subrufa*, has placed herself in position. She hangs suspended from a series of silken lines stretched between two leaves. Her hindmost pair of legs hold the supporting thread and act as a kind of brake and anchor. Between her two pairs of front legs she holds a net of special soft, white silk. Like this, she hangs motionless. But should a small insect, an ant, small beetle or moth crawl or fly within her range her reflexes react instantly. She hurls herself forward or drops down her line of silk, spreads her front legs wide, expanding the net she holds to several times its size, and clamps it over the insect. There is no escape from the sticky silk.

Of the many remarkable spider stories that can be discovered in the Australian bush few can match that of the Hairy Imperial Spider. Other spiders in the grass and bushes around her have built their snares in complex patterns of silken lines. But the Hairy Imperial Spider simply suspends its web in one single viscous drop on the end of a single strand of silk hanging from one hairy leg. For this drop of liquid is in reality the concentrate from which the spider spins her silk through her spinnerets.

The Angler, as she is sometimes called, sits motionless, awaiting prey. From the very few observations made on this spider it appears that its prey is made up of male moths of the family Noctuidae. It is possible that the spider attracts these insects within range with a scent similar to that exuded by female noctuid moths. Other suggestions are that the attraction is the glistening drop of liquid the spider dangles from her leg. But whatever the lure, as soon as a moth approaches within range the spider twirls the drop and its silken line like a lasso. Once the drop has gained momentum the spider directs it and tries to hit the insect. Usually she succeeds. As soon as the moth is hit the droplet bursts and on exposure to

Winter's morning in a wet sclerophyll forest in eastern Victoria. The tall trees are Mountain Ashes. The long strips of shed bark trailing down the trunks are favoured hunting spots for a number of insect eating birds

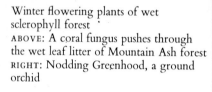

Winter flowering plants of wet sclerophyll forest
ABOVE: A coral fungus pushes through the wet leaf litter of Mountain Ash forest
RIGHT: Nodding Greenhood, a ground orchid

BELOW: Brown Goshawk, hunter of small forest birds

air its content is transformed into silk. Caught in a shower of sticky silk there is no escape for the insect and he is reeled in like a fish by an angler.

For the animals of the night, from the largest to the smallest, life is an unceasing struggle for food and survival. Yet there are moments of relaxation. Each animal eases his tensions according to his nature. A Greater Glider sits facing the breeze in the topmost branches of a tall eucalypt; Sugar Gliders chase each other; Tuans pause at a flower for nectar; a bat glides on outstretched wings; an owl preens; a bandicoot scratches; a legless lizard coils under a bush; a moth flutters through the darkness; a spider opens her egg sac so her young can emerge. These moments are brief.

Searching or defending, tense or relaxed, the animal life at night is ever varied, ever changing and unpredictable.

THE NIGHT DESCRIBED in a southern mainland forest would differ only slightly from a nocturnal visit to a forest in southern Queensland. In the Queensland subtropical forest flowering eucalypts would have been visited by hordes of noisily squabbling flying foxes, but Wombats and pygmy possums would have been absent. There are similar slight differences between forest types. Leadbeater's Possum, for example, is restricted to regenerating Mountain Ash forests while brushtail possums like the more open dry sclerophyll forests and so on.

Differences between the mammal life of Tasmania and that of the mainland are greater. Some species are found only in Tasmania such as the Bettong, Devil and Tasmanian Pygmy Possum. However, the Tuan and all gliders except the Sugar Glider, are missing from the island. Quolls are now very rare on the mainland but still common in parts of Tasmania. But most striking is the difference between Tasmanian and mainland individuals of the one species of mammal. Tasmania's Brushtail Possum is much larger and heavier than the mainland brushtail, also its fur is longer and its tail bushier. The Tasmanian Brushtail forages on the ground much more than mainland individuals. Similarly Tasmania's Bennett's Wallaby, of the same species as the Red-necked Wallaby of the mainland, is heavier and has longer fur. However, mainland forests both by day and by night have a much greater variety of reptiles, rodents, bats, amphibians and invertebrates. These groups in fact increase in number of species the further north you travel and reach their maximum numbers in the tropics.

9 Day in Eucalypt Forest

DAWN UNFOLDS GRADUALLY as the first light infiltrates the mist. The shapes of trees are at first indistinct but soon the smooth Mountain Ash trunks materialise, rising sheer out of a dense layer of dark green tree ferns, blackwoods, Sassafras and Antarctic Beeches. No warmth accompanies the increase in light. The only sound is the gentle tapping of trailing strips of Mountain Ash bark stirring in a gust of wind. Suddenly, without warning, bird calls of unparalleled clarity and volume reverberate through the forest—male Lyrebirds greet the new day with song while perched high in the blackwood or beech in which they have slept.

After his first calls of the new day, the Lyrebird glides down to the valley floor on round, broad wings: the underside of his glorious tail almost the same silvery colour as the mist. Dawn continues to spread its light but underneath the tree ferns, where the Lyrebird alights, it will remain semi-dark all day. The only colours are green and brown. The spreading fronds of the tree ferns filter the light. Their trunks and those of the other trees are covered with mosses, trailing lichens, bryophytes and delicate filmy ferns. Brown is the main colour of the ground which is thickly carpeted with dead leaves, sheets of bark and fallen twigs. They form a moist carpet over the soil and hide earthworms, insects, copepods and other soil organisms, a rich food source for the Lyrebirds. Fungi growing in clumps on tree trunks or pushing through the leaf mould are occasional brighter splashes, mostly yellow and orange.

On landing the Lyrebird begins looking for food by raking the ground with his large, strongly clawed feet. His dark eyes are watchful for the exposed animal life. A slight movement in the damp earth and the Lyrebird snaps up another victim.

His initial appetite satisfied, the Lyrebird becomes restless. Frequently he pauses to give his far carrying call—it is answered from other places up and down the whole valley. At last the Lyrebird cannot contain his energy any longer and runs to one of his display mounds which he prepared in late autumn, in May. The mound, about four feet in diameter, has been scratched completely clear of all debris and growing plants. It is a clear arena for the bird to display on. No vegetation is left to entangle his long tail. Now the bird arrives and, making soft 'chirring' and clicking noises, inspects the mound. Satisfied he launches into his display.

He begins with his own clear notes but as he warms up imitations of other bird calls are woven into the repertoire: songs of the thrush, magpie and butcherbird are punctuated with the ringing notes of a Whipbird; the whispers of thornbills and scrub wrens alternate with the cries of Black Cockatoos and Kookaburras; currawongs and rosella alarm-calls contrast with the sweeter sounds of the Pilot Bird; but the Lyrebird's own notes, the richest and clearest of any songbird, carry the furthest and tighten the whole song into an exciting performance.

Song is only part of his display; before long the bird raises his tail and spreads it forward, covering all of his body and head. Immediately a red-brown and grey bird changes to a shimmering silvery veil. At the climax of the display he makes rhythmic clicking sounds, dances back and forth and sideways on his mound—his tail quivering at every step, its silver startling against the dark green and warm brown of the ferns and soil.

The female briefly visits the mound and elicits this climax to the display. She touches beaks with the dancer then her slim brown form melts away into the gloom. The male continues for a short time, then suddenly the half-hour performance comes abruptly to an end. After a few shakes of his tail and scratches at the mound he too walks off into the forest. He may repeat his performance several more times during the day on any of the dozen or so mounds in his territory.

The whole of the Mountain Ash forested valley is occupied by Lyrebirds; their songs are heard near and far. The valley is a mosaic of the birds' six- to ten-acre territories which the males defend with song and display and into which they attract the females. Each female builds her nest within the territory on a rock ledge, on a stump or in a tree fork and incubates her single egg and raises the young alone.

It is cold, damp and dusky in these wet sclerophyll forests of south-eastern Victoria in winter—yet this is the time when Lyrebirds sing, dance, mate and rear their young.

The Lyrebird is the only bird in full song, but there are many others present. These other birds are not nesting and therefore do not sing but even so they keep in contact with others of their kind with call notes of various kinds. Occasionally a louder alarm call signals a disruption to the routine life of the valley.

The most persistent calls come from high up in the Mountain Ash; non-stop tinkling sounds as if the trees were studded with bells. The sounds are made by Bell Miners, out of sight amongst the leaves of eucalypts where they feed on scale and lerp insects. Occasionally some of the miners sweep down out of the mist to call and chase each other through the undergrowth.

Insect life, on the whole, is not plentiful and the other birds that are heard in the forest have a full time job finding enough food. It is not that the insects have disappeared, it is that they have entered a resting stage during the cold weather. They are hidden deep inside hollows, behind bark or in cocoons spun between leaves or as eggs on trees, shrubs and on the ground. The long ribbons of shed eucalypt bark hanging down from branches and tree forks are favoured hiding places for insects. The resting insect life—with the exception of the lerps and scales—has to be assiduously sought out. This is a task that takes concentration and effort and leaves little time for most of the insectivorous birds to indulge in song or to raise a family.

As the morning wears on, small groups of these birds can be seen busily foraging in all parts of the forest. Around a scramble of fallen branches and twining vegetation at the base of a giant eucalypt a group of eight Brown Thornbills incessantly whisper to each other. The small birds minutely examine every leaf, twig and piece of bark; hanging upside down from the outer foliage or squirming right inside a piece of rolled bark, they find their share of dormant insects and spiders. Sharper, almost hissing notes come from even lower down, from amongst the rotting logs and deep inside a dense clump of tree ferns. These are the scrub wrens. They, too, are tiny and very difficult to see; usually only small shapes darting from one shrub to another.

From a little higher up on the eucalypts comes a mechanical persistent cracking sound. This is not a bird calling, but one systematically tearing a long trailing ribbon of bark to pieces. Jumping over the bark in a flurry of pulling and tearing with its thick, heavy beak is an Eastern Shrike-tit. Its black crest quivers with each new effort. A colourful species in both senses of the word, the seven-inch bird's yellow breast glows in the overcast dimness and its black and white striped head stands out against the dull brown of the tree trunk.

In contrast with the insect and invertebrate life on the vegetation, which is at its lowest ebb at this cold time of the year, the life of the litter layer and topsoil is rich and copious. The reason is moisture. Winter mist and rain keep the ground cover constantly moist and allow the copepods and other litter-decay organisms to multiply rapidly. The small invertebrates are now more numerous than they are in summer when the litter is dry and hot. This food source is, of course, readily accessible to the

Lyrebirds which expose the hopping and squirming animal life with energetic scratching—the result is that the whole valley floor is freshly turned over. But for small birds without strong legs this food supply is locked up. That is, for all except a few opportunists such as the Yellow Robin and the Pilot Bird. They attend the Lyrebirds and feed on the tiny animals exposed by them.

The male Lyrebird which has just left his mound after completing his first display of the day, begins foraging immediately. Wet, decaying leaves are vigorously thrust aside and exposed worms and copepods are quickly picked up. The activity has alerted a pair of Yellow Robins and they draw near. Clinging motionless to the base of a tree they watch the Lyrebird intently. Suddenly one, then the other, robin darts in picking up small insects. They land right underneath the Lyrebird, small bright balls of yellow amongst the sombre colours. The robins are completely ignored; the Lyrebird does not even pause in his scratching as the smaller birds get underfoot and even have leaves and debris heaped on top of them. Pilot Birds are never as insistent and stay out of the range of the Lyrebird's claws.

Deep in the forested valley the daily rhythm is difficult to sense for the light and mist remain an even grey blanket. Time slips by imperceptibly. There is no rising sun or increasing warmth to show that mid-morning has arrived.

But on the valley's northern slope, at a point overlooking the tree ferns and other smaller plants, it is lighter. A Black-tailed Wallaby browses on young plants and the occasional grasses on the slope. His grizzled face is wet from the vegetation and drops of moisture glisten on his warm brown, thick fur. The northern slopes face the winter sun and are drier than the valley floor and southern slopes. The wallaby bounds along his well-worn track up the slope to the shelter of the base of a large Mountain Ash and settles himself down to rest and drowse for the remainder of the day.

But on the slope, as in the valley, birds are the most numerous animals. From the hillside's vantage point it is possible to see treetop species which from the valley had been mere disembodied voices in the mist. The position is now reversed, the Lyrebird's occasional bursts of song drift up from far below while other calls from the treetops make the more immediate impression.

Most insistent are periodic wild cries of 'kee-ah, kee-ah' from the ridge tops, but the owners of these voices are shy and elusive. The mist provides cover and a quiet approach ensures a glimpse of large, dark brown birds. A flock of Yellow-tailed Black Cockatoos is moving through a small stand of wattle trees. The trees are very susceptible to the attack of boring beetles and the cockatoos are searching for the insect larvae. With their powerful, chisel-sharp beaks the birds rip into the wattle stems and then extract the white grubs with their sensitive tongues. Having worked one tree over, a bird flies to another while uttering his wailing cries. As he lands he spreads his long tail revealing pale yellow patches on it. The flock of cockatoos senses something strange or unusual. They fly off in unison, calling loudly in their haste, their feathers beating on the leaves.

Mid-afternoon and a change. The cloud and mist thin out a little and let the afternoon light slant on the northern slopes. The change enlivens the birds of the treetops which until now were prisoners of the mist and were unable to fly any distance. Pied Currawongs shout their clarion calls and King Parrots stop their methodical feeding on gum nuts to make fast sorties through the treetops, their metallic sounds mixing with others of the forest. Currawongs, crow-sized black birds with white patches on wings and tail, are as much part of these forests as are the Lyrebirds and little escapes their steady, yellow-eyed gaze. They are wary birds watching any predators or disturbances from a safe distance, then swooping in if they see an opportunity to seize anything to eat, few things being inedible for a currawong.

The ripple of action precipitated by the change in weather soon settles down. The King Parrots in a whirl of brilliant red and green return to the eucalypts and resume feeding on the seeds. Occasionally they communicate in tinkling notes. The new brightness also highlights the plants.

A variety of prickly-leaved shrubs, wattles and some scrambling plants grow on these slopes. They were crowded out by ferns in the gullies below. Seen closely, brilliant colours glow almost hidden by the deep green foliage. Even in winter a few plants unfold their flowers. Sparsely dotting the hillside is the pink of the Common Heath and the deep red of the bell-shaped Common Correa. At this time of the year with its luminous light, the flowers, covered with droplets of dew, are even more striking in their isolation than if the whole hillside were covered with them. Some of the forest honeyeaters come to gather nectar at these flowers. One of the most common of these birds is the White-naped Honeyeater; he is small, green and white, with a black head. He usually stays high in the trees. But like most honeyeaters he is versatile and now visits some of the flowers. He comes so close that the bare red patch above his eye is distinctly visible.

The honeyeater is suddenly alarmed and flies off. The cause of the interruption is not far off; the undergrowth shakes and there is a sound of breaking sticks. The movement stops at the edge of the clump of plants and a long leathery nose tests the air in all directions. All is judged to be safe and the nose followed by a spiny, prickly body bulldozes out of the undergrowth. The Echidna which has just broken cover is a short-legged, but powerful animal about 16 inches long. His emergence has attracted the attention of the ever watchful currawongs and one of them swoops down. Without even looking up the Echidna immediately retracts his head and digs his strong claws deeply into the soil. The circle of outward pointing spines holds no interest for the bird; he hops around the mammal a few times and then flies off. Some time passes before the Echidna slowly, cautiously uncurls and tentatively extends his nose from under the protection of his spines. No further threats are sensed and clambering over the ground debris the powerful little figure continues. The Echidna seems to have lost some of his caution for he now has his nose to the ground—no longer is he testing the air. He is searching out the nests of ants or termites. These insects are amongst the most numerous in Australia and before long the sensitive nose has found its mark. With muscular shoulders heaving, the Echidna tears into the soft earth and guided by his snorting, snuffling nose has soon exposed an ants' nest. The insects swarm all over the anteater but his spines and thick skin make him virtually impregnable from the ants' stings and bites. Thrusting his nose deep into the nest galleries the Echidna sweeps eggs, pupae and adult insects into his tube-mouth. The pink, sticky tongue is extended six inches into the nesting galleries. The Echidna has no teeth but crushes his victims between hard plates on the base of the tongue and the roof of the mouth. He has soon exhausted the first ant nest and ambles up the ridge to find another.

The late burst of light has little effect on the other, southern side of the ridge. The lower slopes on this side never receive direct sunlight in mid-winter. Even when there is no mist it is moist here for the dew does not evaporate. The reduced winter light has little effect on the trees as they grow tall enough to rise above the slope's shade. However, it severely curtails the growth of the shrubs and certain ground plants. But what restricts one group of plants leaves the way open for others and the constant winter shade and moisture nurtures an intriguing array of plants, mostly dark green species capable of photo-synthesizing at very low light levels. Ferns are the most obvious and the tallest, and tend to hide the others, the miniatures. To find them needs close attention to detail and a thorough search of the ground. But once the first signs are found the eye soon becomes accustomed to the shapes and colours and a world of fantastic shapes slowly impresses itself on the mind. There, amongst green moss-covered rocks and brown wet leaves is such a sign; from a rosette of small leaves rises a green stalk which supports a translucent green, almost spherical flower. Once this first flower of the Nodding Greenhood Orchid is spotted others are noticed flowering all over a small flat area surrounded with an amphitheatre of mossy rocks. A further search of the slope is rewarded with finds of more of these unexpected hidden corners of perfection—many terrestrial orchids flower at this time of the year. Helmet Orchids, their small pink flowers resting like eggs on their dark green leaves crowd together between the exposed roots of a tree; Bird Orchids have pushed their leaves and dark red-brown flowers through a patch of moss. The variety of intricate shapes of the orchid flowers is highly functional for, as is discussed in a later chapter, they are designed to attract pollinators in a host of different and highly ingenious ways.

Days are short in June. The search for ground orchids has been so absorbing that time passed quickly and unnoticed. But already the Lyrebirds have launched into their last display for the day. As the mist closes in once again and the light gradually drains away, the valley is filled with the sound of the world's most accomplished song birds. The birds stop their song just before darkness. In a series of jumps they spring from branch to branch till they are settled for the night in the protection of the trees.

The winter months are always cool but on occasional days the sun comes through but not strong enough to warm the forest and activate the dormant insects and reptiles. They become active in spring when most of the forest birds begin nesting, including many migrants which spend the winter in the warmer regions to the north. Snakes such as the Copperhead and Tiger Snake will hunt for frogs around permanent waterholes. Spring will be a livelier, busier time of the year. Yet here, in winter, even with the lesser diversity of life, the performance of the Lyrebirds in the mist-muted forests of deep green undergrowth and glistening Mountain Ash trunks creates a majesty found at no other time of year.

SUCH WAS a winter's day in a wet sclerophyll forest in Australia's temperate climate. To contrast both climate and forest type it is worthwhile to look at a dry sclerophyll forest in the subtropics 800 miles to the north somewhere in the New South Wales-Queensland border area. Time is advanced by about two months, it is a day in August which, here, is early spring. Overcast and rainy days are few. For weeks on end the weather is warm with balmy days and invigorating nights. Cold weather is felt on only a few days when a cold penetrating wind blasts in from the west. Spring flowers are already out in profusion, nesting has begun for many birds.

A HEAVY DEW fell overnight. In the first light, under a cloudless sky, it lies like a silvery blanket over grass and shrubs and drips from the leaves of trees. As the first rays of yellow sunlight stream over the horizon the scene changes instantly from silver to gold. Grass stems, spider webs, the weeping branches of casuarinas all sparkle with drops of dew. Not a breath of wind disturbs the droplets.

The forest has an open structure, the result of fire. Ground cover is a yellow carpet streaked with green and is made up mainly of grass. Dotted here and there is the grey-green of shrubs and young eucalypts. Some of the shrubs are in flower; a wattle makes a splash of intense yellow against the muted green of the surrounding foliage. Rising out of the tall grass are the trunks of eucalypts—the rough, black and furrowed ones belong to the ironbarks. Occasional bloodwoods stand out as warm brown stems covered with flaky bark. The smooth trunks of Forest Red Gums glow with a dull sheen in the early sun; their bark is white streaked with blue-green and red-brown. It is not a tall forest. The average height of the trees is 60–70 feet with an occasional ancient giant about 100 feet in height.

The first rays of light are warm and dispel the damp chill of the few hours before sunrise. The Grey Kangaroos which are grazing in a small mob on a grassy flat lift their wet, dripping faces. For a while they just stand letting the warmth penetrate their fur. Mature bucks and does begin their first grooming session of the day. Leaning back on their massive tails and with eyes half-shut they scratch their chests with lazy, slow strokes of their front claws.

One of the females in the mob of about fifteen kangaroos has a well-grown young in her pouch. During the night's grazing the joey poked his head out of his mother's pouch and half-heartedly nibbled at the grass. At the slightest noise he retracted his head and disappeared into the depth of the spacious pouch. But with the first warmth of the day he, too, is being groomed and cleaned. His mother first thoroughly licks the joey's head and shoulders and then unceremoniously dumps him out of her pouch. His mother holds him with her front paws and continues to groom him but the joey has had enough of keeping still and begins to wrestle with his mother, embracing her and grappling and kicking with his feet. But this does not hold his attention for long either and suddenly he dashes off at high speed, almost tripping over his outsize feet. His mother quickly scans the forest for possible danger to the joey, but every-thing is tranquil on this perfect morning. She uses the brief moment he has left her in peace to thoroughly clean the inside of her pouch.

At this age the joey, though inquisitive and spirited, is still very in-secure when more than two hops from his mother. Every now and again he becomes panic stricken at his own audacity and races back and tries desperately to get into the pouch. But there is no real danger and his mother refuses him entry. She does this simply by standing upright. No matter how hard he struggles he can get no more than his head and shoulders into the pouch. But his panic soon passes. Hiding his head for a minute or so, and perhaps a quick drink, reassures him and he dashes off again. Should real danger exist, perhaps a hunting Dingo or eagle, the mother would call her joey with soft sucking noises. These are instantly obeyed and as soon as he arrives his mother leans forward and the joey climbs quickly into the pouch head first, does a tumble-turn inside and confidently pokes his head out. There are no dangers this morning and the joey gets his full share of high spirited exercise.

Besides adult males and females the mob has five newly independent young. Their behaviour this morning includes some adult quiet groom-ing intermixed with liveliness of the young. The young bucks in par-ticular are very energetic and wrestle each other. Their sparring match looks very vicious, the sharp claws of the front feet reach out for the opponent's eyes and ears, and to counteract this offensive the wrestlers bend their heads back as far as they can. In another tactic they raise themselves high on their toes and tail tips and then lash out with the hard, sharp nails of the hind feet. But for the young it is all in fun and only practice. However these same fighting tactics used by the fully mature males, which have immensely powerful chests and arms, can result in serious ripping wounds. Grey Kangaroos are fast, agile fighters and old bucks usually show scars such as split ears and strips of fur missing from the chest and abdomen.

But full-scale, serious fights are rare and the adult bucks, towering broad and tall over the does and young, are content to just stand and warm their muscular chests in the early sun.

The early sun also warms a small metallic-shiny skink stretched out on the sunny side of the trunk of a Forest Red Gum. The Snake-eyed Skink is one of the few reptiles active at this time of the day. Most of them, together with the terrestrial insects, are still in the grip of the dew and the cold which clings to the ground till the sun has risen well above the horizon.

The kangaroos' early morning period of contentment is enacted against a chorus of bird songs. Noisiest, most strident calls come from the crown of a flowering ironbark, about a hundred yards from where the joeys race through the grass. So profuse are the eucalypt's flowers that they almost hide the foliage. Their nectar and pollen act like magnets in attracting flower feeding birds—mostly lorikeets and honeyeaters. Early this morning, flock after flock of screeching lorikeets, mostly Scaly-breasteds, but also Rainbow and Musk Lorikeets, arrive at this plentiful food supply. The noisiest, largest flocks cause panic amongst the baby kangaroos away from their mothers.

A flock of Scaly-breasted Lorikeets approaches the ironbark over the treetops in a tight fast flying formation, the birds screeching to each other. The low angle of the light illuminates the brilliant red on the undersides of their wings which contrasts with the intense green of their upper sides. Hardly seeming to slow down the flock of about twenty birds hurtles into the treetop. Immediately after landing each bird walks along a branch and begins feeding on the flowers. The feeding is almost frenzied. Having exhausted one cluster of flowers each gives a few screeches to keep in touch with others in the flock and makes his way to fresh ones. If it were not for this constant screeching the lorikeets would be difficult to detect for they blend perfectly with the leaves.

The lorikeets do not have the flowers to themselves but share them with a host of honeyeaters. One of these is just as noisy and his cackling voice can be heard clearly from up high in the ironbark. Like all honey-eaters the Noisy Friarbird has a slender, slightly down-curved beak and a tongue with a brush tip. With this tongue he extracts the nectar in a part-lapping, part-sucking, motion without damaging the flowers in any way. The Noisy Friarbird is pale brown above, almost white underneath, his head completely bald and dull black in colour. A horny knob adorns the top of his beak. At his throat he has a ruff of white feathers. About 14 inches long, he is one of the larger honeyeaters and besides being noisy he is aggressive, tolerating few other birds in his domain. In between nectar gathering and calling he dashes through the tree's crown in pursuit of other, smaller honeyeaters, cuckoo-shrikes and any other birds he can bully. He seems to have come to terms with the lorikeets and feeds with them peaceably side by side.

But the ironbark's crown is wide and has many flowers. Other honey-eaters visit the tree. A pair of White-throated Honeyeaters twitter un-molested and probably undetected in one of the outer branches. These smaller birds, very similar to the White-naped Honeyeaters of the Vic-torian forests, are searching for insects as well as gathering nectar. The nectar is for themselves, but is not rich enough in protein for the growing young in the nest. The honeyeaters seek this protein in the form of insects.

Gradually it becomes warmer. The dew dries and releases the larger insects from their encumbrance of water droplets. They begin to move about to gnaw, suck or drill the eucalypts or to lay eggs on bark, leaves and flowers. These insects, of which tens of thousands live on each tree, are the most numerous organisms in the forest but because, with a few notable exceptions, they are mostly silent and small, escape attention. The setting is dominated by the birds not because of their numbers but because of their colour, their action, their song and their size.

The Forest Red Gum is heavily infested with lerps and scale insects, so heavily that the older leaves are thickly coated with the insects' sticky exudations. Pardalotes, weebills and warblers are busily extracting the lerp insects from their shelters, often swinging upside down from leaves larger than themselves. But they must be careful for the leaves sometimes become so sticky that the tiny birds can become irretrievably glued to them. But the small birds are more concerned with maintaining their territory or, for those whose nesting season is further advanced, with feeding the young in the nest. Seldom are these birds seen for they live high up in the tree's outer foliage but their soft, often wistful songs float down from the tree crown. The gentle calls are a constant background sound. Even though the dawn chorus has now subsided somewhat the sweet sound of the White-throated Warbler's descending scale of notes occasionally drifts through the forest. Pardalotes, small rounded birds with short tails, also call throughout the day—the Black-headed Pardalote's 'chip-chip-chip' and the colourful Spotted Pardalote's casual 'sleep-ba-by'. The weebills, smallest of all the foliage birds are just over three inches long but their calls are more insistent, less wistful—mostly a chattering song or a single clear whistle.

The forest's most pleasant songster sings at his best at this time of the year. Ever since daybreak he has poured forth his song from various trees in his newly-established territory. The Rufous Whistler pauses only briefly to catch a few beetles and spiders among the red gum's leaves before selecting another perch; raising his beak he starts his song anew, his white throat fluffed out, vibrating with the effort. After a few resounding 'echongs' he launches into his full rippling song. He is only a small bird, six and a half inches in length, but his voice carries far. A voice which issues a warning to all males of his kind to stay away from his territory but an invitation for the females to share it.

Not all the forest insects are small. Stick insects, larger beetles, cicadas, caterpillars of certain moths, longhorned grasshoppers range in size from one to ten inches. Many of them are already increasing in numbers as the result of the spring's first warmth and they are attacking the Forest Red Gum's rush of new growth.

A Crested Hawk, one of the most handsome birds of prey, closely scrutinizes the outer foliage of the Forest Red Gum for these larger insects. From his vantage point in a neighbouring bloodwood, bobbing his head up and down, concentrating hard, the hawk studies a stick insect he has just spotted. He launches out and lands briefly with slate-grey wings outstretched on a clump of red gum leaves and snatches the stick insect from the tree with his talons, returning to the bloodwood with his catch. This hawk's elegantly barred chest, yellow legs and yellow cere shine in the morning light. The crest on the back of his head vibrates with every tearing movement as the insect is daintily eaten. The Crested Hawk, which is about 15 inches long, is virtually insectivorous, only an occasional mouse or lizard varies his diet of stick insects, beetles, grass-hoppers and cicadas. With his beak and talons, smaller and weaker than those of other birds of prey his size, he is better suited to this kind of hunting. He is expert at spotting prey from the outer leaves of the eucalypts.

Another forest hawk, the Brown Goshawk, is also making her way to the red gum, but by contrast she has large, steel-trap claws and a heavier beak. She is more ruthless and fierce than the gentle Crested Hawk. The female goshawk is considerably larger, more heavily muscular, than the male which would be about the same size as the Crested Hawk. She is hunting and stealthily flits from tree to tree intent on moving towards the red gum unseen. If one of the honeyeaters should spot her the smaller bird's alarm call would cause panic and all vulnerable birds would race for cover. For this reason the goshawk must make a surprise attack from some distance. Skirting the flowering ironbark she waits her chance hidden in another bloodwood.

The Rufous Whistler, a little less cautious than usual in the urgency of his song, is singing from an exposed branch low in the red gum. Seeing her chance the goshawk bursts from cover. Lorikeets and honeyeaters scream their alarm and scatter but for the whistler it is too late. Inches from the safe cover of a clump of shrubs the goshawk's trap-like claws close on him.

Once the goshawk has made her swooping strike alarm calls cease. There is instant silence amongst the birds living in the patch of shrubs. They are hidden deep in the cover. But the birds are highly active and are not intimidated for long. A few minutes after the whistler was struck down all is back to normal. First to break the silence are a pair of Blue Wrens. Irrepressible birds, they soon resume their hunt, examining grass blades and leaves for tiny insects and spiders. They have two young in their nest carefully hidden deep in the thickest part of a prickly shrub. The young have an insatiable appetite and the two wrens keep up a constant shuttle service to feed them, but never do they leave the patch of shrubs—an island in a sea of grass. The female wren, a plain brown bird, built the nest and incubated the eggs unassisted, and is even now more conscientious than the brilliant male in feeding the young.

Singing in defence of his territory is the male's main preoccupation. Since the young hatched he has taken a more active part in raising the family and now makes frequent trips to the nest with beakfuls of small insects. No matter how often he visits the nest he is always greeted with at least one hungry mouth. But still he pauses frequently to sing through-out the day. Shortly after the goshawk has passed he perches on top of the dark green shrubs and reels off his excited twittering call, his brilliant blue feathers shining in the sun, his tail cocked straight up at right angles to the three-inch body.

The wrens are not the only ones to have a nest in the isolated patch of bushes, and every now and again brown-coloured honeyeaters with brilliant yellow head markings, drop quietly out of the trees and un-obtrusively make their way to a dense clump of grasses and ferns. The Yellow-tufted Honeyeaters—so named because of the bunches of feathers behind their ears—catch their insect prey high in the treetops but have hidden their nest, which now contains young, close to the ground.

A Kookaburra, always on the lookout for an easy meal in the form of nestling birds, has noticed the honeyeaters' regular pattern of movement and is now perched on a dead eucalypt branch overlooking the bushes. He is motionless in concentration. Only an occasional cocking of the head and raising and lowering of his crown feathers show his interest in living things to pounce on. But he cannot see either of the nests from his vantage point. The parents of the threatened young have spotted the menace and stay away from their nests, they do not want to lead the Kookaburra to it. The wrens twitter their apprehension and act as though they are busy at a nest, but are actually a safe distance from the true nest site where the young squat quiet and motionless. The honeyeaters are not content to merely deceive the large kingfisher, they actively dive-bomb him, all the while uttering their alarm call. Alarm spreads fast through the forest and soon the Yellow-tufted Honeyeaters have attracted re-inforcements in the form of a band of Noisy Miners—the most aggressive and persistent of all in harrying predators. The miners are fearless and frequently make direct hits in their dives. Noise and abuse become too much for the Kookaburra and he moves on without finding the nests. He lands about a hundred yards further on and throwing back his head, opening his heavy beak wide, utters his wild, laughing call.

Now that it is mid-morning the sun has dispelled even the ground level chill and the insects in company with other litter invertebrates are active, providing more bird food. Most enthusiastic of all the birds in seeking out this food source is a party of Grey-crowned Babblers. They started nesting early this season and have three small young in a large, domed, stick nest in a sapling eucalypt. While one of the party of nine birds stays in the nest to keep the young warm the rest are busily searching for ground spiders, crickets, centipedes and worms. They constantly call to each other in an undertone as they prise under logs with their long curved beaks, turn over stones and smaller branches and hop over fallen trees. When most of the birds have some food item to take to the nest there is much bubbling and whistling and all take off for the nest together. More excited calling as the whole party lands in the nest tree accompanied by posturing with tails fanned and wings trembling—a noisy high spirited spot of activity in the forest.

Not all the birds which animate the forest this morning are closely linked to a particular niche such as flowers, foliage, shrubs or ground cover. Some, while confined to the trees, move all over them, others merely use the trees as perches—landing places for sorties after ground animals or flying insects. Above the treetops, swallows, martins and swifts cut through the air and catch their food on the wing.

A Grey Fantail sings its soft song from the vantage point of a low eucalypt branch. One of the most charming of all the forest birds, this tiny soft-grey sprite fans his long, broad tail, droops his wings and postures from side to side as he calls. He only pauses in his song to dart at a passing insect. With sudden twists and turns, his beak snapping audibly, the fantail picks up moths, mosquitoes, flies and other small fry. After each sortie he returns to a favoured perch to continue his quiet warble. At this time of the year the fantails are nomads, making their way slowly southwards to begin nesting, perhaps in southern Victoria, in a month's time.

Many other migrants are moving through the forest, pausing only to forage. One of these uses a strategic perch as a lookout like the Grey Fantail. He sits perfectly still, no tail-fanning, no sound. It is a Sacred Kingfisher intently watching the ground below. He spots something, a few quick jerks of the head and he dives down into the grass in a flash of intense blue and green. Moments later he reappears, a small skink struggling in his beak. The kingfisher flies to a eucalypt branch and there bashes the unfortunate lizard in a series of bone-breaking jolts against the branch. Finally the kingfisher throws his head back and swallows the small lizard.

Cuckoos too are moving southwards—the small Golden Bronze Cuckoo with its metallic green and gold back, the somewhat larger Fan-tailed with its chestnut underside and slate-grey on the back, and larger still the Pallid Cuckoo. The migrant cuckoos mostly feed quietly, seeking out caterpillars more than other insects.

Towards noon all corners of the forest are warm and dry, no dew remains. The direct sun is hot and an Owlet Nightjar that had been basking and dozing in the entrance of a hollow eucalypt limb, now retreats inside. Bird activity slows down. Only an occasional cuckoo's call or wren's soft twitter is to be heard. Most are quiet in the midday's drowsy warmth.

Cold-blooded animals react very differently. During this warmest period of the day they are free from the slowing effect of the coldness—a coldness less and less recurrent since the passing of winter. Snakes and lizards which earlier soaked up the warmth of direct sunlight now are actively hunting. Skinks race after flies and leaf-hoppers on the tree trunks. A large legless lizard, the Scaly-foot, hunts more slowly, staying close to a pile of dead branches under which he has his home. Only during the very hottest part of the day does the Lace Goanna come out of hiding. He pushes through the grass with a free-swinging sinuous gait, his forked tongue, a sense organ, swishing right and left in front of him. Everything in his path is investigated—holes in the ground, hiding places under bushes or logs and on occasions the trees themselves, for the goanna is an excellent climber. But this midday he stays on the ground, stops and makes an unsuccessful attempt at digging out a small marsupial mouse from its nest under a log and then continues on his way. The large lizard, almost six feet long, is beautifully marked in dark charcoal-grey with irregular bands of yellow.

The warmth has also coaxed various snakes from their hiding places. A green and yellow Green Tree Snake, smoothly and easily coils its way up a young eucalypt in search of insects. On the ground a Yellow-faced Whip Snake, one of the fastest of all snakes, rushes through the grass chasing a small lizard.

Earlier this morning a Death Adder, a short thick snake banded in earth colours of grey and brown, slowly eased out from the cover of thickly piled branches and dead leaves to warm himself in the sun. Thoroughly activated and alert, the venom warm and free-flowing in the glands bulging behind his eyes, the Death Adder moves once again.

A male Grey Kangaroo, largest of the forest inhabitants, lif his head while grazing. Mature males have massive shoulde

A seven foot long Taipan, the largest and most dangerous snake in Australia

A Squatter Pigeon feeds one of its young. The young are only a few days old and are still fed almost entirely on pigeon milk

In a patch of dappled light he works himself into the covering of fallen leaves till he is half buried, only his hooded eyes and the thin white tip of his tail above the leaf litter. He is now virtually invisible—his colours blending with those of the ground. The snake lies absolutely still—though ever alert.

As soon as one of the party of Grey-crowned Babblers comes within sight, the Death Adder begins to move the thin, worm-like end of his tail gently. The Babbler's attention is attracted and he moves towards the wriggling snake's tail. The closer the bird comes the more vigorous the reptile's tail tip wriggles. When the bird is within six feet the tail tip stands up vertically and vibrates furiously. The inquisitive babbler stabs at the possibly edible morsel with his long beak. Instantly the ground explodes. The snake strikes. There is no escape for the babbler. The snake hangs on biting and chewing and with each movement of his jaws he injects more venom. The stricken bird dies almost immediately and at first his death affects the other babblers. They gather around the snake and, calling constantly and loudly, hop around for some minutes. But their concern does not last long; soon they move off to resume their search for food for the three young in their nest.

And so the afternoon unwinds. Insects buzz around the flowers, ants gather seeds or capture other insects and carry them to their nests in ceaseless activity. By late afternoon when the sun is low on the horizon and shafts of yellow light slant through the leaves, trunks and grass, the reptiles slow down and seek the shelter of hollows and tussocks. The spring afternoon is still too cool for them to stay active. Later, in the warm summer months, many will move about only at night.

Where the morning was cool and damp with dew—late afternoon is crisp and dry with clear light. Colours stand out brightly, shapes are sharply outlined. Birds again burst out in song and visit their favoured feeding spots.

The sun is almost down but darkness is still a few hours away. In a grassy gully a Rufous Rat Kangaroo eases himself out of his grass nest at the base of a thick tussock. He moves out carefully so as not to disturb his grass nest.

A few other marsupials of the eucalypt forest begin to stir themselves in readiness for the night's feeding. A Koala, which slept all day wedged in a tree fork, lifts her head sleepily and surveys the forest. A well grown young, too large to fit in her pouch, slept between her front paws, but he too has woken. The young is very lively from the moment he wakes and is soon off on a short exploratory climb away from his mother. She is unconcerned, and still sleepy-slow, grooms herself using her teeth and the large sharp claws of her feet. When it is almost dark she climbs higher into the Forest Red Gum and begins the main business of the night—eating the eucalypt's leaves. She will consume over two pounds of them. From her perch the Koala sees a Red-necked Wallaby slowly bound through the undergrowth. Rat kangaroos, kangaroos, wallabies and Koalas, these are the only marsupials to be active during daylight hours. The others will emerge when darkness is complete.

With food in its beak, wings spread, and tail fanned, a Grey crowned Babbler displays to other birds in its closely-knit flock

III WOODLANDS

1 Tropical Woodlands

IN THE FIRST HALF of May the monsoon has petered out into an occasional afternoon shower and the summer's heat has diminished.

After a full wet season's growth the extensive low-lying areas of water-logged soils of the southern part of Cape York Peninsula are choked with bright green ground plants. These shallow bogs are already beginning to dry up and after a few weeks without rain will be completely dry.

It is early morning, cool and invigorating. Yesterday afternoon's heavy shower, probably one of the last of the season, has refreshed the swamps and renewed the activities of the frogs. All night they have been calling and now with the first light are burrowing underneath grass tussocks and fallen logs. One tiny species seems to have forsaken its nocturnal habit and in full daylight hops over the sandy ground and lassos passing insects with lightning flicks of its pink tongue. *Notaden melanocephus*—it does not have a common name—is a small almost spherical frog. Its rough textured back is spotted with brilliant colours, yellow, orange and deep maroon. This brilliant colour may be a signal to would-be predators that the frog is unpalatable, even poisonous, for it can secrete an unpleasant milky substance through glands on its back. Thus being invulnerable to the attacks of birds and lizards it can move about unmolested in broad daylight.

In these open woodlands there is no continuous tree canopy and soon the sun warms the herbaceous plants growing amongst the grasses and sedges. The small plants' flowers make splashes of white, yellow, deep red and many other colours amongst the general greenness. Some of the flowers last only one day and open rapidly and simultaneously with the first warmth. Within half an hour a patch of ground that was green and brown, the colours of plants and soil, becomes dotted with the delicate mauve flowers of the creeper *Jaquemontia* and the large pink and white blooms of an hibiscus.

The warmth that has stimulated the many flowers to open has also roused the reptiles. Small long-tailed dragons, Tommy Roundheads and Jacky Lizards, rush through the ground cover after insects. A pair of courting Black Whip Snakes, heads bobbing and bodies twined around each other, writhe and wrestle through the dew-laden grass. A large Sand Goanna pushes through the undergrowth; now and again he raises himself on his hind legs to look over the lush growth, then ambles on. He may look relaxed but he is ready to strike at any living thing, snake, lizard, bird or mammal, that comes within his reach. A Taipan, Australia's most dangerous snake, is also hunting amongst the grass tussocks, testing hollows and burrows with his forked tongue for rats, bandicoots and other small, warm-blooded animals. An average mature Taipan is eight feet long, though he is known to grow to eleven feet, is lightly built and lightning quick in his movements. His venom is extremely potent and is stored in his venom glands in large quantities and injected with inch-long fangs. He is mostly dark brown with a pale yellow underside.

The dominant features of these waterlogged plains are termite mounds. Not the ochre or yellow rounded and smooth structures found in the eucalypt forests, but pale grey mounds with darker patches, sharply spired on the top and with fluted surfaces. Most are six to eight feet high and ten feet or more long. They are very thin, only a few inches, but sometimes thickening to a foot in places. A few of these termitaria are of a different shape, a single round spire tapering towards the top and about eight feet tall, like a gigantic witch's hat. One such mound near the edge of the swamp has a circular hole two inches in diameter about two feet from the ground. Shortly after midday, when it is hot and steamy, a green bird appears at the hole from within the termite mound and it quietly looks out. A female Golden-shouldered Parrot is ready to leave her nest to feed on the seeds ripening on the many grasses.

Golden-shouldered Parrots, which are found only in parts of Cape York Peninsula, always lay their eggs and rear their young in a termite mound. They make a tunnel one to two feet long into the mound with their strong beaks and then excavate a nesting chamber about seven by six inches. The cavity is not lined and the four to six white eggs are laid on the powdery bottom of the nesting chamber. At this time of the year the female is incubating her first of perhaps two clutches of eggs, a job she does alone. At about midday she leaves her nest to feed out on the plains. The eggs are well insulated in their dark cavity and will not cool during her absence.

Grass seeds, now half ripe, are the food of many other birds with eggs or young. Finches swing from the seed heads of the tall clumps while quail feed on smaller grass plants. The ground-dwelling Squatter Pigeons stride majestically through the grasses and reach up to their full height to pick off the seeds.

Still near midday and still hot, a Squatter Pigeon rises from her feeding area in a loud clatter of wings and flies fast and low to a spot ten yards from a particular clump of grass growing on one of the slightly higher ridges between the boggy plains. As soon as she lands she freezes, her head raised to peer over the grass plants. Suddenly she jerks her head down and runs through a well worn tunnel through the vegetation. After a while she halts again and standing perfectly still takes in her surroundings with a steady gaze from her dark eyes. No danger is detected. She gives a deep soft coo, fluffs out her feathers and shuffles to her nest where she broods her two tiny young. Her nest is a mere scrape in the ground, lined with a few pieces of dry grass.

The young pigeons, only a few days old, are hungry and they push their heads up through their mother's breast feathers. The parent now lowers her head and the young insert their beaks into that of their mother's to feed on the pigeon 'milk' she regurgitates. A quiet tender episode amongst the grass, sand and ants, in the midday heat under the eucalypts.

Meanwhile the female Golden-shouldered Parrot has been joined by her colourful mate, attracted by her constant whistles. He is the same slim build but of an entirely different colour. His chest and sides are brilliant blue with a suffusion of turquoise around his beak. On his underside is a patch of orange, each feather edged with pale yellow. The top of his head is dark brown and there is a band of yellow above his beak. His back and wings are pale brown except for the brilliant golden-yellow on his shoulders which gives him his name.

The pair of birds, chirping quietly to each other, continue to feed amongst the grasses, pulling a seed-head down now and again and stripping it with their strong beaks. Then suddenly the two fly off together and in a flash of colour land on top of the termitarium in which they have their nest. In flight the female shows added colour—turquoise on her rump and tail feathers. Still chattering and whistling the male bows in front of the female and vigorously swings his head from side to side. She takes no notice and after a little preening she drops down and lands at the nest entrance. Before squeezing into the tunnel she has a careful look into it, perhaps to see if a goanna or snake has entered to rob her eggs; reassured she disappears inside. The male remains on top of the mound for some hours, his blue feathers shining in the sun and visible from far away. Mostly he warbles his sweet whistles, now and again pausing to scratch or to yawn. The male's song is not completely reassuring to his mate for she appears at the nest entrance from time to time and scans the surroundings for possible danger. Nearly always she returns quickly to the interior of the mound, backing along the narrow tunnel.

Later, when the parrots' young have hatched, they enter into an unusual relationship with the moth *Neossiosynoeca scatophaga*. Parrots, like kingfishers, do not clean their nests of the droppings of their young. But the Golden-shouldered Parrots' nest is kept perfectly clean at all times by the larvae of the moths. They feed on the nestlings' droppings and even keep the birds' feet and plumage immaculate. When fully grown the moth larvae pupate together forming a honeycomb of silk on the floor of the nesting chamber.

Towards mid-afternoon clouds begin to gather. The increasing coolness and promise of later turbulence seems to excite the animals. A flock of Galahs, pink and grey cockatoos, rise and, screeching loudly, wheel and turn in perfect unison low over the treetops. A small group of White Cockatoos, brilliant against the dark clouds, rise high over the distant stony ridges then tumble straight down in a series of quick turns around their own axes.

The exuberance is cut short by a brief but heavy downpour, which clears the heat haze from the air and freshens the vegetation. A fragrance of eucalyptus leaves and nectar floats on the gentle breeze. Squatter Pigeons, wet and bedraggled, preen themselves and are soon sleek and dry again.

The distant ridges on closer inspection are a series of low rounded hills with rocky, gravelly soils, and wide valleys between. The trees are on average only twenty to thirty feet tall, widely spaced; the ground cover shorter and not as untidy-looking as in the lowlying areas. Many trees are in flower. *Acacia hemignosta's* weeping branches are covered with yellow flowers, the fineness of their structure contrasting with the dark, rough bark of the tree. The pale yellow flowers of the stringybarked *Eucalyptus tetrodonta* push through blue-green long leathery leaves. *Grevillea glauca's* leaves are tinged with even more blue, with golden tips on new shoots. Its flowers cascade down the branches. From a distance the hills are a patchwork of various colours, green, yellow and brown but never the emerald green of the moist temperate climate. The grass is streaked with yellow, the green shoots hidden underneath the older blades. The foliage of most trees has a bluish tinge and that of others such as the fine-leafed grevilleas is a very dark green. At the end of the wet season these colours are largely hidden by fresh new growths of a lighter yellow-green but they soon mature to their dry season colour. Most of the flowers such as the creamy-white of the eucalypts and *Grevillea parallela* and the pale green of *Grevillea glauca* do not stand out in the landscape. But here and there is a bright red or orange patch. The red patches are flowering shrubs of *Grevillea decora* and the orange ones the six to ten inch flower spikes, in the shape of a toothbrush, of *Grevillea pteridifolia*.

After the shower the sun soon reappears.While the raindrops, glistening and dripping, dry from the foliage, the many birds shake the water from their feathers and preen themselves for a short while before searching for food. For many of them nectar is the main attraction. The Helmeted Friar Birds chattering in their raucous voices dip their polished black beaks in flower after flower of *Eucalyptus tetrodonta*. Not far away a Blue-faced Honeyeater, a green and white bird, buries its electric blue face in the orange flowers of *Grevillea pteridifolia*. The black and white Banded Honeyeater is so small that it almost disappears into a bunch of *Grevillea glauca* flowers, and showers itself with nectar. A flock of screeching Scaly-breasted Lorikeets, the red undersides of their wings flashing in the late sunlight, skims the treetops and lands in a flowering eucalypt. As soon as they land they begin to feed, clambering all over the flowers and swaying on the thin outer twigs.

Honeyeaters and lorikeets are adapted to feed on nectar and have tongues and actions designed to feed rapidly on the flowers—they can drain an individual flower in a fraction of a second with a flick of their brush-shaped tongues. But so rich is the flow of nectar that even birds whose usual diet is very different will turn to the sweet liquid. They are not used to gathering nectar and their methods are slow and awkward. The Red-winged Parrot usually feeds on seeds, but now turns his attentions to the eucalypt blossoms. He nips off one flower at a time with his beak, transfers it to his foot then slowly licks the nectar, drops the flower, picks another one and continues like this for hours. He could never get a full meal from the nectar. Woodswallows, insectivorous birds, also swarm over the nectar-rich flowers and besides picking off visiting insects, dip into the flowers themselves.

Some of the ridges are very rocky and boulder strewn with a thin film of soil trapped between the larger outcrops. The slopes of a gully form an amphitheatre, a miniature landscape with its own wildlife drama, one on a small scale and integrated into the stark environment.

Rough textured rocks and the shaggy bark of the larger eucalypt trees growing amongst them are the backdrop for the drama. The gully faces west and the setting sun floods it with yellow light. A grass tree has managed to get a foothold between two rocks which it hides amongst its dark green 'skirt'. It is in flower; a tall single spike six feet tall is covered for half its length with minute white, star-shaped flowers, each filled with nectar. In a flash of brilliant green, orange and blue amongst the sombre rocks a Rainbow Lorikeet lands on the spike and methodically drains one flower after another.

Small patches of colour among the gravelly soil are provided by the flowers of many ephemerals: a tiny lily's scarlet flower; the mauve of a sundew sustained by the moisture seeping from under the bigger rocks; white and yellow of the paper daisies rustling in the afternoon breeze.

Grasshoppers leap from one grass tussock to another and are often snared in the strong golden webs of a large *Nephila* spider. Another large spider hunts at night but now the only evidence of his presence is a large silk-lined tunnel in the ground. Smaller spiders, stalking and snaring the myriads of flies, beetles, wasps, bugs and other small insects, lie in wait amongst the leaves and cracks in the rocks or bark. Jumping spiders like tiny jewels walk on the leaves and jump from one to another always searching for prey. A small fly may land nearby. The spider immediately spots it and faces it with his two large front eyes. He stalks, then in one long leap, but anchored by a silken thread, he catches the insect in his jaws. Another small spider which lives amongst the dark rocks does not actively hunt its prey. It builds a web across a hollow or a crack in the rock and waits for an insect to blunder into it and become entangled.

On the furrowed trunk of an ironbark, another hunter has made a kill. A Praying Mantis on elegantly slim legs has darted in and snatched an ant from a line ferrying between the flowers in the tree top and the nest on the ground. Holding the ant in his scissor-like front legs the mantis eats it. The mantis in turn is being chased by the large soldier ants from the nest. But the plodding chase by the ants is easily dodged by the fast manoeuvres of the mantis.

The sun has almost set. A python slithers from a cavity amongst the rocks to catch the last of its warmth. His head and neck are jet black and the rest of his eight-foot body is banded in browns and yellows. His skin is like the shiniest enamel. The Black-headed Python hunts mainly at night; even at this time of the year it is too hot amongst these rocks for him during the day. Only when it is overcast does he emerge in daylight and relentlessly hunts any living animal large enough for him to crush in his coils—goannas, dragons, birds, rodents, but above all, other snakes.

A few Rock Wallabies also shuffle from their rock shelters, they come out earlier than usual in this crisp afternoon. Sitting on their favourite rock shelf they go through their waking-up ritual of grooming and yawning. Some lie down for a while on the still-warm rocks. These are harsh surroundings for mammals, particularly towards the end of the dry season when what little grass remains is powder dry and has poor food value. Except for their thickly padded hind feet, these small wallabies are the very antithesis of toughness. Their grey-brown fur is silky soft and their features are finely moulded; large sensitive eyes with long lashes, well shaped ears edged with black, a delicate black, moist nose above a soft muzzle. How they maintain their condition in the heat, the drought and the meagre food of the spring and early summer is a mystery. In spite of their looks they must be tough and some of this toughness is evident when the wallabies are seen in action amongst the rocks of their habitat. They are absolutely fearless as they bound from rock to rock even up seemingly sheer cliffs. Sure-footed, they can stop in an instant while in full flight, flinging their short arms out to keep their balance.

But Rock Wallabies are not common and mammals generally are scarce. There are few animals about at night in the rolling hills of central Cape York Peninsula.

The termite hill plains, the eucalypt woodland, and the paperbark woodlands discussed later, are the main habitats of the vast area of open woodland in northeast Queensland though they are not the only ones.

Of these four types, the termite hill plains are the most restricted in area and occur only on Cape York peninsula between Laura in the south and the Watson River about three-quarters of the way up the Peninsula. These extensive shallow basins with their ill-drained soils collect the wet season rains which drain slowly into the sluggish creeks and rivers.

During the wet season they are shallow swamps, though not to be confused with the deep lagoons and marshes of the river systems. In a matter of weeks after the wet the water has disappeared and the soil baked hard. These conditions do not promote tree growth and the main vegetation is made up of grasses and sedges with a very occasional paperbark or grevillea tree. The few aquatic animals to live in these temporary swamps are mostly frogs, and they are really only dependent on the water during the breeding season. As soon as the rains end they dig themselves underground deep enough to remain cool, with a supply of water stored in their bodies. The same soil which does not allow the wet season rain to percolate to the rivers now insulates the frogs from dehydration.

At least one animal, the spectacular Golden-shouldered Parrot, *Psephotus chrysopterygius*, is found only in the restricted areas of termite hill plains of Cape York Peninsula.

The low rounded hills and gravelly ridges with intervening gently sloping valleys extend almost the length of Cape York Peninsula and for most of its length constitute the Great Dividing Range. We have seen how this sparsely vegetated country looks like a park at the end of the wet season; the skies are clear; the animals are prolific and active all day long. But towards the end of the dry season, in November, it becomes unmercifully hot and it seems that the country has died. It is hot, silent and the sky shimmers and is hazy. The new shoots which gave the trees a green appearance have now matured into long leathery-grey-green or blue-grey leaves, which droop in the heat. The grass has turned completely brown. Other ground plants have long since shrivelled and most birds have deserted the hills for the river flats. Only in the early morning can an occasional call be heard on the ridges. In summer these hills are forbidding, inhospitable places.

Woodland of the Atherton Tableland with taller trees of fifty to sixty feet high, experiences a more equable climate. There still is a definite dry season in spring but it is of much shorter duration. Being on higher ground than the Cape York woodlands it also escapes the extremes of summer heat. In a few places of better soil and on the higher slopes of the Tableland the eucalypt woodlands give way to forests as dense and almost as tall as those of the southeast of Australia.

Grass grows up to seven or eight feet tall on large stretches of mixed eucalypts, pandanus and paperbark woodlands, along the coast. The grass is impenetrable, even in the dry season, and the Aborigines used to burn it each year not only to flush wallabies and other game but merely to be able to travel, which, because of their nomadic existence and the hardships of the dry season, was of the utmost importance to them.

This mixed woodland is the type that mostly adjoins the monsoon forests of Cape York Peninsula and some animals come out of the rainforest at certain times of the year to feed on the nectar of gum blossoms or the fruits of other trees. Two species of flying fox frequently leave the cover of the rainforest to feast on the flowers in the open woodlands. Neither of them is well known, though it cannot be said with certainty that they are rare. The larger of them is *Dobsonia magna*, the Spinal Winged Fruit Bat, which has a wingspan of about three and a half feet. In Australia it is found only on the eastern side of Cape York Peninsula but it is widely distributed in New Guinea. Its main differences from the common Australian flying foxes are that *Dobsonia's* wings meet in the middle of its back forming a distinct line and that it has a small but distinct tail, whereas the common flying foxes of the genus *Pteropus* have no tail and their wings grow from the side of the body. The behaviour of *Dobsonia* is also different; it is a more skilful flyer amongst the dense rainforest foliage, being able to hover with loudly flapping wings and dodge branches and leaves. *Pteropus* bats seldom fly below the canopy unless there is a clear flight path. They have more speed but less manoeuvrability.

The other nectar-eating flying fox is the tiny Queensland Blossom Bat,

Syconycteris australis, with a combined head and body length of only two inches. Occurring all along the Queensland coast it has been observed on very few occasions, yet in its chosen habitat is not rare. We saw about twelve flying around a food tree like overgrown bumble bees, their large eyes brightly reflecting the beam of our spotlight. The Blossom Bats have a tubular snout and a very long tongue in the shape of a brush and it was thought that with those adaptations for feeding from flowers their diet was exclusively nectar. They certainly feed on it with practised skill and there is some evidence that they are nomadic in habit, following the flowering of certain trees. But there are records of them as fruit eaters and we saw them eating figs in the rainforests of Cape York.

During the day a few birds usually found in the monsoon rainforest and nesting there, also venture into the open. Honeyeaters visit flowering trees. The black Palm Cockatoo using its huge chisel-like beak rips open the tough seed cones of the pandanus palms and feeds on the kernels. The large Eclectus Parrots eat the small shining black seeds of a wattle tree.

In a few places of infertile soil along the east coast of Cape York grows a short but dense type of vegetation very much like the heath lands or Wallum of coastal southeast Queensland. There is the same association of *Banksia*, *Melaleuca* and *Casuarina* with a few eucalypts. The appearance of the two widely separated kinds of heath is very similar, though the species composition of the Cape York woodlands is less complex and does contain a few tropical species such as *Grevillae pteridifolia* which are absent from the south.

A very interesting plant is found in association with the streams and swamps of this heath-like country and other wet areas of poor soil. This is the Pitcher Plant, *Nepenthes mirabilis*, which grows as a tall climbing plant amongst the sedges, paperbarks and pandanus palms. *Nepenthes* is a genus of plants found over most of southeast Asia, but in Australia is found only on Cape York. The only other Australian Pitcher Plant is the unrelated *Cephalotus* of southwestern Australia.

The Pitcher Plant derives its name from the shape of the insect trapping device it develops at the end of its leaves. Almost every leaf terminates in a pitcher but only a small percentage of them are in use at the one time. Some, at the lower portion of the plant, have withered and died and others on young leaves at the top though perfectly formed, are too small to function and their lids are still tightly shut. The mature pitchers, which are as much as seven inches long, have their purple lids open in readiness for their function; to trap insects. Insects, particularly ants, seem to be attracted to them, whether by the scent of a chemical, the purple spots on the lid and inside of the pitcher, or the thickened bright yellow-green rim is not known, but frequently a large pitcher is covered with ants. If they go beyond the lip they are doomed, they will slide down the smooth waxy sides and be digested by the enzymes in the liquid at the bottom of the pitcher. The more the insects struggle to escape the less chance they have, for in their frantic movements they scrape waxy scales off the wall of the pitcher which coat their feet. This soon makes it impossible for them to walk up the inside walls.

Ants are not the only victims; one pitcher contained small cockroaches, beetles, grasshoppers and numerous other unidentifiable insect fragments. The soils in which the *Nepenthes* grow are infertile and generally lack nitrogen. The plants extract extra supplies of this essential plant food from the insects they trap. If they are grown in fertile, well drained soils the pitchers do not develop.

THE ESSENCE of the open woodlands, particularly those of Cape York Peninsula is not the sum of exciting glimpses into the lives of colourful and interesting species. It is the power of growth and life which manifests itself so forcefully at the onset of the wet season. The whole countryside which has virtually turned to dust in the heat and drought of early summer then suddenly bursts with vigour and vitality.

A Pitcher Plant in flower

2 Mangroves and Paperbarks of the Tropics

THE MAJOR RIVERS of northeastern Queensland, the Herbert, Johnstone, Mulgrave, Barron, Daintree and others empty their waters and silt into shallow, muddy bays. The silt and the saltwater create the specialised world of the mangrove swamps. From high tide mark to the edge of the mudflats is a succession of different kinds of mangrove trees. The best known of these are probably the two species of *Rhizophora*. These grow in the softest mud furthest from the shore; at low tide their characteristic silt roots are exposed as impenetrable thickets. Fresh silt and flotsam is trapped and settles amongst these roots and the mangroves constantly migrate further and further from the shore. The outermost shrubs are constantly submerged for about a quarter of their height and are suspended in soft mud rather than rooted in soil.

Mangroves grow in the tropics throughout the world and in Australia line river estuaries and bays from the Queensland-New South Wales border in the east along the northern shore to Shark Bay in Western Australia with isolated patches on the southern coasts. Mangrove swamps are extensive in total area and numerous animals have become adapted to live in the habitat created by them and the salt mudflats. Mangrove species of tree snakes and goannas hunt Mangrove Warblers, Honeyeaters, Kingfishers, and mangrove insects. Mosquitoes and biting midges breed in the mud pools left by the tide. In the tropics these mangrove forests are hot, humid and often filled with the stench of gas bubbling from the mud. Anyone venturing into them is immediately attacked by myriads of biting insects. Yet once these discomforts are braved, the mangrove forests and woodlands are found to be fascinating places with highly specialised plant and animal life. A closer look at the mangroves and mangrove animals has been left for another occasion. In the present context these woodlands are important as the last breeding places for the once super-abundant Torres Strait or Nutmeg Pigeon.

The pigeons have a remarkable life history. They nest each year in huge colonies on selected islands off the northeast Queensland coast, travelling to and from the mainland to feed on rainforest fruit. On most islands they have been exterminated by man. Only in inaccessible mangrove forests do they remain but even here in drastically reduced numbers. From personal observations at Low Island, from interviews with local residents with observant minds and long memories, and from the writings of E. J. Banfield, writer-naturalist and long-time resident of Dunk Island, it has been possible to work out the story of the Torres Strait Pigeons on a nesting island as it would have occurred at the turn of the century when the birds were common. The place is Low Island, off Mossman.

BETWEEN AUGUST 7th–12th the first pigeons arrive in north Queensland's lowland rainforests from New Guinea and other islands to the north. First there is a trickle of two or three hundred birds, but in a few days this swells to a steady stream and soon the forests throb with the slap and clatter of wings, the continuous murmur of soft coos and the pulsating 'roo-ca-hoo' of the courting males: with heads bent low, chests inflated almost to bursting point, they boom out the last 'hoo' of their mating call. Around their favourite feeding trees, the quondongs, nutmegs, palms and figs, the noise is so constant and loud that it drowns out all other sound. Hundreds upon hundreds of the pigeons are packed tightly together on the spreading branches. In the sunshine their immaculate white plumage, with charcoal grey flight feathers and tail tip, shines in the treetops. Not a feather seems out of place and their contours are as smooth and as rounded as an ivory carving. The males are most majestic; they have imposing powerful chests and are of much heavier build than the females which are about half as large again as a homing pigeon.

After a few weeks or more of feeding and courting, the birds late one September afternoon set course for Low Island. This fifty-two acre site of coral rubble and mangroves is their nesting island and focal point of their lives for the next five months. Flock after flock of thirty or forty birds clatter out of a tall tree, then fly with strong steady wing-beats first over the dark green forest then dip right down and fly inches above the dark blue water in a straight line seven miles to the island. Another week or so elapses while the nesting site is chosen, the nest is built and the single white egg is laid. The nest is much more substantial than those of other fruit pigeons which are but a few sticks put roughly together. The Torres Strait Pigeon makes a structure of dead branches or, more frequently, of the green twigs from a small-leaved species of mangrove. Throughout the breeding season the ground underneath these trees is carpeted with twigs broken and dropped by the pigeons. Nests are never lined with feathers, grass or other soft materials.

The large lustrous egg is incubated by one of the pair while its mate flies off to feed. Even now with only half the number of pigeons the mainland forests are filled with their sounds, a constant monotone, like the pounding of the surf, punctuated with the throbbing calls of the males. At night the pigeons return to their sitting mates. The returning partners have their crops bulging with fruit; a reserve supply for the next day when it is their turn to remain on the nest and incubate the egg.

By the end of November activity on the island reaches its peak. Young of all sizes, from the small pink and helpless ones only a few days old to fully feathered white birds ready for their first flight, occupy the tens of thousands of nests. Only a few contain eggs, those of pairs starting their second brood or that may have lost an egg or young in the now frequent thunderstorms. The pigeons have settled down to a well regulated routine, but the daily afternoon return from the feeding grounds is still a time of excitement in the colony.

The first flocks arrive at about 4.30 in the afternoon. From the western edge of the island they can be seen approaching—small white dots on the horizon skimming inches above the dark water. The flocks vary in number from two or three to as many as 150 but average between thirty and forty. Flock after flock flies from as far north as Cape Tribulation or as far south as Mossman—an average distance of seven miles of open rough water. Mountains and storm clouds building up are a perfect backdrop to the flocks of white birds. They fly fast in powerful, controlled wingbeats easily overtaking the terns also returning to their nests on the coral island. By about 5.15 the flocks come in so rapidly that they form a continuous stream from those landing overhead to white specks in the distance. The numbers gradually diminish until at 7.00 p.m. the last birds arrive in darkness.

As a flock arrives, the pigeons drop one by one down to their nests. All day there had been an undertone of 'oos' and 'ooms' but now the volume rises till the whole island throbs. The first sign of the mass arrival is the whistle of wingbeats, then a clatter and slapping as bird after bird drops down amongst the mangroves to its nest. The returning mate is greeted with a peculiar nasal 'cleck'. As excitement mounts 'roo-ca-hoos' and 'oom-ooms' come from nests all over the island and mostly spaced only a few yards apart. Where there had been a scene of boredom—birds quietly sitting on their nests, pecking at sticks, yawning, snapping at mosquitoes, accompanied by an occasional soft call—now there is noise and excitement. More and more pigeons clatter to their nests and are greeted by their mates. Thousands upon thousands of plump white birds flutter, bow and climb in the dark green gloom of the dense mangrove forest. After the initial excitement the new arrivals sit quietly grooming; for short periods they even doze squatting on a branch.

Towards dusk the pigeons that have young make their way to the nest. They hop from branch to branch, then walk to the nest with dignity and, to human eyes, even a flair for the dramatic; no slinking through the leaves to make an unobtrusive approach. Gently the pigeon now touches her young which shuffles under her ample breast. The nestlings also are dignified without the insistent clamour and begging for food of most young birds. When the parent pigeon, her crop bulging with food, has had a careful look around, she signals to the young, hungry after a full day's fasting, that feeding can commence. The young now inserts his beak into that of his parent's and feeds. Both males and females feed the young but on alternate days. It is almost dark. At night all is silent.

At dawn the island once more throbs with sound. A pair of White-breasted Sea Eagles glides low over the trees—at this time of the year the giant birds of prey live on pigeons, not fish or other marine life. The swift, compact pigeons can easily out-manoeuvre the larger birds but flying only a foot or so above the mangroves the eagles overwhelm their prey before these can gather speed or gain room to take evasive action. Dawn is the time when these attacks are most successful, for pigeons about to leave for the mainland congregate in the treetops and in their panic at the sight of the approaching predator get in each other's way and are more easily struck down.

The tallest mangroves are white, packed solid with pigeons that have left their nests and are ready to leave for the mainland. For a few minutes they soak up the warmth of the sun. They lean over on one side then raise one wing letting the sun shine on the underside. With eyes half closed they sit in apparent ecstasy. After half an hour the sun becomes too hot and a group of about six to eight birds flies up from a tall mangrove and sets off to the mainland. They fly over other trees and are joined by more and more birds till fifty white birds rise high into the air and fly swiftly to their feeding grounds. Flock after flock rises and the noise of their wings drowns out the quieter 'coos' and 'ooms' of those left behind. Departing birds are lighter than the arrivals; they fly higher and faster and soon have disappeared in the pale blue sky. As it becomes hotter the colony gradually settles down till soon it is only a murmur of subdued calls.

By the end of November the island has been occupied for nearly three months. The mud and coral rubble under the trees are carpeted with the undigested seeds of many kinds of native fruits. In a few places above high tide mark some seeds have germinated and form a mosaic of soft

green with patches of red and blue made by ungerminated seeds. But the seedlings are doomed for soon their roots will reach down to salt water when they inevitably die.

The pigeons leave the nesting colonies by the end of January when some birds will have raised as many as three young and most at least two in succession. The pigeons, both parents and young, spend another two months in the rainforest, putting on condition for their journey to New Guinea at the end of March.

ON THE FLAT intermittently submerged mangrove islands like Low Island the breeding success of the pigeons is extremely high—much higher even than in mangrove forests in river estuaries or on the continental islands such as Dunk and Hinchinbrook to the south. The reason is a lack of predators on eggs and young. Snakes, goannas, rats, but mostly the Black Butcherbird, *Cracticus quoyi*, which takes such a fearful toll of eggs and young of birds in the lowland rainforests, are absent altogether. They are still present, though less numerous, in mangrove forests in river estuaries and on continental islands which have a fauna similar to that of the mainland.

The choice of nesting in colonies on islands no doubt contributed to the exceptionally large numbers of Torres Strait Pigeons that once inhabited these coastal lands. The fact that they have all but disappeared from one half of their former range and have been reduced to a mere shadow of their earlier numbers over the other half, is not due to the predation of snakes, lizards or birds, but the greed and thoughtlessness of humans. The reasons why the Torres Strait Pigeon—whose afternoon return to its nesting island is one of the most breathtaking spectacles in natural history—may join the fate of another, now extinct, pigeon we will examine in a later chapter.

WHERE THE MOUNTAINS RISE straight from the shore, and on fertile well drained flood plains, the mangroves change abruptly to rainforest just above high tide mark. But there are large tracts of coastal flats where the soils are boggy and infertile, conditions which in spite of a favourable climate exclude rainforest. Instead there are paperbark woodlands. In sharp contrast with the rainforest where there is tremendous diversity of trees, these flats are completely dominated by a single species, *Melaleuca viridiflora*, a kind of paperbark. Another contrast with rainforest is the light and brightness of the woodlands. Paperbarks do not usually grow so close together that their crowns interlock and therefore do not create the gloomy damp microclimate that rainforests do. As a result they have a dense understorey of grasses and sedges. The trees have pale trunks with thick bark composed of many layers of paper-thin tissue and so add to the impression of brightness. Here and there other trees grow: a few stunted eucalypts, several species of *Grevillea*, grass trees, *Xanthorrhoea*, pandanus trees and an occasional casuarina break the monotony.

The most remarkable feature of these forests is the great abundance of epiphytes; every tree has at least some growing on its spongy papery bark. As we have already seen, epiphytes have a difficult enough time getting their supplies of moisture and nutriment in the humid rainforest. Their difficulties are even more intense in these places with their hot sunshine and much higher evaporation rate. They have had to adapt further. The Tea-tree Orchid, *Dendrobium canaliculatum*, has even larger bulbs and fleshier leaves in which to store water than have the rainforest orchids. The other common epiphytes, two species of the Ant Plant, *Myrmecodia* sp. are still better adapted. They have developed large bulbous, succulent tubers in the tissues of which they store enough water and perhaps nutrients to carry them through several hot, dry months. These bulbs can grow to a tremendous size, occasionally up to ten pounds in weight, but they can be seen from tiny ping-pong ball size to larger than a football on the trunks and branches of the trees. When a bulb is cut through, a maze of dark brown tunnels running through the white spongy tissues is revealed. How these tunnels may benefit the plant is not known; perhaps they aerate the tuber. To a species of tiny brown ant, *Pheidole* sp., on the other hand the benefit is unquestionable—they use the galleries as their nests. Almost every ant plant over the size of a tennis ball has ants living in it. They enter the bulbs through small openings on the outside. The plants suffer no ill effects from the ants' activity but they do not derive any benefit either for they grow equally fast without them.

Ants of many kinds have a mutually beneficial relationship with a family of butterflies, the Lycaenidae, comprising the blues, coppers and jewels. The ants look after the butterfly's caterpillars, protecting them from some parasites and in return are supplied with a sweet sugary substance exuded through special glands by the caterpillars. The kind of ant that inhabits ant plants has such a relationship with a Copper Jewel, *Miletus apollo*, a small orange butterfly with metallic red and green patches on the undersides of its wings. The caterpillars of this butterfly live inside the ant plant bulbs and feed on their spongy tissues.

At the end of the wet season when most of the swamps have partly dried, paperbark woodlands are at their most attractive. The shaggy paperbark trunks rise out of tall deep green grass; Agile wallabies disturbed in their feeding bound away, splashing through bogs. The honey flow is on; *Melaleuca, Eucalyptus, Grevillea* all have flowers rich in nectar and attract nectar feeders. *Melaleucas* are loaded with pale yellow-green bottle-brush flowers; cream coloured, cup shaped flowers droop in tight bunches from the twigs of eucalypts; grevilleas give splashes of brilliant orange flowers. The forest hums with the wingbeats of countless insects. Honeyeaters and parrots sing and chatter as they climb over the blossoms. Flycatchers and cuckoo-shrikes snap up insects in swooping dives through the trees. But by August, particularly in the monsoon areas north of Cooktown, these forests gradually become drier and drier. The grass withers and the hot sun beats down on the bare ground. Birds are only heard during the cooler mornings and evenings. Wallabies lie in the shade and have to travel further during the night to get enough to eat. By the end of November the first storms bring rain, and the cycle begins anew.

A White-breasted Sea-Eagle. A pair of these birds nest on Low Island and catch many pigeons during the breeding season

3 Eucalypt Woodlands of the Southeast

THE NEW ENGLAND TABLELAND of New South Wales is on an average 3,000 feet above sea level. As a result winter in the plateau's woodlands has cool days and cold nights. But many freezing nights develop into warm, sunny days, when the air is still and crystal clear.

A cracking frost overnight has spread a white sheet of hoar frost over the grass and isolated shrubs. Every blade and every leaf is studded with white crystals of rime. The whiteness contrasts with the rough-barked lower trunks of Yellow Boxes and New England Peppermints, and with the blue-grey foliage of the trees' widely spreading crowns. The short-trunked trees do not crowd together in forests but are generously spaced leaving wide expanses of grass. At dawn sunlight scatters uninterrupted over the park-like, spacious woodland, sparkling and winking on the ice crystals.

The cloudless, windless dawn seems to remind some birds of spring and they burst into a chorus of song. Not just the twittering, chirping chorus of innumerable small birds whispering in the undergrowth, but the clear, far carrying carolling and fluting of magpies and Grey Butcher-birds singing with full force from the treetops. This dawn beauty is shortlived for on these clear winter mornings the sun soon becomes warm. The rime melts, congeals into dew which rolls down grass blades and drips from leaves. Birds cease to sing and begin the day's search for food. For a few birds the feeling of spring may persist longer—magpies carry sticks to a nest site, a pair of Red-backed Parrots preen each other, a Blue Wren with feathers fluffed trembles with the effort of song.

There is no wind. In the shade of the wide eucalypt crowns the frost persists till mid-morning. But in the sun it is warm enough amongst the grasses, on the tree trunks and in the foliage for insects to emerge from their shelters and to feed. Most reptiles remain in their retreats under logs or in hollows till spring and only a few small lizards come out to bask in the sunshine. A family group of wallaroos grazes on a sunny hillside. The male, clothed in almost black long fur stands upright, alerted by a distant sound. There is no danger and as he scans the hills he lazily scratches his chest with his front claws. With each stroke, powerful muscles ripple on his arms and shoulders. Beside him the more slender female, pale grey in colour, continues her grazing uninterrupted. Her joey-at-heel races up and down the slope; at his age he is still carefree. A Red-necked Wallaby basks in the warmth on the edge of a patch of denser vegetation.

Reptiles and invertebrates are fewer in number than in the warmer season, but enough are to be found to sustain a great variety of birds. Winter is not so severe that it eliminates this food supply and there is no mass migration of birds away from the tableland. Certain nomadic and migratory species such as cuckoos, bee-eaters, fantails, woodswallows, kingfishers and others move to warmer places, but this is only a fraction of the total population. On this warm morning birds are everywhere.

Most conspicuous are the black and white birds, an unrelated group, which with the parrots, are most typical of the woodlands.

After their carolling dawn chorus the Black-backed Magpies fly down from the treetops and begin foraging. The members of the family group, consisting of a pair and their three young from last year's nesting, stride through the grass. They pause frequently, look and listen intently, then pounce, with a quick stab of the powerful beak on grasshoppers, beetles and other insects. Leaves, small branches and stones are turned over with a quick twist of the bill—the speed of the movement surprises worms, centipedes and other soil organisms before these can crawl away. All the magpies in the group have an air of confidence about them, but none more so than the adult male. He is a shiny, jet black with patches of pure white on the back of the neck, rump, tail and shoulder. His stride is deliberate, never hurried—his head is held high. The female and young have some grey in their plumage and do not radiate so much confidence, holding their heads not quite so imperiously. Except for brief pauses when preening or singing in the treetops, the magpies can be seen pacing the ground all day.

The magpies' singing companion, the fluting Grey Butcherbird, hunts very differently. He still gets his food on the ground, but because he is smaller and has shorter, weaker legs, he cannot find his food by walking through the grass. Instead he watches from vantage points, low branches or rocks, and makes his attacks from above. Though his legs are comparatively weak, the butcherbird's beak is even heavier than the magpies and has a stout hook on the end.

A pair of butcherbirds inhabit the same patch of woodland as the magpies. Every so often one of them dives to the ground and returns quickly to his perch with wriggling prey—perhaps a small skink or insect larva—in his beak. The victim is killed with a few sharp bashes against the branch and is then swallowed. Both magpies and butcherbirds on rare occasions pursue and kill small birds. Sometimes a pardalote or thornbill is flushed from cover and the larger birds give chase. Nearly always the little bird regains the safety of dense foliage. But very occasionally he tries to outfly his pursuers—rising higher and higher, circling wildly. The magpie or butcherbird then usually wins.

Another black and white bird, the much smaller Willie Wagtail, also hunts his insect food from a vantage point such as a low tree branch. A pair of Willies hunt only two trees further along from the butcherbirds. The two species never seem to clash. The butcherbirds never attempt to catch the Willies and the Willies, who aggressively divebomb such nest robbers and predators as Kookaburras, crows, hawks and eagles, never direct their aggression towards the equally predatory butcherbirds. This morning the wagtails frequently cross the paths of the butcherbirds but the birds ignore each other. The 'wagtails', which are really flycatchers, are black with white undersides and white patches over the eyes. Their long tails are perpetually fanned and ceaselessly swish from side to side. The wings are constantly flicked out from the body. The pair of wagtails are never still: if they are not darting after a flying insect they are singing, or scolding a passing crow, or chasing each other, or diving on a Kookaburra which absorbs the punishment motionless and in silence.

Part of the particular area of woodland is a small marsh with muddy banks, choked with dark green grasses and sedges, a striking difference from the yellow winter grass surrounding it. This little island of green is the haunt of a pair of Peewees or Magpie Larks. They are about the same size as the butcherbirds, but with longer legs and shorter beaks. Their plumage is black and white. The birds are ground feeders and walk, magpie-like, around the small swamp in search of insects and worms. Occasionally they leave the damp spot to make insect-hunting forays into the surrounding woodland.

With the arrival of spring the Magpie Larks stay even closer to the swamp for they will then use the mud from its shores to build their nest.

In the warmth of the day all seems peaceful, even somnolent. But the many birds never relax their vigil, not even during the drowsy midday period. A dark shape slicing through the air over the treetops is instantly recognised as a Peregrine Falcon and a wave of alarm-calls spreads through the woodland. A family of Brown Tree-creepers are the first to spot the danger—their penetrating 'peeng-peeng' rings through the clear air and spreads the alarm. A group of ten Yellow-tailed Thornbills rises in haste from the short grass seeking cover in a dense bush. As the tiny brown birds fly up, their yellow rumps flash in the strong light. They look more like butterflies than birds. As the raptore skims overhead such foliage birds as Fuscous Honeyeaters, Striated Pardalotes and even the larger Red Wattlebirds give their alarm calls and shrink away into thick clumps of leaves.

On this occasion the Peregrine is not hunting and quickly passes out of sight. For the birds out of sight is out of mind. Almost immediately the tree-creepers hop once again along the tree trunks, the thornbills fly down to the grass and resume feeding, twittering and calling to each other. The Red Wattlebird pauses briefly to give his rasping call before resuming his search for insects amongst the leaves of a Yellow Box.

Since early morning, even before the grass completely dried, the seed eaters have been quietly busy. The abundant supply of grass seeds ensures that these woodlands are unusually well endowed with parrots and finches which are amongst the continent's most colourful birds.

Overnight the parrots roosted in trees, the finches in the dense wattles and prickly shrubs that are sparsely dotted over the woodland. While the frost was still thick over the ground the flocks of parrots flew in fast formations over the treetops, twittering to each other all the while. A few landed at the small swamp and drank. The water was not completely frozen overnight.

First to scatter over the ground in search of seeds were Diamond Firetail Finches arriving in a chirping flock of about thirty birds. As they landed they looked like a shower of fiery red flower petals raining down. The four-inch birds begin feeding, shuffling and hopping between grass tussocks and picking the fallen seeds from the ground. Every now and again a bird flies up, grabs a seed head in his feet and tumbles to the ground with it. Holding the thin stem under his foot he extracts the seeds.

From a distance the finches' brown backs blend with the drab colours of the ground but on close inspection they are most colourful birds. Their heads are dove-grey, the beaks are pinkish-red and their black flanks are boldly spotted with white. Their brightest plumage is on their rumps. While the flock is busily feeding the birds have their wings folded and this largely obscures the bright colour. But the feeding flock is nervous about predators, mostly those that strike from the air, and every now and again, as if a signal were given, the flock takes wing. Then the red bursts into view. Mostly these sudden explosions of movement have no apparent reason; no falcon or hawk is within view, no snake is to be seen gliding through the grass.

Scattered throughout the woodlands are further flocks of Diamond Firetails. They are not as conspicuous as the more numerous and even more colourful parrots. The ground cover is not tall and by scanning the plain the small green or red heads of these birds are seen peering over the grass.

In the drowsy midday warmth a flock of about sixteen Red-rumped Parrots is feeding in a patch of sunlight. In the heat of summer they will be active only in the shade. As they feed they busily scamper over the ground, the flock gradually spreading out. But they always disperse in pairs, for even in these winter flocks mated males and females stay close together. Frequently they offer each other food or indulge in mutual preening. Members of the flock, though dispersing, never lose touch. In between picking up grass seeds and small green herbs they twitter incessantly. Any danger is signalled quickly and the birds, rising into the air, lose no time in forming a dense protective flock. The female Red-rump is not very conspicuous—her drab yellow-green tones do not contrast with those of the grass. The male, however, is resplendent in brilliant greens and yellows with a patch of blood-red colour on his rump.

Scattered amongst the slim and elegant Red-rumped Parrots are pairs of a larger, more robust parrot, the Eastern Rosella. Both male and female rosella are of the same pattern but the male's colours are much deeper and more intense. He is undoubtedly the most colourful bird to be seen in the woodland. His head and chest are a brilliant red, except for white cheek patches, and the rest of his plumage is a pattern of black, yellows, greens and blues.

All these birds and several species of honeyeaters, birds of prey, parrots and finches are residents on the tableland: they live there all the year round, most of them in well defined territories.

But two other outstanding birds invade the tableland's woodlands mostly in winter. These are the Scarlet and Flame Robins. They are nomads, travelling away from the more severe climate of the high peaks and ranges surrounding the tableland. Now the small birds are studded over the woodlands like so many ornaments—particularly the males. They give the appearance of decorations because of their habit of sitting motionless on conspicuous rocks, blackened tree stumps or the outer twigs of shrubs. The male's colour, in the Flame Robin, truly like a small fire, adds a new dimension to these perches. Lichen-covered rocks seem more interesting when the small rounded Flame Robin perches on them. A tiny shrub is worth a second glance with a scarlet, black and white bird clinging to it. These birds are no mere decoration of course, they, like the others, are part of an integrated natural system and their perches are mere taking off points for quick dashes after insects.

The open nature of the woodlands and its abundance of birds is a double inducement for such raptores as kites, kestrels, hawks, falcons and eagles. The landscape's open structure allows these hunters more room for attack and the bird life is a ready food supply for them. Woodlands support many more raptores than do forests.

The larger birds of prey, particularly the Wedge-tailed Eagle and the Whistling Kite catch few if any birds; they are carrion feeders. The Wedge-tail also hunts the introduced rabbit with great effect.

Several of the woodland raptores can be seen from the one vantage point. A pair of Whistling Kites soar over the small marsh. Far in the distance the dark characteristic shape of the Wedge-tail rises effortlessly on the air currents. A Black-shouldered Kite hunts over a clear stretch of grass; his grey wings beat just fast enough to keep him hovering in the one place. He studies the ground thirty feet below. Little escapes his dark red eyes. He spots a movement in the grass. It is a small skink slowly crawling from cover to bask in the sun. With adjustments of wings and tail the kite drops vertically down till he is about ten feet above the ground, his yellow legs extended below his white body. The skink suspects nothing. Suddenly the kite plummets down into the grass— reappearing moments later with the lizard in his claws. He flies to the top of a dead tree to eat his catch.

Apart from the appearance of the Peregrine Falcon the scene has been quiet but busy all afternoon. The kites and eagles are either too small or too far away to pose a threat to the many birds which continue to forage. There is no actual shortage of food, but it is scarce enough to keep the birds busily searching all day.

Quiet though it has been in the particular woodland setting, the afternoon does not simply fade away into an equally quiet evening. Just as the light begins to fade, the Peregrine Falcon, this time hunting in earnest, storms in to shatter the peace. The falcon, a large powerful female about eighteen inches long, flies in fast over the treetops. As she appears over the more open patch of woodland, birds utter their alarm cries and scatter for cover. The loose flock of feeding Red-rumped Parrots and Eastern Rosellas rises twittering from the grass; as the birds become airborne they bunch tightly together. Twisting, turning, undulating in flight the birds seek safety in numbers and evasive action. But already the falcon has risen steeply into the air and circles above the flock—she is hungry. She has singled out an Eastern Rosella which straggles behind the rest of the flock. In a steep power dive the falcon attacks. The rosella's laboured flight is too slow, he is struck out of the sky and is dead before he hits ground. The falcon circles once then lands on her prey, with wings outspread she utters her shrill cry—then begins to pluck the rosella before eating his flesh. The last rays of light, streaming over the grass strike the Peregrine's barred chest as she finishes her meal.

With the disappearance of the sun the winter chill is felt at once.

At dusk a few winter breeding frogs raise their voices from beneath grass tussocks and from under logs along the edge of the small marsh. The temperature there must be close to freezing, but even so these tiny cold-blooded amphibians, froglets and toadlets, have enough mobility to deposit their eggs in burrows and under logs. There the eggs remain till the spring and summer rains flood the small swamp. It is not till early morning, when the frost is at its most intense, that the amphibians finally fall silent.

Not all days on the tableland are sunny and windless. There are cold days with blustering wind, sleet and snow. Birds may then suffer real hardship, and if the bad weather persists a few may die. However, on balance, the tableland's winters are not harsh and its inhabitants mostly survive the few short spells of severe weather.

SUCH WAS A DAY on the crest of the Divide, a place where the east and west meet. In these regions of transition, between the comparatively humid east coast and the dry inland, plant and animal species from both quarters mingle. Some, such as the Eastern Rosella, the Scarlet Robins and certain eucalypts, are found almost exclusively in these parts. Along this top of the Divide it is drier than on the coast and it is also cooler in winter, conditions which exclude true forest. Instead there are wood-lands where trees have short trunks and wide, spreading crowns and are widely spaced.

This pattern of vegetation covers large tracts of southeastern Australia, from the Darling Downs in Queensland through the New England and the Southern Tablelands of New South Wales to northern Victoria and into parts of Tasmania. It is a remarkably uniform stretch of land in the kinds of plants and animals found there. Yellow Box for example is a common woodland tree from southern Queensland to Victoria. Parrots, finches, honeyeaters, robins and a host of other birds are found the full length of this 1,200-mile stretch of the Divide. Though generally uniform in species make-up there are differences from place to place: it is never monotonous. First of all the country's topography may vary greatly, from upland plateaux to rugged granite ranges. There is also some variety in plants and animals. On the Darling Downs, the Pale-headed Rosella replaces the Eastern; in Tasmania and southern Victoria the elegant Blue-winged Parrot is to be seen while the largest honeyeater, the Yellow Wattlebird, and the Green Rosella are found exclusively in

Tasmanian woodlands. South of Canberra the White-backed Magpie becomes more common than the Black-backed, and north of the Queensland border the Pied Butcherbird is more often found than the Grey. Similar variations exist among the plant species.

JUST NORTH OF ROCKHAMPTON in central Queensland, lies a woodland of special interest. Most of the area's drama is played out in limestone caves situated in Mt Etna, near Rockhampton in Queensland. The surrounding woodland supplies the food requirements for the main cave dwellers—the bats.

Cone-shaped Mt Etna rises 930 feet out of the flat, woodland plain. On one side the mountain is covered in low, shrubby rainforest, the other is bare limestone with a scattering of rainforest plants—umbrella trees and figs whose roots go deep into fissures and caves. Here and there a few vines and shrubs add to the assemblage—they are all rainforest plants, and though they are too sparse to form true forest, they do give the mountain a touch of the tropics.

The limestone itself is a flat, pale grey, hard and with a metallic ring when struck. Innumerable seasons of rain have creased the stone into razor-sharp ridges and numerous caves have been worn in the mountain's rock. Many of these are homes for thousands, and at times, hundreds of thousands of bats. One cave is of particular interest; it is called Bat Cleft. It consists of a long fissure which is the entrance to a cave 80 feet straight below.

The cave is a closed chamber with no other entrance. It is the focal point for as many as 200,000 Bent-winged Bats of two species; mostly *Miniopterus australis* with the larger *M. schreibersi* in very small numbers.

The bats, all pregnant females, begin to arrive in the first half of November and cluster on the walls of the cave during the day. At night they fly off to catch insects in the surrounding woodlands. Before this time the bats were dispersed in hundreds of smaller colonies scattered through a vast area in the Rockhampton district. During the cooler months they were torpid during the day. They were cold, with slowed pulse rates and breathing to conserve energy. Only at night would they warm up and fly out for food.

But now, in early summer, inside Bat Cleft they remain warm all day and do not go into torpor; their body warmth raises the cave's temperature. When they arrived the cave's temperature was 71°F, and in about three weeks the activity of the many thousands of bats causes the temperature to rise to 31°C (88°F). The natural increase in temperature would have been only a few degrees.

It is by then early December, a good time to see the spectacle of Bat Cleft. Inside the cave the temperature and humidity are now just right for the bat nursery and during the first two weeks of the month the young are born. At birth they are pink, blind and helpless. The clustering of hundreds of thousands of bats in the enclosed cave produces the incubator-like conditions needed to keep the baby bats warm during the mother's absence at night. Few caves of this nature exist and therefore all the female Bent-winged Bats of the district congregate in this one cave. The males remain dispersed.

Bat Cleft is about halfway up the mountain, its entrance is surrounded by Umbrella Trees and figs. A faint murmur and an almost overpowering smell of ammonia rises from below. The fumes of many breeding seasons have reacted with the limestone, have pitted it and bleached it white. At dusk, near the cave entrance, scores of butterflies have settled on the trees. A brown Rock Wallaby scatters the insects as he bounds along the rocks. It is a wonder the soft-looking marsupial is not cut to ribbons by the sharp limestone, but he jumps from ridge to ridge with complete comfort and unconcern.

As the last light washes yellow over the surrounding plain, the murmur below increases as the bats leave their young. First they fly in circles inside the main chamber—then a solid column spirals upwards. A small dark brown bat flits out of the cleft, but dashes straight back again. It is still too light. A few moments later, when darkness is almost complete, the first bat leaves. She is followed by a trickle of others. The trickle swells to a solid column pouring out of the cleft. For three-quarters of an hour the bats stream out in undiminished numbers then it steadies to a trickle and soon the last one is off. Once out of the cave the Bent-winged Bats fan out under the tree canopy, each one needing to catch hundreds of tiny insects to replenish her energy. All find their quota.

But before they reach the safety of tree cover, they run the gauntlet of several predators.

As soon as the sun went down Carpet Snakes (as many as nine have been sighted) emerged from cracks and hollows surrounding Bat Cleft. They reached the entrance just as the first bat flew off into the twilight. Quickly the snakes find a spot to anchor themselves. From there they strike out time and again into the dense column of bats. Those bats caught in mid-flight are soon devoured and the snake is ready to strike again. Some of the snakes are unlucky and catch nothing, but one of them has already swallowed two bats and has a third caught in his coils.

Attack on the column comes from the air as well. Three much larger, pale coloured bats dive again and again into the mass of flying shapes.

These False Vampire or Ghost Bats occasionally catch the smaller ones and eat them. Ghost Bats have their nursery in another cave about a mile away. The spectacular animals have a wingspan of over two feet, and appealing faces with outsize ears and large eyes. Usually they prey on frogs, lizards, small birds, mammals and large insects which they pick off tree branches and foliage. But the solid column of bats is an irresistible target for them. Ghost Bats are not common anywhere and the Mt Etna colony of about 200 individuals is the largest known.

Deep down below, the hundred thousand or so baby bats are left all night clustered together on the cave walls. Sheets and sheets of blind, pink bodies drape the vertical rocks. Sometimes a baby puts a foot wrong and he, with several others clinging to him, falls to the ground. Before they can climb back they are grabbed by several brown beetles which weigh them down and eventually devour them. Later in the season another, smaller beetle will have bred up into millions and move over the cave floor consuming the accumulated droppings or guano.

Outside all is soon dark. A constant whisper is the only sound made by the bats leaving. Other species have left nearby caves. Sheath-tailed Bats, larger than the Bent-wings, zip overhead on broad wings at tremendous speed. The only sound made by a Horseshoe Bat as he hovers over shrubs is the soft clicking of his echo-locating.

Before sunup all the Bent-winged Bats which have survived the night pour back into the cave and reclaim their young—which begin to suckle immediately.

In about four weeks at the end of December, the young bats are furred but still unable to fly. In February the young are independent of their mothers and must hunt for themselves. At this time there are some 300,000 flying bats at Bat Cleft. The temperature in the cave is close to 38°C (100°F) with a humidity of 100 per cent. It is time to disperse. By the end of March Bat Cleft is virtually deserted—only about 1,000 Bent-winged Bats remain through the winter.

IV MOUNTAINS AND HEATHS

1 *High Mountains of the South*

TASMANIA and the southeastern bulge of the Great Dividing Range contain the only true high mountain environments in Australia. These environments are distributed over three states and the Australian Capital Territory. Tasmania is the most mountainous and has 2,500 square miles of highlands. There are 1,000 square miles in New South Wales, 870 in Victoria and 140 in the A.C.T. In total that is 4,500 square miles of land above the winter snowline. This is only about 1/700th of Australia's total area, but it embraces two of its most distinctive habitats—the alpine and the sub-alpine.

The high mountain habitat is defined as having a continuous snow cover for at least one month of the year. The lower limit, called the winter snowline, adjoins tall wet sclerophyll forests or, in certain parts of Tasmania, temperate rainforests. The height above sea level of the winter snowline varies, of course, with the area's distance from the equator. In Tasmania it is roughly at the 3,000 feet contour, in Victoria it is between 4,500 and 5,000 feet and in New South Wales and the A.C.T. it is between 5,000 and 5,500 feet. Most of the high mountain country falls within the category of sub-alpine, the area where winter snow lies continuously for one to four months of the year. This is the habitat of the snow gums, *Eucalyptus pauciflora* on the mainland and *E. coccifera* in Tasmania. Snow gum woodlands form a broad band across the mountains but do not extend to the very highest peaks. In positions sheltered from the hurricane winds and greatest temperature extremes, snow gums may grow at altitudes of 6,500 feet but in most places they cannot grow above the 6,000-foot contour.

Above the treeline is the true alpine environment, subject to the most severe climatic conditions in Australia. Mt Kosciusko, at 7,316 feet the highest peak in Australia, has an annual precipitation which is the equivalent of 90–100 inches of rain. For several months of the year the temperature does not rise above freezing point. Snow may blanket the area for as long as eight months and in sheltered places snowdrifts persist throughout the year. Frosts may occur on any clear night, summer or winter. In summer the difference between the daily maximum and minimum temperatures may exceed 28°C (50°F). Frequent gales are one of the mountain's outstanding climatic factors. Most come in winter, accompanied by snow, and on occasions reach hurricane force. But even in winter there are short spells of fine, sunny weather.

However severe these conditions are, they are not as tough as those that exist in the high mountains of other continents—such as the European Alps or the Canadian Rockies. This milder climate combined with the generally flat terrain, particularly on the mainland, gives Australia's alps a very distinctive character.

The comparatively mild winter means that the soil, protected by a thick blanket of insulating snow, does not freeze. The average depth of the snow is seven feet but in certain valleys it collects into drifts 150 feet in thickness. Above the snow cover, a howling gale may whip sleet, snow and mist over the plains and the temperature may fall below 11°C (20°F). Those conditions, particularly the wind, make it impossible for life to exist above the snow. But at the same time, underneath the snow there is no change in the steady 0°C (32°F); there is no wind and no frost. Many living organisms continue their life. This is the first great difference from high country in other continents; life under the snow does not come to a halt, animals do not hibernate. In Australia the ground freezes only on exposed mountain ridges where the protective snow is blown away by the strong winds.

The second great difference is the result of comparative mildness in association with the general flatness of the high country; its gentle rounded contours instead of jagged, sheer peaks. The gentle terrain allows the build-up of a considerable amount of soil and the fact that this soil does not freeze allows greater, year round, activity of the ground organisms that cause litter breakdown and soil aeration. The soil, therefore, is deep and fertile. The effect of this is most obvious in the midsummer months when much of the land above the treeline is covered with what is called tall herbfield. This vegetation type is characterised by masses and masses of wildflowers. Australia's alps are richer in flowers than those of any other country.

In the sub-alpine lands, life continues above the snow in winter. The animal life even in July, the coldest month, is most surprising. It is related to the same factors as those that prevail above the treeline.

On a July day in sub-alpine woodlands the tinkling calls of a few froglets and toadlets may even be heard around a small pool of water formed by the run-off from snow melted during a sunny period. Parrots and cockatoos feed in the snow gums. Wombats push through the snow and nibble at the snow grass underneath. At night ringtail possums come out to eat the leaves of snow gums. A few moths even take wing, and, most surprising of all, a Long-eared Bat may swoop down to catch them. Bats are usually the first animals to cease activity in cold weather.

Even when it is actually snowing some animal life is about. White-backed Magpies search amongst snow-covered shrubs; a Lyrebird scratching amongst snow-covered ground litter, pauses briefly to sing. Most, but by no means all, of this above-snow activity takes place in the lowest levels of sub-alpine woodland, in the areas where they border the montane eucalypt forests.

Underneath the snow, as well as above it, animal life continues actively throughout winter. This life, completely hidden, was unexpected and its full extent was not realised until the CSIRO Division of Wildlife Research began a survey in the Kosciusko National Park in the late 1960's. They then found that a whole host of small mammals and insects lived active lives in winter under the snow blanket. The activity was confined to places where rocks, shrubs and snow grass prevented the snow from packing down hard. This life, in contrast to the above-snow activity, was found to exist in alpine as well as sub-alpine habitats.

Most of the surprises came from the study of mammals. It was found that two species of marsupial mice, a pygmy possum and two rodents all remain active under the snow in winter. They live there in extensive networks of tunnels through the dense ground cover of snow grass, shrubs and boulders. When not foraging in the tunnels the small mammals rest in grass nests in burrows in creek banks or in hollows between boulders, but they do not hibernate.

The two marsupial mice are part insect eaters and part carnivores and probably live mostly on the rich insect fauna. They may occasionally catch one of the rodents or a Mountain Pygmy Possum though there is no direct evidence of this.

The other three mammals are vegetarians and feed on snow grass and the numerous fleshy fruits, leaves and bark of the alpine shrubs. In many places dead sticks and detached blades of grass can be seen sticking through the snow. In these places the mammals have eaten the bark or stems from the lower portions of the plants. This is the only indication of the presence of these mammals to be seen above the snow.

Three of the five mammals are found over large areas of Australia besides the alpine regions. One, the Southern Bush Rat, occurs on virtually the whole of the east coast, including tropical rainforest; it is the most common of the alpine mammals. The Brown Marsupial Mouse extends from the subtropics to the southern coast and the Dusky Marsupial Mouse, a tough little carnivore, is found in damp, cool habitats

LEFT: A male Golden-shouldered Parrot stands on top of a termite mound inside which his mate is incubating her eggs

ABOVE: A male Eastern Rosella emerges from his nesting hole

BELOW: Brown Snake coiled ready to strike. Large—up to seven feet long—highly venomous easily aroused and instantly ready for attack, this species is highly dangerous

ABOVE: A flower of the Tasmanian Waratah briefly holds summer snow

RIGHT: A bush of the Tasmanian Snow Berries in transient summer snow

BELOW: Spagnum bogs of southern New South Wales at altitudes over 4000 feet are the only habitat of the Corroboree Frog. The inch-long frog is here seen deep down in the burrow it has dug for its eggs

in the southern and eastern mainland and in Tasmania. The other two species are quite rare and not so widely distributed. Perhaps of all five the Broad-toothed Rat is most specialised for life in the high country. He has exceptionally dense, long fur and can live in quite damp situations. He needs this tolerance during the spring thaw when most of the animals' tunnels are waterlogged. Outside alpine areas in the Snowy Mountains and in Tasmania this rodent is even rarer and is always found in damp, cool spots with a thick grassy undergrowth.

The fifth species, the Mountain Pygmy Possum, *Burramys parvus*, is the only true alpine mammal in Australia, in that it occurs only above the winter snowline. Of the five it is the rarest. So far it has been found only in areas above 5,000 feet at Mt Hotham and in the Snowy Mountains. *Burramys* is further distinguished by perhaps the strangest history of all Australia's mammals.

Burramys, a marsupial, first came to be noticed in 1896, but only as a fossil found in the Wombeyan Caves in New South Wales. Other fossil remains were later found in caves in the Buchan district of Victoria. The strange turn of events came in 1966. In that year a small possum, which later proved to be *Burramys*, was caught alive in a ski lodge at Mt Hotham, 5,800 feet above sea level. Subsequently in 1970 the CSIRO's Hans Dimpel and his co-workers in the field, found colonies of *Burramys* in the Snowy Mountains at altitudes of 5,050 and 5,850 feet. The little possum, whose combined head and body length is between four and five inches, was always caught on the ground amongst low shrubs and rocks and it appears likely that they do not climb trees like other pygmy possums.

No birds live above the treeline in winter and comparatively few stay in the sub-alpine woodlands. All reptiles and all but a few amphibians hibernate.

All this points to the fact that amongst the vertebrate animals there are few which are specially adapted to the cold environment and consequently live nowhere else. In fact there are only four: *Burramys*, and three species of frog. Apart from these exceptions the vertebrates of the high country are hardy species that have learnt to tolerate a wide variety of climatic conditions. The most versatile, the Southern Bush Rat, has already been mentioned. Others include the Wombat, the Echidna, such birds as Gang Gang Cockatoos, Crimson Rosellas, Little Ravens, White-backed Magpies, currawongs and a few migrating species of robins, honeyeaters and the Pipit. There are only two snakes, the White-lipped and the Copperhead, and about a half dozen lizards found in the alps.

In times of prolonged bad weather many of these animals suffer badly.

The birds leave for lower altitudes and the cold-blooded animals become torpid—but for such animals as Wombats, blizzards of long duration can mean death from starvation.

The three high mountain frogs are of particular interest. They are unrelated species living in widely separated mountains yet all have the same habitat—sphagnum bogs at altitudes above 4,000 feet. All three lay their eggs in burrows dug deep into the damp moss.

The most northerly of the three species, the Sphagnum Frog, lives at altitudes of about 5,000 feet, at Point Lookout, on the eastern edge of the New England Tableland. This area, under the strict definition, just fails to qualify as sub-alpine for snow never lies there for more than a few weeks. On the other hand it is high enough and cold enough to support snow gums. This isolated small plateau is the only known home of the Sphagnum Frog.

In summer this species goes through its entire reproductive cycle, from calling and egg-laying to the development of tadpoles, while hidden deep inside the sphagnum moss. The moss grows in waterlogged depressions which it covers in soggy carpets a foot or more deep. The moss is always moist. Sphagnum Frogs, about one and a half inches long, are a rich reddish or orange-brown in colour with black markings on the side and on the back.

Four hundred miles to the southwest of Point Lookout, in the Brindabella Ranges of the Australian Capital Territory and the Snowy Mountains, lives another of the 'bog frogs'. The Corroboree Frog, in a brilliant pattern of yellow and black bands, lives there at altitudes as high as 5,500 feet. Brilliant in colour as this species is, its secretive habits of living entirely hidden in the moss have meant that it was not recorded till 1952, and only in the 1960's was it established that in certain sphagnum bogs Corroboree Frogs are extremely numerous.

One of the most remarkable aspects of this tiny, inch-long frog is the enormous volume of the eggs laid by one female. The eggs number as many as forty and after being laid swell enormously. In summer it is possible, by gently parting the moss, to see a female Corroboree Frog sitting on top of her eggs. All the eggs together are several times her own size in volume.

Another 140 miles further to the southwest, at Mt Baw Baw and nowhere else, lives the third of the sphagnum frogs, appropriately called the Baw Baw Frog. At about two inches long it is the largest of the three. It is dark brown in colour with irregular yellow patches on the back. Like the other two it breeds in sphagnum bogs at altitudes over 4,000 feet.

Although the alpine insect fauna has not been studied extensively, enough is known to establish that it is the only part of the high country fauna that is specifically adapted to it. Insect life in the alps, of the mainland in particular, is rich and spectacular. There are many species that are found only in the alpine environments. One of the most interesting is the Kosciusko Grasshopper which can compensate, to a small degree, for temperature fluctuation by changing its colour from dark blue to a light blue-green or vice versa. Another insect unique to the high country is the cicada *Tettigarcta crinita*, the only one of its kind in which both sexes can produce sound; in all others only the males emit sound. There are several species of alpine butterflies and most other major insect groups have species specially adapted to the cold country.

However one of the high mountains' most interesting insects is not one specifically adapted to its climatic extremes, rather it uses the comparative summer coolness as a sanctuary from the heat and food shortages of its breeding grounds. These breeding areas are the grassy plains sloping west from the Divide in New South Wales and southern Queensland.

The insect in question is the Bogong Moth, a small, plain, brown species with a wingspan just under two inches. The females lay their eggs in autumn when the winter herbs on which the caterpillars feed begin to grow amongst the grasses. Throughout the cold winter months the caterpillars develop slowly. They pupate in spring. A month or so later the moths emerge—but instead of renewing the life cycle as the vast majority of moths would do, the insects leave the breeding areas, flying southwards or eastwards. They migrate to the high country of the Australian Capital Territory, the Snowy Mountains and the high plains of Victoria. The reason they leave is that the food plants on which the caterpillars depend are disappearing with the onset of hot weather. During the dry summer only the grasses remain and they are not the right food for the caterpillars. Neither the moths nor their eggs can survive the summer heat of these plains to await the growing season of the food plants. So the moths leave for the mountain coolness. Their migration is not a haphazard movement of insects scattering from the plains to the mountains. They follow a specific pattern, migrating to a small number of caverns at specific points on the highest peaks. These summer camps have been occupied by successive generations of moths since time immemorial. The floors of the caverns are in some places covered with moth remains over one foot in depth. Aborigines feasted on the moths every year long before European man established himself in Australia.

Known summer camps of Bogong Moths occur on about eight high peaks. All the camps are over 4,000 feet above sea level, and some are at altitudes over 6,000 feet. Best known of all the camps is the one at Mt

Gingera in the Australian Capital Territory. It was here that Dr I. F. B. Common documented the moth's extraordinary life history.

During the spring migration to the mountains, the moths sustain themselves on the nectar of flowers found along the way, and if necessary, draw on the generous supplies of fat in their bodies. Fat reserves constitute 61 per cent of the dry weight of males and 51 per cent of the females.

En route the moths rest periodically in small cavities among rocks, in holes in trees and similar retreats. Towards the end of October the first moths arrive in the summer camp set in small caves between giant granite boulders. They move into the darkest parts of the caverns, some of which are only cracks a few inches wide, and settle on the walls. The first few arrivals form a rosette on the rock wall, their heads pointing to the centre. The early trickle soon swells to a stream. The newcomers settle on the walls in a well organised manner. They push their heads underneath the moths already settled, lifting the abdomens of the earlier arrivals from the rock surface so that each moth only clings to the rock with its front pair of legs. The two pairs of hindlegs rest lightly on the neighbour below. This way many moths can pack together in a small space and each insect's large, sensitive eyes are hidden underneath its neighbour, and are protected from the light. In this formation all that can be seen of the moth cluster is a tightly imbricating pattern of wings. As many as 1,500 moths crowd together on a square foot of cave wall.

Between mid-December and early January maximum numbers are reached in the Mt Gingera caves. By this time all the walls are covered with carpets of moths. The main camp at Mt Gingera contains about 150,000 moths at this stage.

For the next month or so numbers remain constant. During this time the majority of the moths do not leave their caves at all. They are aestivating. A small number will make wild random flights over the rock outcrop at dusk and dawn. During these flights the moths may take in some moisture, but they do not feed. Neither is this a mating flight for the moths are still sexually immature.

During the height of summer, numbers decline slightly. Parasites and a few hot spells of weather take a heavy toll. At Mt Gingera numbers increase again in the camp in February and March. This is the result of moths moving in from the south, from camps in Victoria and in the Snowy Mountains. Nightly new arrivals come while those that aestivated at Mt Gingera have already dispersed in the return flights to their breeding grounds. By early April all the moths have left. Many predators, from bats to Little Ravens, ate the moths during the summer but they make little impression on the numbers. Adverse weather and a parasitic nematode have a far greater effect.

On the journey back to the breeding ground the moths must take in food in the form of nectar if they are to mature sexually. Their fat reserves are almost exhausted.

The same moths that left the plains in spring return in autumn. How successive generations of these small, lightweight insects can make these journeys of up to 500 miles, to precise points in the high mountains and back again is one of nature's great mysteries.

AS THERE are few strictly alpine species amongst the vertebrates, and because the invertebrates are very inconspicuous, it is not the animal life that gives the high mountains their very special appearance. Neither are the animals primarily responsible for the unmistakable high country atmosphere, or for the exhilarating feelings the mountains generate in anyone visiting them.

It is the physical environment, the mountains themselves, the broad valleys, the small lakes, the rocks, the snow and weather that dominate. The plants, because of their spectacular flowers and their close harmony with the physical features reinforce these special high country qualities. At the same time these plants give a unique character to the Australian high mountains which distinguishes their alpine tracts from those of all other countries.

Foremost amongst the characteristic plants are the snow gums. These are broad-leaved evergreen trees and nowhere else in the world are trees of this type found above the winter snowline. In other countries the sub-alpine trees are either deciduous, or more commonly, they are conifers of some kind. Apart from being evergreen the snow gums add character to the sub-alpine lands by the elegant shapes of their smooth pale-coloured trunks—straight in sheltered areas, or leaning and twisting where exposed to the savage winds. Every autumn and winter the Alpine Snow Gums shed their bark in long strips. The fresh bark is then exposed in patchworks of red and pink that only later bleach into the characteristic creamy colour.

Another special plant, one that grows wherever there is sufficient soil, is the tussocky Snow Grass. It grows as a ground plant in the snow gum woodland but is also found in the high alps right beside the persistent snowdrifts. It is an invaluable food source for many of the mammals and insects.

There are many other vegetation types in the alpine lands. The plant associations are determined by soil, drainage, rockiness, and the exposure to wind and sun. These various elements may combine to give rise to heaths, bogs, fens, alpine herbfields and, on the very highest exposed slopes, to feldmark, an association of low creeping shrubs, mat plants, mosses and lichens.

In the high treeless alps the tall alpine herbfield is the most interesting and most characteristically Australian vegetation type. It is best developed on the gentle rounded slopes of the Snowy Mountains near Mt Kosciusko and is the result of the special types of soil found there, as mentioned earlier. The herbfields are at their best in mid-summer from late January to mid-February. Whole mountain slopes are then covered with meadows massed with these wildflowers. Yellow Billy Buttons, white Snow Daisies, yellow and white everlastings, pale mauve Glacial Eyebrights mingle together in colourful lush fields of flowers. Here and there are clumps of bright pink Trigger Plants and in places where the soil is thinner, or there is a rocky patch, tight mats of white Snow Purlane and the sweet scented Alpine Stackhousia creep over the ground. Dotted amongst the taller flowers are small tussocks of Mountain Gentian and the less conspicuous Leek Orchids.

Unlike the animal life, the plants are specifically adapted to the high mountain environment. They are tough plants that can cope with the short growing period, the crushing weight of winter snow, the severe frosts during snow-free periods in spring and autumn, the flooding when snow is melting, the intense solar radiation of summer, and the short summer droughts. The outward signs of these adaptations are dwarfed and rock clinging habits, small spiny leaves, development into tussocks and a covering of fine downy hair.

The most difficult condition for the plants to deal with is the constant, strong wind. On the highest slopes, those fully exposed to hurricane winds that blast in from the west, few plants can grow. One of the few that manage a precarious foothold in these rugged areas is the heath *Epacris petrophila.*

It establishes itself in the lee of small rocks, rocks which must be well anchored, for the winds are so strong that small, free stones are rolled along the slopes. In five years the heath grows to a height of one to two inches and is no longer fully protected by the stone. The wind now forces it to creep along the ground surface. Creeping on at the rate of half an inch per year the *Epacris* continues to spread. Where there are suitable places the stems, pressed to the ground, send down new roots. Eventually it will have moved away from the rock that initially protected it and the winds will begin to erode the tussock. The dead, windward side of the bush for some time protects the outward growing portion, but growth cannot keep pace with wind destruction and in about 26 years the tiny creeping shrub dies, its cycle completed. On these exposed slopes few, if any, other plants can survive.

Most of the features and characteristics mentioned, apply to alpine lands on the mainland. While many of them also apply to the Tasmanian habitat, the island's high country has many unique features. Most of these can be traced to Tasmania's different climate and terrain.

Even though it is in colder latitudes, Tasmania's alps do not experience quite such temperature extremes nor such fierce winds as those that prevail on the mainland mountains. This is because the island is under the moderating influence of the oceans. In Tasmania's mountains snow does not persist as long as on the mainland, nor does it bank up in drifts so deep that they do not melt entirely in summer. Winds, though constant, are not as severe.

Tasmania's mountains, mostly composed of dolerite, are much more rugged than the gentle, rounded domes of the Snowy Mountains. The island's high country consequently lacks the well drained, fertile soils that give rise to such vegetation types as tall alpine herbfield. In fact this vegetation type is virtually lacking in Tasmania where the alpine soils, shallow, waterlogged and rocky, mostly support heaths.

Tasmania's high country fauna is very low in species and has no purely alpine forms amongst the vertebrates. But the plant life is most distinctive and quite different from that of the mainland. Soil types and a higher rainfall, particularly in the sub-alpine tracts, are responsible for this.

Sub-alpine woodlands are not dominated solely by snow gums. Many temperate rainforest trees and shrubs reach the treeline in Tasmania. Antarctic Beeches, King William Pines, *Richea* Grass-trees mix with the snow gums.

Above the treeline, in the island's mountains, cushion plants are a common component of wet heaths and dwarf, often creeping, pines form a major part of the dry heath communities. Both the cushion plants and conifers are absent from the mainland. On the mainland the alpine lands with their tall herbfields may be more colourful than the sub-alps, but in Tasmania the reverse is true, the sub-alps, supporting shrubs and small trees of Hakea, Tasmanian Waratah, Mountain Rocket, Snow Berries, *Richea* and *Orites*, are the more colourful and varied.

Each mountain environment has its own characteristics; they all have a special grandeur and an untamed wildness in common.

2 Heathlands

AUSTRALIA is a land of flowers—often bright and always distinctive. The eucalypts and wattles, the continent's main forest and woodland trees, flower more brilliantly and more profusely than their counterparts in almost any other part of the world. The highlands in summertime, as we have seen, are carpeted with flowers. But the most varied and dense concentrations are to be found on the heaths of the sandy coasts and on the skeletal soils of the rocky ranges along and east of the Divide. It is here that the flora is dominant. Other forms of wildlife are not as numerous but the flower pollinators, mostly insects and birds, are conspicuous exceptions.

Heathland plants, their flowers and fruits, can be appreciated from any number of different aspects: their relationships with their pollinators; massed displays of brilliant colours; intimate details observable in close-up studies of tiny flowers; shapes and textures; interplay with habitat as evidenced in the contrast between fragile flowers and the harsh, rough rocks and tree trunks; interplay with weather such as when flowers take on new brilliance viewed against the sun. No matter what the point of view there is fascination and interest to be found amongst the heathland plants.

HEATHS ARE DENSE plant communities, having no trees and growing on ill-drained, acid soils very low in plant foods.

The coastal heaths, which grow in deep sand, are subject to the same limiting factors as those of the rocky plateaux, for pure sand is as inert and as devoid of food for plants as is solid rock. In both sand and the skeletal soils of stony ground, plant foods of very limited quality and quantity are restricted to the top few inches of soil.

Sandy heaths once formed an almost continuous narrow strip along the east coast from about Gladstone in Queensland, south to Wilson's Promontory in Victoria and into northeastern Tasmania. Here and there the line was broken by rocky outcrops, by river estuaries or by flood-plains. In places there were very large complexes of sandy heaths such as in southeast Queensland, where it is called wallum. Included in this

TOP: A Southern Bush-rat has been flushed from its tunnels under the snow, perhaps by a fox or an antechinus

BOTTOM: Summer or winter the Broad-toothed Rat remains active in the alpine regions of the Snowy Mountains and Tasmania

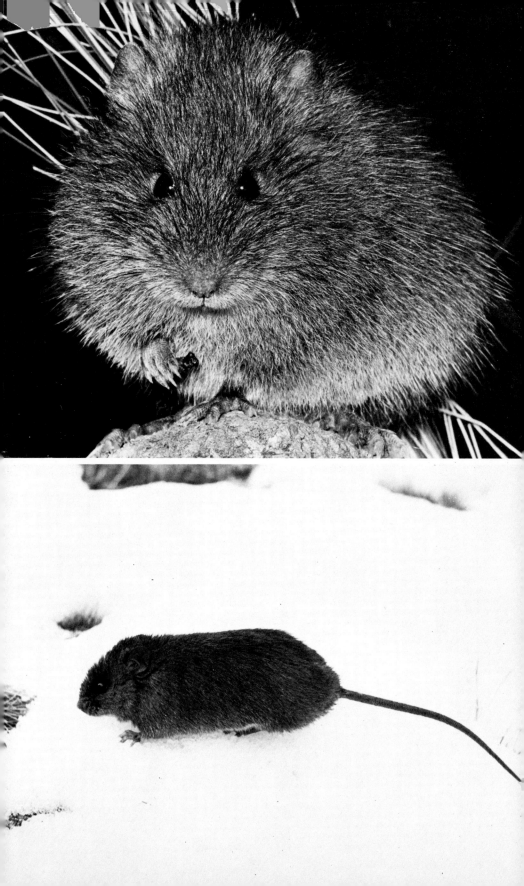

LEFT: Bat cleft, Mt Etna, by day. The c
leads 100 feet down to a cave
BELOW: The Ghost Bat or False Vampi
this is the largest of the carnivorous and
insect eating bats
BELOW LEFT: A small nursery of about
baby Little Bent-winged Bats
BOTTOM: A female Little Bent-winged
with her young
RIGHT: Bent-winged Bats emerging at
nightfall. Ghost Bats capture the smalle
species

ABOVE: A pair of Black Rock Skinks sun themselves on a slab of sandstone in the Grampians. During courtship, in spring, the pair stay closely together, often touching each other and sometimes biting gently

RIGHT: Tryon's Gecko perfectly matches its granite rock surroundings. Its velvet-soft feet are so structured that it can walk with ease on the underside and vertical slopes of smooth rock boulders. Geckos are nocturnal, retiring to rock crevices and fissures

Queensland area are two of the most extensive sandtracts of the east coast—Fraser or Great Sandy Island, and the Cooloola Sandmass. Other large areas of coastal heaths occur north of Newcastle, in southern New South Wales and along the east coast of Victoria. But heaths are fast disappearing as a result of land clearing operations.

Mountain ranges composed of rocks that weather slowly and give rise to thin soils are also quite extensive. There is the granite belt in southern Queensland and neighbouring areas in New South Wales; the Hawkesbury Sandstone area; the Blue Mountains; the Grampians in Victoria. In Tasmania mountain height and climate tend to produce the more specialised alpine heaths rather than those of the type found in the ranges of the mainland.

The vegetation of the sandy coasts and rough rocks is not solely made up of heath, but rather is a patchwork of woodlands of various types with true treeless heath in the swampy depressions. Drainage, aspect and topography bring changes. Along the edges of the swamps, encircling them on slightly higher ground, grow shrubs with an overstorey of banksias, she-oaks and woodland eucalypts. Here and there, where the soil may be slightly enriched, paperbarks and tea-trees form dense growths even in waterlogged areas. For the purposes of this discussion we have somewhat stretched the definition of heath to include these types of woodland and tea-tree thicket.

To gain a deeper understanding of the heaths and all their subtleties it is useful to examine their components and special qualities. Firstly let us look at which plants are involved and secondly how these have successfully adapted to what is a very difficult environment for plant life.

The significance of just what plants are present in the heaths can be better understood by a brief look at how plants are classified. Botanists have classified plants into a system of several divisions which to some degree show relationships between them. The base unit of these divisions is the *species*, which is a natural entity containing plants all of which have the same physical appearance and are capable of reproducing themselves exactly from seed. A group of closely related species, their relationship based on physical characters, is known as a *genus*. The next step up the scale of classification is the *family* which contains a number of related genera. Each step up embraces broader characters till the end division is reached, the plant kingdom which includes all plant life.

About eight families of flowering plants dominate the heaths and each contributes one or more special facets. All facets together create the unique atmosphere and feeling of the east coast heathlands.

The family Proteaceae gives the heaths much of their texture, their feel, their Australian-ness. To this family belong the genera *Banksia*, *Grevillea*, *Hakea*, *Petrophila*, *Telopea* (the Waratah) and others. These are woody shrubs, some growing to small trees, with hard, often prickly leaves. Their distinctive flowers vary from the stiff wire-like cones of banksias to the small, fine flowers of hakeas. Many have large woody seed capsules, knobbly nuts or shaggy cones.

Each spring the heaths are covered with a cloak of yellow. The numerous plants responsible for this spectacle belong to the family Leguminosae of which two main branches are found in the heaths. One branch includes the genus *Acacia*, the wattles, of which many distinctive species, from small woody shrubs to trees, occur in and around the heaths. The other branch contains the most profuse and most common group of heathland flowers—the peas. Many genera are involved such as *Bossiaea*, *Pultenaea* (Bush Peas), *Dillwynia* (Parrot Peas), *Daviesia* (Bitter Peas), *Gompholobium* (Wedge or Glory Peas) and others. All are woody shrubs, many with prickly foliage and most have yellow flowers; a few have pink or red flowers.

Poised between the 'Australian' textured Proteaceae and the soft flowered Leguminosae (which we have just mentioned), is the family Myrtaceae: poised between them in the sense that they have both heavy textures, mainly in their woody fruits and bark and so imparting an Australian quality, and that they are soft flowered. Among the Myrtaceae (which also includes the eucalypts) are perhaps the best known of the heaths' genera, *Callistemon* (Bottlebrush), *Melaleuca* (Honey-myrtle or Paperbarks), *Leptospermum* (Tea-trees), plus several others. Unfortunately the common names given to these three genera are often interchanged, for example *Leptospermums* are known as tea-trees in Victoria while certain species of *Melaleuca* are known by that name in Queensland. Both these genera are known as paperbarks. But whatever their name they are an important part of the heathland vegetation. Again they are mostly woody shrubs with some *Melaleucas* growing into quite tall trees. They all have woody fruits which are particularly well developed in *Callistemons*. Bottlebrushes produce some of the most brilliant patches of red while flowering. Paperbarks and tea-trees flower profusely but are mainly responsible for the fields of white and pale yellow.

Proteaceae, Leguminosae and Myrtaceae together make up the bulk of the woody plants and wildflowers of the heaths. However there are a few other outstanding families which lend unusual interest.

Of these the family Rutaceae is of interest because even though its species are few, individuals are very numerous. In fact most of the large patches of purple and pinks in the heaths come from the flowers of the rutaceous genera *Boronia* and *Eriostemon*. These two genera are found only in Australia.

Heath as well as being the name of an ecosystem is also the name of one of its constituent plant families, the Epacridaceae. In the coastal and rocky heaths its most common genus is *Epacris* which grows in dense low masses of woody-stemmed, prickly-leaved plants. At times these masses are so dense that they are impenetrable. Epacrids of several genera flower in white and in bright pink.

Not very conspicuous yet present in large numbers are the orchids—members of the family Orchidaceae. They grow in small unobtrusive clusters hidden underneath the woody shrubs or amongst the grasses and sedges of a particularly damp patch. Terrestrial orchids though, are spectacular in a different way as we shall discuss later. The orchids are soft stemmed plants growing from an underground bulb in sharp contrast with the woody shrubs around them.

Two genera of conspicuous plants common to the heathland do not fit into any of the above families. One is of the iris family. The native iris, known as the Purple Flag, belongs to the genus *Patersonia*. It flowers periodically in great profusion. The plants which look like grass tussocks, are then transformed to deep blue-purple masses. This flowering is short-lived and spasmodic but 'Patersonia days' in the heath are memorable for their mass of brilliant colour.

The other conspicuous plant, the grass tree, belongs to the family Xanthorrhoeaceae. Several types of grass trees, of the genus *Xanthorrhoea*, occur on the heaths. The species range from those growing as small tussocks with flower spikes only a foot or so long, to others with trunks twelve feet tall topped by stout flowering spikes six feet in length.

These are the main families of plants which give the heaths their atmosphere, colour and character. Other families and species are present but not so conspicuously. These include the trigger plants, the tiny insect-trapping sundews, numerous sedges and many others.

This brings us to the second point; how have the families of plants mentioned adapted to the low soil fertility?

The genera of plants discussed, though belonging to worldwide families, are entirely or predominantly endemic—that is all or most of their species are unique to Australia. This uniqueness of occurrence on the generic level is paralleled by a uniqueness of appearance; an appearance which is the result of the plants' adaptations to the heath's two most potent ecological forces, low soil fertility and fire. It is from the success and efficiency of these adaptations that the answer to the paradox of profuse growth on poor soil derives.

The plant foods in lowest supply in the heathland soils are phosphates. The plants' adaptations are mostly an ability to survive, even thrive, in conditions of extremely low phosphate levels. Many of these adaptations are inherent in the plant, in its genetic makeup and in its physiology, and are not immediately visible. The plant's inherent tolerance to low fertility, its efficient recycling of plant food by withdrawing it from dying leaves and branches, special root systems and root physiology are particularly noteworthy features. Also of importance is the ability of many heath plants to stay alive in a static condition without putting on new growth for up to two years. In this way they survive periods of zero supplies of phosphorus and nitrogen in the soil.

These internal adaptations are reflected to a certain degree in the plant's outward appearance. The leaves are reduced in size, they are hard, stiff, often very prickly; the stems are woody and thick. Many species, particularly those of the families Proteaceae and Myrtaceae, develop woody fruits. Banksias, hakeas, bottlebrushes, dwarf heathland eucalypts and she-oaks all have stout seed capsules in shapes that vary from small buttons to large cones. The ultimate in this development is the Woody Pear, *Xylomelum pyriforme*, which has pear-shaped fruits up to four inches long and two inches across. This hard fruit, made of solid wood, encloses two winged seeds. Its outside texture is like soft velvet. The variety of textures of the plants, fruits, leaves and barks—knobbly, shaggy, prickly, velvet soft, paper flaky, furrowed or fluted—are one of the heath's most outstanding qualities. In the true heaths the plants are dwarfed, growing no more than two to six feet in height.

In outward appearance the heathland plants' adaptations to low phosphate levels is one of harshness and durability. But one of the heath's greatest attractions is that this harshness is frequently overlaid with delicately fragile flowers and soft, velvet shoots of new growth. Harshness and delicacy then emphasise each other.

Under normal conditions growth of the heath plants is comparatively slow once they are established. If the heaths remained undisturbed the plant communities would become increasingly simplified. Year after year more and more plants would be eliminated, suppressed by the more vigorous and hardy of the component plants, which would take over completely in 20–30 years. Geography and soil determine which plants will become dominant. In Queensland's wallum *Hakea gibbosa* and *Melaleuca sieberi* take over; on the sandy heaths of Victoria's Wilson's Promontory the Coast Tea-tree, *Leptospermum laevigatum*, may form dense, single species stands.

If it were not for the other major force, fire, heath would become continuous thickets of tea-tree, paperbark or hakea. Fire maintains the great diversity. It is fire that allows the less vigorous and less persistent species, or those with a naturally shorter life-span, to renew themselves.

The plant families discussed are as well adapted to recover after fire as they are to low soil fertility, though not all in the same way. The main adaptations to survive fires are devices to protect and store the seed crop; lignotubers and dormant buds protected by thick bark. Some species have all three kinds of adaptations.

The heath's major plant groups have heavy seed crops. Some groups, like the pea flowers and wattles, shed the seed soon after flowering but the hard impervious coats which protect the seeds resist the attacks of fungi and insects—for some decades in the case of wattles. The seeds of these plants are stored in the ground. Other plants, mostly of the families Proteaceae and Myrtaceae store their seeds on the bush itself. A hakea bush, for instance, may be covered from the ground to the tips of its branches with all the knobbly capsules it has produced during its entire lifetime. Bottlebrush shrubs similarly store their entire seed crop. The fruits of their first flowering are woody knobs on the trunks near the ground and those of successive seasons grow at various intervals up the stems. Certain species of banksias also retain their shaggy seed cones for many years. Plants such as tea-trees and eucalypts do not retain their full seed crop but shed the seeds from their small nuts every one, two or three years. But these myrtaceous shrubs and trees flower so profusely that their seed crop of one year may exceed that of a bottlebrush or hakea that has all the seed it ever produced stored on its bush. A bush of the tea-tree *Leptospermum scoparium* for example, may have 50,000 seeds on the shrub —the result of one year's flowering. A mature shrub of a *Banksia ericifolia* has about 2,500 seeds on the shrub and a *Hakea gibbosa* only about 100. Banksias and hakeas on the other hand have a higher germination rate of their seeds. The seeds of all these plants, in strong contrast with those of plants of other habitats, can withstand high temperatures and are unaffected by the rapid passage of a bush fire.

Many of the plants have well developed lignotubers, like the eucalypts, but there is no pattern as to which plants have lignotubers and those which have not. Species with and without are found in the same genus, but they seem to be restricted to the families Proteaceae and Myrtaceae, the 'Australian' families. As we have seen with the eucalypts, lignotubers are a striking and eminently successful adaptation to fire.

Fire rages fast through the heath's dense accumulation of woody material. All the above-ground plant material is killed with the outstanding exception of the protected and fire resistant seeds and stems protected by thick bark. All that remains after fire has passed through is bare sand, ashes and skeletons of the toughest shrubs.

Evidence of recovery will be visible within days if the weather conditions are right. First to sprout new green leaves are the grass trees; new shoots appear within weeks and within the following twelve months their tall flowering spikes will appear all over the heaths. Fire seems to trigger the flowering process. Next to appear are red and gold velvet stems, pushing up through the soil; these are the new shoots of those banksias which have lignotubers. Other lignotuberous plants, tea-trees, hakeas, angophoras also put out new growth. Many plants, particularly the angophoras, push out brilliant red new shoots from dormant buds protected by the bark. Recovery of all these plants after fire is a hundred per cent.

The fire has freed millions of seeds imprisoned either in their own tough coats or held in woody nuts. Fire splits the seed coats and moisture can then reach the embryo plants. The fire also dehydrates the woody cones causing them to open and broadcast the seeds. The woody fruits are either waxy or made of wood of very low flammability.

All those plants without lignotubers and without dormant buds on the trunk are killed outright. But their seeds are so numerous that these species may actually increase in number immediately after the fire. The countless millions of seedlings carpeting the heath with new green after fire will go through a cycle of fierce competition and in perhaps four to five years, depending on the seasons, the heath will be exactly as it was before the fire.

Heaths are probably at their most spectacular one or two seasons after being incinerated. Orchids, which survived as underground bulbs, show a dramatic increase with their competitors temporarily removed. The new shrubs and tussocks put on an extra burst of flowering.

Having discussed the major plant groups and their adaptations, it is of interest to examine how the plants perpetuate themselves and maintain their vigour. The perpetuation is a process of actual reproduction of species and is not to be confused with the recovery of individual plants from such disasters as fire.

The vast majority of the heathland plants are flowering plants which are species that reproduce from seeds. There are few non-flowering types such as algae, bryophytes, mosses and ferns which reproduce from spores or by other primitive methods.

The key to the successful reproduction of flowering plants is that as many flowers as possible are pollinated; that is that the pollen(male part) finds its way to the stigma (female part) of a flower of the same species.

It is this aspect of the heathland plants' reproduction that is emphasised in this chapter.

As most of the flowers of the heath contain both the pollen-bearing stamens and the stigmas, this pollination appears, at first, to be simply accomplished. But this is not the case. This type of *self-pollination* would result in inbreeding, a weakening of the genetic make-up of the species and would lead to eventual extinction. Self-pollination is rare amongst the vigorous plants of the heaths, instead nearly all have their flowers *cross-pollinated*.

Cross-pollination is the process whereby the pollen of one flower is deposited on the stigma of another of the same species, but situated on another plant. It is this process that maintains the species' vigour and flexibility to adapt to new situations for it ensures a constant mixing and interplay of its genetic types. For animals this cross-fertilisation is easy, but plants being securely anchored to the soil, need the intervention of a third party—it may be wind, water or an animal. Flowering plants employ many ingenious devices to ensure cross-pollination. The entire structure of the flowers—their shape, colour, pattern and arrangement of floral parts—is directed to finding and encouraging this third party. Methods range from the quite simple to the most ingenious and a great variety can be seen amongst the heathland plants.

One of the most striking features of the heath is the unusually large proportion of animals associated not with just the plants but specifically with their flowers. These animals, from insects to birds and mammals, are the agents of cross-pollination. The heathland flowers are showy and brightly coloured, a showiness which attracts their animal pollinators. Basically the structure is that the flower attracts a pollinator by its colour, structure or perfume or a combination of all three. Once the insect, bird or even mammal is attracted to the flower, the pollinator has to be lured exactly to the right place—and be given a reward. The lure is often in the form of series of dots or protuberances of a bright colour directing the flower visitor to a landing spot. Further markings then lead to the reward, the nectar which is placed in such a way that the visitor, attempting to reach it, will bend over the stamens and collect the pollen. At the same time the visitor deposits pollen already collected elsewhere on the flower's stigma, and the act of pollination has been completed. Self-pollination is avoided either by different rates of maturity of the male and female parts (that is, the stigma would be receptive only after the pollen of its own flower has been shed), or by such cunning placement of the pollen and stigma that the pollinator cannot possibly deposit pollen on the stigma of the same flower.

For all these flower visitors nectar is the great attraction; the flowers do not get something for nothing. The result is that the heath has a very rich honey flora. In spring when the maximum number of flowers are out simultaneously the air is filled with the sound of birds and insects, for birds and insects are the main pollinators.

At first all this animal life buzzing, twittering and fluttering gives the impression of a gigantic chaotic movement. But things are not as haphazard as they appear. Not every bird and every insect can get nectar from just any flower. The flowers have developed in such a way that they attract and make their nectar available only to those visitors which are best suited to pollinate them.

Many bottlebrushes and certain Proteaceae, for example, have bright red or orange flowers—colours which attract birds. The birds lured to the flowers are honeyeaters and lorikeets which have brush tongues specialised for sweeping nectar and pollen from flowers. The birds attracted to these flowers have beaks of the right size and shape to penetrate deeply into floral parts where the nectar is hidden from short-beaked birds and insects. The birds will also feed on the pale off-white and yellow-green flowers of banksias, honey myrtles and eucalypts. But red and orange are common components of Australia's bush flowers and Australia's flora is bird pollinated to a greater degree than that of most other continents. Lorikeets and honeyeaters, found almost exclusively in Australia and New Guinea, are specialised to feed on the nectar and pollen of an equally unique flora. In the heath these two elements combine to maximum effect.

Birds—noisy, colourful, conspicuous as they flit about banksia cones and bottlebrush flowers—are the most obvious of the nectar gatherers. However, not all flowers are bird pollinated and bees, wasps, flies, beetles, moths, butterflies and ants are just as busy—some on the very same flowers as the birds. Many more are at flowers whose nectar is in too small a quantity or too well hidden to be of interest to birds. Some of these flowers are non-specialists which attract all insects. Examples of this type are the open flowers of tea-trees and eucalypts. Many plants, however, are specialised to attract particular groups of insects. Yellow and blue flowers are mainly attractive to bees. White or pale flowers, whose colour is most noticeable in the semi-dark, are visited by moths. Flower structure also plays a part in selecting the pollinator. Some have the nectar hidden deeply within the flowers so that only animals with long beaks or tongues can reach them. In this way the heaths are a mosaic of bird flowers, bee flowers (some for long-tongued, some for short-tongued), beetle flowers, fly flowers, moth flowers and so on. Each

LEFT: Rose Boronia, of the rocky heaths
ABOVE: Wedge Pea, of the sandy heaths
BELOW LEFT: Seed pods, backlit, of a heathland wattle
BELOW: Flower and woody seed cones of *Banksia ericofolia*
BOTTOM RIGHT: Silky Purple Flags, a native iris

ABOVE: Male Scarlet Honeyeater at its very fragile nest. These tiny honeyeaters, just under 4½ inches long, are one of the very few to feed their nestlings on nectar.

RIGHT: A preying mantis of the genus *Orthodera* devours a bee it has caught on a flower of *Banksia collina*

BELOW: A small skipper on paperbark flowers

animal group concentrates on those flowers which have the colour, shape and scent that specifically attracts it. It is blind to the others. Only man has the capacity to appreciate the full spectrum.

Most advanced and most intimate flower-pollinator relationships are found amongst the orchids. Cross-pollination in orchids is no haphazard spraying of pollen over a range of visiting insects or birds. The flowers of each species of orchid attract exactly the right insect which is lured or guided to exactly the right place to get pollen deposited on exactly that part of its body which will be in contact with the stigma of the next flower it visits. Unwanted visitors are kept out by barriers, narrow entrances and other devices.

Every orchid group has its own story, each is more astonishing than the next.

But before setting off to unravel some of these stories it is of value to look briefly at the flower structure common to the world's 20,000 presently known orchid species. The flowers are made up of three sepals and three petals. One of the petals has been transformed into a completely different structure, the labellum. The labellum is the flower's most striking feature and is elaborately ornamented with patterns, shapes and colours (different in each species and directed towards attracting or trapping the insect pollinators). Only a very few, such as the Sun Orchids, have no labellum. There are even fewer exceptions in the way in which the orchids' reproductive parts are arranged. Male and female parts are joined together to form the column. The pollen grains are not shed as a loose powder, as in nearly all other flowering plants, but are held together by elastic threads to form a bundle. When an insect visits a flower the bundles of pollen grains, known as pollinia, are glued to the insect by a sticky disc. Then when the next flower is visited the pollen bundles are deposited by the insect on the equally sticky female part of the flower, the stigma. The adhesive disc remains attached to the insect. There is great economy in transporting the pollen *en masse* instead of a haphazard spraying of grains. Depositing all the pollen at once ensures that all the ovaries in the plant's seed container are fertilised, for each ovary needs one pollen grain to develop into a seed.

Within this basic arrangement there is an infinite variety of twists and turns making up the most intricate devices known in the plant kingdom. The object of the devices, which devolve mainly around the labellum and column, is to effect cross-pollination. Orchids may shoot darts, half drown, trap, or even make their visitor mate with them to gain these ends.

Some of the most astonishing relationships between orchids and their pollinators are hidden in secluded corners of Australia's heaths.

Deep in a grove of paperbarks on a sandy ridge, broad leaves several inches long have pushed through the ground cover of fallen leaves and mosses. The strap-like leaves are dark green with reddish margins. Here and there a flower spike about a foot high has pushed its way up. About three or four bonnet-shaped flowers have unfolded their purple, tartan-striped labellums. These are the plants and flowers of the Tartan Tongue Orchid. They are easily overlooked by humans—no strong scent or brilliant colour attracts attention. But to the male Ichneumon wasp of the species *Lissopimpla semipunctata*, the attraction is irresistible. The flower exudes exactly the same scent as the female of his own species. He in fact cannot distinguish the two and approaches a flower as he would a female wasp. He attempts to mate with the flower. As he withdraws, two yellow, club-shaped bundles are stuck to his abdomen—the orchid's pollen bundles. As the wasp proceeds from flower to flower he exchanges bundles of pollen and in the process cross-pollinates the orchids.

In winter and spring many of the sixty or so Australian species of greenhoods can be seen flowering. Mostly small species whose greenness matches that of the mossy corners they favour. Seeing their small balloon-like flowers amongst the ground litter, it is difficult to imagine the intricate co-ordination of flowering parts and pollinators. One of the flower's sepals and two of its petals form a hood-like cavity. The other two sepals, growing upwards in some species and downwards in others, enclose the chamber in which the column and labellum are hidden. The labellum in greenhoods is irritable—that is it can be triggered to slam against the wings protruding from the sides of the column. Pollinators can enter the flower's chamber only when the labellum is in the relaxed position. These pollinators are small, fragile insects, gnats, and mosquitoes. It is not known what attracts them for there is no bright colour nor scent discernible to humans to draw attention. Obviously the attractions are more subtle.

When a mosquito enters a greenhood flower it moves down to the labellum, reaches the bottom where it releases a triggering device which slams the labellum forward, pressing the insect against the stigma. Any pollen bundles it might have collected are thus put on the female part of the flower. There is only one escape route open to the trapped insect—straight up through a tunnel formed by the labellum and the column wings. As the visitor squeezes through this narrow passage he collects the pollen bundles on his back. These will be pushed on to the sticky stigma of the next flower he crawls into. After twenty minutes or so the labellum relaxes to open the flower again. It is a neat device to ensure that a flower's pollen never fertilises its own stigma.

These are only two of the several score of intriguing stories of cross-pollination to be found amongst the heathland's orchids. Most of them devolve about a fantastic shape accompanied by a most subtle chemical attractant. These chemicals are mostly unknown but some insects, such as certain flies that visit Leek Orchids, seem completely hypnotised by them for long periods, oblivious to anything else.

Some of the stories are still to be told. It is not known just what the function of the Bearded Orchid's beard is or why the hinged labellum of an Ant Orchid trembling in the breeze is exactly shaped like a black ant. But for every shape there is a story.

Birds and insects are the only flower pollinators to which heath plants are specifically adapted through particular chemicals, colours, structures and devices. These two groups are in fact the main pollinators. The only other kinds of animals that visit the flowers are a few species of mammals. In the heaths of southwestern Australia lives a tiny possum that feeds almost exclusively on nectar. It has specialised mouth parts which enable it to probe deeply into banksia, bottlebrush and other flowers. On the coast of the southeast no such specialist mammal exists, rather there are a small number of opportunists that take advantage of the rich nectar flow when it is available. These include the Pygmy Possum, the Yellow-footed Marsupial Mouse and, in the surrounding paperbarks and euca-lypt woodlands of the northern section of the region, the flying foxes. But these animals are straight-out nectar feeders, and no neat, close rela-tionships exist with the flowers which are only incidentally pollinated.

This chapter so far has been mainly concerned with explanation and analysis of the nature of heaths and their inhabitants. It is hoped that the information will enhance the reader's own experiences when he sets out on journeys of discovery. In the remaining pages of this chapter we leave analysis behind and attempt to put down what certain days spent in the heaths are like. First a day in a coastal heath somewhere in the wallum in the Queensland-New South Wales border regions, then a day on the rocklands of the Sydney Sandstone.

IT IS A MORNING in early spring. The dew has dried, the animals are slightly relaxed after their first foraging of the day. The sun is warm, but without the sting it will have later in the year. No wind tugs at the shrubs. Sounds are clear and far carrying. Against the monotone of surf pound-ing the beach beyond the dunes rise the sounds of birds in the trees around the heath and of insects on the flowers close by.

A flock of screeching Rainbow Lorikeets cuts through the air, their green, blue and orange sharp and clear against the cloudless sky. The small parrots land on a flowering Coast Banksia and immediately clamber over cone after cone, burying their faces deeply into the flowers as they drink the nectar. Along this edge of heath and banksia woodland other birds are busy. Male Scarlet Honeyeaters pause frequently on the tops of banksia cones and broadcast their 'deedle-dum' songs. Then they resume feeding, delicately probing the flower cones with their long beaks, the colour of their tiny bodies blazing intensely in the dull green foliage.

Bronzewing Pigeons, not yet breeding but already in pairs, walk sedately through the ground cover, pecking side by side as they feed on fallen seeds. Suddenly they rise simultaneously. In a clatter of beating wings and a flash of gold and purple from iridescent wing patches they speed away among the trees.

A corner of the plain was burnt last autumn and there is now an army of tall flowering spikes of grass-trees. It is a noisy corner. Friarbirds, their bald, black heads contrasting with their white neck ruffs, cackle to each other as they hang on the flower spikes. The honeyeaters use their glossy beaks alternatively to dip for nectar and to snap up insects. A White-cheeked Honeyeater, neatly striped in black and white, is replete for the moment and calls from his perch on top of a flower spike.

Another bird, now very rare in these heaths, does not join in this general exuberance. He had his moments of calling and fast flights early this morning and tonight he will again utter his sharply rising notes. Dusk and dawn are times of activity for the Ground Parrot; now he is hidden, green amongst the green foliage, perhaps searching for seeds of grasses, sedges and heaths.

The heathland plants reach, on the average, only knee height. In occasional patches, perhaps fertile pockets or places missed during earlier fires, they grow to about waist height. Looking to the horizon the flowers of these plants appear like a sea of colour in varied patches of purple, yellow, blue, white, pink—mingling, separating. Brilliant blue Sun Orchids and equally bright Red Bottlebrushes punctuate the pattern of colour. That is the overall picture. But look lower down at the plants closer at hand and patches of colour come into focus and take shape.

With your back to the sun, looking with the light, the Pink Wax Flowers and boronias are a flat pink and purple; the flowers of bush peas are deep yellow and orange; the paler larger ones of Glory Peas are like so many smooth butterflies transfixed in mid-flight. Between them is a taller long cane of a bottlebrush, adding a splash of brilliant scarlet. Guinea Flowers glow like pale yellow buttons amongst their silver-grey foliage.

Turn around quickly—look against the light. The same plants are there but the light filtering through the branches, leaves and flower petals heightens the colours—the textured petals of Pink Wax Flowers in particular sparkle as if they were covered with sugar crystals.

Lower your eyes still further, squat down and examine the ground cover closely. A tea-tree bush, its green foliage hidden by the white stars of countless flowers, is an insect battleground as well as the source of sugary food. Flower wasps of the subfamily Thinninae buzz from flower to flower in a never ending search for nectar. Males are strong fliers with long yellow-banded abdomens. Many of them carry the smaller females clasped to their undersides and stop now and again to feed them. Colourful bugs, beetles, flies and dayflying moths are also busy gathering nectar. Hidden in denser clumps are the Assassin Bugs, their weapons—their long probosces—at the ready. As an insect draws near the Assassin rushes out and pierces the armour of the flower visitor with a stab from his proboscis. Immobilised with venom the victim is then sucked dry. Praying mantises stalk amongst the flowers in a more active search. They use no venom but seize and hold flies, bees and moths in large raptorial front legs.

The ants, by their constant untiring movements, draw attention to the life and activity on the ground. Not far away is the nest of a species of Bulldog Ant; large ants about an inch long and fiery red-brown in colour. At the first approach they stop and point their long, serrated jaws at the intrusion; they are ready for action, ready to jump on anything that threatens and to drive their painful stings firmly home. If the nest is not directly in danger they soon resume foraging. Ants leave the nest, fan out, and return with spiders, wasps, flies, beetles; anything small enough to be carried by one or two ants. They both kill and scavenge for their food. Other Bulldog Ants emerge from the nest and bring out the hard indigestible parts of their prey such as beetle wings and grasshopper legs.

Other species of ants, mostly very much smaller, are also active. Some are 'milking' sugar from scale insects, others hunt or gather plant seeds. Grasshoppers and crickets, burrowing bees and wasps dash about or dig into the soil. They are stalked by a long-tailed coppery skink. Striped and glistening like highly polished metal, the Copper-tailed Skink races in pursuit of insects and spiders.

While you are making these close observations of the life around you, you may notice for the first time some tiny flowers on low woody shrubs. It takes a magnifying glass to see the beautiful textures; furry flowers of the Beard Heaths or the delicate bells of the *Lissanthe*.

Time passes. The sun warms. A strong breeze springs up. With them comes an almost imperceptible change. The birds, less vocal, retire. Some flowers fold or droop. Insects withdraw deeper into the foliage.

In heaths in other parts of Australia there will be different species present and some will be missing. Heaths to the south will have the added charm of the delicate Emu Wrens, the strong songs of Bristlebirds and the endless warbles of the Heath Wrens; all most elusive species like the Ground Parrot. Tasmania's heaths are favoured by Scarlet Robins, and so on. We have described only one mood of one heath. The variety of both moods and heaths along the coast ensures that each visit will be a new and refreshing experience.

HEATHS IN THE rugged ranges along the coast and the Divide have an added dimension, and extra force—rocks. In these heaths, rocks arranged in sheer cliffs, square blocks, rounded boulders the size of houses, or in gigantic heaps and tumbles are an ever present backdrop to the plant communities. The rocks are never uniform—granite is coarse grained, rough textured, rounded, grey or with a covering of black lichens. Sandstone is fine textured, angular and ochre-yellow and orange, occasionally banded with purple. Whatever the rocks, they are a perfect foil for the delicate, bright flowers.

Rocks also mean lizards. The many cracks, fissures and caverns in the weathering stone provide safe and cool hiding places for skinks, dragons and geckos.

Some of the rock lizards seem to have assumed the toughness of their surroundings. The dragons are rough and prickly. One of the larger skinks, Cunningham's Skink, is also rough textured, particularly around the tail, and is heavily built. The nocturnal geckos on the other hand are slim, velvet-soft and, with their large eyes, have none of this toughness of exterior.

Rock Wallabies and the much larger wallaroos are as tough as the rocks, except for their large soft eyes. Fearlessly the marsupials jump up and down cliffs, balancing with outstretched arms.

Each type of rock outcrop, granite, sandstone or limestone, has its own plant associates and each rock-plant association has its own moods.

Consider the interplay of these components during a spring afternoon and evening in the Hawkesbury Sandstone near Sydney.

THE SLOPE down to one of the countless inlets of Broken Bay is a series of giant steps of sandstone shelves. It has been a good season and each terrace is covered with vigorous, healthy plants. Most of them are now in full flower. The afternoon has clouded over, the wind has dropped.

The duller, even light and stillness allow a greater awareness of the flowers. Bright sunshine would burn out some of the colours, particularly the reds, oranges and yellows. And a wind whipping through the shrubs would constantly distract attention to moving shapes and dancing colours. Now, overcast, in the quiet stillness of the afternoon against a backdrop of angular blocks of muted purple, grey and brownish tints, their beauty can be absorbed.

Tall shrubs grow in a patch of soil, surrounded by a semicircle of sandstone rocks. No less than three species of grevillea grow so close together that their branches intermesh. Grey, furry flowers of *Grevillea buxifolia*, smaller pink ones of *G. cericea* and the fleshy brilliantly red flowers of *G. punecea* all mingle together. A few paces away two banksias crowd side by side. The tall needle-leaved *Banksia ericifolia* towers over a smaller shrub with grey-green serrated leaves. The taller shrub has its flowers hidden in the foliage and in the subdued light their orange glows inside the deep green of the interior of the tree. Dark, shaggy seed cones • brood beside the gay flowers.

The smaller bushes are also vigorous. Boronias, wax flowers and tetrathecas display their flowers on long stems draped over the sturdier bushes around them, enlivening the sombre greens with pinks and purples. A wattle with sharp prickly foliage and covered with countless brush-like flowers, has taken root in a crack between two boulders and looms over the patch of flowers.

Towards the edge of the amphitheatre the soil is thinner. Smaller shrubs grow here. *Epacris longifolia* displays its intense pink, white-tipped flowers against the sandstone like a burst of sparks. Bush Peas and Parrot Peas add dashes of yellow. On an exposed ridge of gravelly soil is a blaze of blue-purple where thousands of Purple Flags have unfolded their flowers on the tussocky plants. Straight below them is a soakage where an impenetratable thicket of heaths and sedges has taken advantage of the regular water supply; red-leaved sundews grow along the wet, rocky margins.

Along a sheltered gully a few stunted trees have taken root. Amongst them the sandstone's most startling flower—the large, intensely red Waratah commands attention. Each Waratah's stem is crowned with a dome-shaped flower surrounded by the equally brilliant bracts. Because of their size, shape, texture and colour, Waratah flowers dominate their surroundings wherever they grow.

The whole slope is covered in flowering plants from tall Waratahs to tiny orchids. Each shelving terrace, each corner of piled blocks of sandstone is a natural garden.

Many kinds of animals appreciate this natural profusion of flowers. Most of them are attracted to the rich nectar flow and others to the ready supply of insects. Some, such as a variety of honeyeaters, utilise both sources of food—snapping up insects and dipping into the nectar with equal skill and alacrity.

The White-cheeked Honeyeater is especially well adapted to feed on the nectar of banksia flowers—its beak is of just the right length to penetrate the cones deeply and get at the nectar quickly and easily. It is so dependent on this source of food that it times its nesting to coincide with the peak flowering of *Banksia ericifolia*. But while a diet of nectar and insects can sustain the adult bird, it is not the right combination for the growing young in the nest. These young are fed on insects only. Another honeyeater of the area, the strong-voiced White-eared Honeyeater has a much shorter beak. It is not nearly so closely tied to the flowers—nectar in fact is only a minor part of its diet. Insects sought out from behind bark and amongst leaves are its mainstay.

During the afternoon the clouds have built up. Suddenly there is a heavy downpour; the soft spring rain falls straight down, there is still no wind to slant the heavy drops. The shower rejuvenates the plants; they smell fresher. There is a new tang in the air. Flowers and foliage are even more brilliant, mosses are a deeper green, lichens on the rocks have revived. Frogs bonk, trill and tweet in response to the new rush of water in soaks and ponds.

The sky clears and the sun breaks momentarily through. Drops of water sparkle on leaves and branches, adding brightness to the freshness. Birds for a moment become wildly excited. A male Blue Wren emerges, perfectly dry, from deep inside a shrub and sings enthusiastically, with feathers fluffed out. Five Yellow-tufted Honeyeaters, dry and bright yellow, crowd together on a dead branch, contrasting with the dark, wet wood as they sing. A pair of Willie Wagtails chase each other in and out of the foliage. Two Kookaburras shake the water drops from their backs and preen. During the shower they gave forth their loud laughing songs.

A breeze springs up again, shaking water drops from leaves. Another cloud passes over the sun. Excitement dies down and everything is back to normal.

Shortly after dusk a few marsupials appear. A Pygmy Possum comes out from its dry nest in the heart of a grass-tree. He stays in the bushes and concentrates on catching insects, though he too will occasionally probe the larger flowers for nectar. Marsupial mice forage mainly on the ground and ringtail and brushtail possums emerge and feed in tea-tree thickets and the timber in the gullies. A Black-tailed Wallaby thuds through a swampy area. A bat swoops low over a flowering grevillea. But on the whole, compared with the eucalypt forests, night animals in the heaths are few.

SO MANY TYPES of rocks, so many moods. The Grampians of Victoria, like the Hawkesbury area, are made up of sandstone, and the flora is rich, colourful and profuse. The rocks are of the same appearance but form higher cliffs, many showing dipping strata. The plant groups are also similar but vary enough in species make-up so that each area has its own special stamp.

In the heaths, plant vitality and plant adaptation create communities of vigour and diversity in spite of low soil fertility. At the same time the heaths imbue the eastern areas of Australia with their own special character.

Cunningham's Skink is a sturdily built lizard about one foot in length. It is commonly found amongst granite boulders

V CONSERVATION

THE PREVIOUS CHAPTERS were descriptions of plants and animals in their pristine state. In this condition the wildlife is always in balance with its physical environment. This balance however, is not static, it is ever dynamic and flexible and capable of adapting to any natural changes that may occur in soil or climate. This stability has existed in patterns of self-perpetuation and adaptation since time began. Only man can, and does, disrupt this balance and in doing so destroys nature.

This destruction is gathering pace at an alarming rate.

During the 1970's it is still possible to see nature in its original state, as described in the foregoing chapters, provided you have the time to travel and the patience to find out the hidden corners and the hitherto forgotten lands. In some instances it is necessary to put the picture together from visits to several different places. But this situation may not persist for much longer. Many of the forests, heaths, beaches and caves described and depicted in these pages are doomed to disappear; more about this later.

In the 1970's nature conservation in Australia, and particularly in its southeastern corner, finds itself at the crossroads and in a position of some paradox and irony. By this time Australians had stopped open seasons on the Koala and Platypus and saved these mammals from extinction. The Cape Barren Goose appeared to be on the way to recovery to a healthy population. Australian Fur Seals abounded at Seal Rocks where once they seemed to have been hunted to the point of no return. Leadbeater's Possum, after being 'lost' for fifty years, was re-discovered in some numbers in 1961. There were reliable reports of Thylacines having been observed in Tasmania. The beautiful Parma Wallaby was re-discovered near Gosford in New South Wales. A new mammal, *Burramys parvus*, previously only known as a fossil, was discovered live in the Victorian Alps in 1966 and subsequently in the Snowy Mountains. Quolls and Devils were on the increase in Tasmania. Turquoise Parrots, once thought to be extinct, were also on the increase. Only the Paradise Parrot was still missing and the Black-breasted Quail's status was uncertain. Looking at the bare list of names of plants and animals the picture was optimistic. It is a false picture. In the same period of time as these encouraging signs come to the fore, the mechanical age with its unlimited capacity for mindless destruction of the environment is about to make its presence felt in full. Destruction of complete habitats is imminent. This destruction will be of entire habitats including all their animals and plants and although these are protected by law, there is no effective law to stop the total destruction of all land of a given area including its plants and animals. As a consequence animals saved from extinction, and many more besides, are now plunged into new and greater dangers. Large-scale habitat destruction is of two kinds—direct and indirect.

The direct destruction completely eradicates the natural Australian environment. Some of these destructive projects include removal of heaths and forests to establish plantations of exotic pines and to create pasture land; destruction of beaches, dunes and heaths for sand-mining and resort development; destruction of caves, including important bat colonies, for limestone quarrying; destruction of forests and woodlands for the wood-chip industry; drowning of wilderness areas for hydro-electric schemes.

Forestry, grazing, mining and housing developments are, of course, necessary activities for any country that wishes to maintain a high standard of living. But in southeastern Australia the unfortunate situation has arisen that the commercial and industrial considerations and values override all others. The resource of wildlife, as important as any in the country, is pushed aside and is in real danger of being seriously and irrevocably depleted. Should this depletion be allowed to occur, and there is every indication that it will, there will be a corresponding drop in the standard of living. No matter how much material wealth is gained, with each species, each ecosystem that disappears, the quality of life will drop.

The indirect destruction of habitats is more insidious. It is a slow, creeping but inexorable force that undermines slices of the environment that may be even larger than those affected by direct destruction. Foremost of these indirect forces is the abuse of fire. Significant areas of rainforest are annually destroyed by fire. Under natural conditions, heaths, woodlands and eucalypt forests recover after fire. But as so often happens when man interferes in nature, some balance is destroyed and the system, working to perfection under its own influences, collapses under man's heavy hand.

In many parts of the east coast huge tracts of heath and dry sclerophyll forests are deliberately burnt each year—year in, year out. The causes of these fires is carelessness: cigarettes thrown from cars; camp fires allowed to escape; burning rubbish.

While the heaths and forests can cope with fire at longer intervals, annual fires eventually undermine their vigour and sap their vitality. Permanent, undesirable changes take place. Rank blady grass and bracken ferns replace the tussocks of the more succulent Kangaroo Grass and ground herbs and shrubs. Gullies, stripped of their protective covering of plants, become eroded, bare gutters. Regenerating trees and shrubs in forest understoreys are eliminated. The soil is diminished in fertility.

Plant and animal species accidentally or expressly introduced from other countries also constantly undermine Australian habitats. Introduced weeds suppress native plants along roadsides, where most people see the environment. In the temperate areas the introduced blackberries choke acres and acres of forests and heaths in impenetrable masses of thorny branches. In the subtropics Nagura Burr and lantana have taken over entire mountainsides and river flats.

Rabbits, introduced from Europe, have laid waste natural grassland and forest undergrowth and in the process have pushed many native mammals to the brink of extinction. Starlings, sparrows, Indian Mynahs, Asian turtle-doves, Domestic Pigeons, blackbirds, Goldfinches and other foreign birds have supplanted native species in cities and towns. The foreign birds are spreading and are ousting birds in country areas. Over large tracts of the east coast's woodlands, for example, the aggressive starlings have taken over the nesting hollows of parrots and other native birds. The introduced fox, and the domestic cat gone wild, take a tremendous toll of native birds and mammals. Cane toads, introduced to combat cane beetles in Queensland, are wiping out native reptiles and amphibians.

Collectors of native orchids and ferns and other operators who gather vast quantities of wildflowers, add further to the depletion. The indiscriminating broadcasting of pesticides and the pollution of air and water have added a new dimension to the creeping desolation in recent times.

All these indirect assaults on the environment leave it sadly depleted and debilitated, its subtle beauties vanished. There are vast areas of these devitalised habitats along the Divide and most of them are around the centres of population. The sad result is that most Australians see this undermined landscape as typical of their country—they do not realise that what they see is but a poor shadow of the original countryside.

Much needless direct and indirect destruction of the Australian habitat takes place in the four States we visited while gathering material for this book. Some of it is unnecessarily large in scale and other operations are so destructive of the resource of wildlife that the public interest is better served if they are curtailed or abandoned. There are many sound reasons why wildlife conservation is essential for human welfare. The bush supplies aesthetic needs and economic advantages of many kinds.

The economic advantages include the fast growing numbers of visitors who inject new money into the economy; wild plants and animals that inject new life into domesticated species.

Most crops and animals on which our very lives depend have a long history of domestication but from time to time, when production falls for no obvious reason, the stock needs genetic rejuvenation. New vigour is then injected into a plant or animal strain by crossing it with a wild species. Recently a new grain of greatly improved yield has been bred by scientists who used some wild plant species in the development of the new cereal. This is only one example. Every habitat has the potential of increasing the production of vital products and if it is destroyed these potential benefits disappear with them. Also the key to a particular area's maximum productivity in the form of crops or animal products can often be found only in the original ecosystem. If this is destroyed man may never realise this effectiveness.

Many important drugs are first discovered as compounds in wild plants. North Queensland rainforest plants have already yielded substances which show promise in fighting cancer and heart disease.

Man has always seen something in a tree more than its timber; something in an association of plants that transcends a cold enumeration of the constituent species; something in the seemingly purposeful, constructive inter-relationships between organisms that elicit awe and wonder. He is affected by a sight such as a Golden Bower-bird at its playground as he might be by an artistic masterpiece. These enriching feelings sharpen his sensitivity and recharge his imagination. They allow him to relax and unwind and are an effective and important counter to the tensions and pressures of everyday life. Only in large nature reserves can they be experienced.

Tourism is a fast growing industry and in some areas of Australia it is already a major income earner. A large number of these tourists come for the change and aesthetic qualities provided by the bushland. But this change can only be provided where there is the minimum of interference; the bush does not have to be 'organised' and recreated in the image of man. Catering for tourists may eventually surpass some of the destructive mining and clearing operations as a money earner and will benefit a far larger number of people than the few companies that now clear the forests, heaths and woodlands, the chief tourist attractions.

Bushland once lost can never be regained. Wildlife conservationists are often accused of impeding progress, but no society is truly progressive in its overall planning unless it includes a farsighted conservation programme. If the abuses of the natural environment, often masquerading as progress, are stopped the area will be richer not the poorer.

All these considerations are anthropocentric—but wildlife must be allowed to exist in its own right.

Space permits us to mention only a few of the numerous cases where the value of the natural environment should, but does not, take precedence over commercial interests. We were fortunate that we began this book when we did: four or five years later some of the most spectacular and most interesting subjects would have disappeared. Lowland rainforests of north Queensland would have been converted to biologically sterile grasslands. The Mountain Ash forests in Tasmania could have lost their tallest trees and most impressive forests. The bat nursery at Mt Etna's caves would certainly have gone as may the turtle breeding ground near Bundaberg. Rainbow Beach has changed already and unnecessarily intrusive human activities make it no longer the exhilarating place it was only two years previously.

LOWLAND RAINFORESTS between Townsville and Cooktown are the most seriously threatened of north Queensland's habitats. In 1961 about 60 per cent of all the rainforest which originally existed here was still in the hands of the crown. But much of it in the form of State Forests and Timber Reserves on which trees are harvested for timber, and as vacant crown land which can be opened up for clearing or subdivision at any time, which is in fact what is planned for the Cape Tribulation area, the last extensive tract of lowland tropical rainforest in the whole of Australia.

By far the greatest portions of rainforest still remaining are on steep mountain slopes and areas of poor soil. Hardly any of the optimum rainforest that once grew on the extensive basalt soils between Tully and Babinda now stands. So little that a survey conducted by L. J. Webb in 1966 could find only twenty acres at Clump Point near Mission Beach and about 2,600 acres at McNamee Creek near Innisfail. The McNamee Creek area has since been declared a National Park. So there is less than 3,000 acres of the most complex plant community in Australia left. Other types of lowland rainforest such as the palm swamps are not much better represented. Most are small remnants of once large tracts. It is in these remnants that many of the important drug plants have been discovered. Some occur only in small pockets a few acres in extent. The annual careless and irresponsible burn-off of grasslands, and cane fires allowed to escape wear away these remnants destroying forever small but important.pockets which remained along creeks and rivers.

Many potentially important plants have probably already disappeared. The animal life too is endangered. The White-tailed Kingfisher, a specialised nester, occurs only in lowland rainforest and is disappearing with it. There is evidence that in some areas there are already more king-fishers than available nest sites, doubtless the result of habitat destruction. The surplus birds cannot reproduce and eventually perish without leaving offspring; year by year the numbers of these spectacular birds dwindle.

Mossman Gorge and hinterland, the mountains Bartle Frere and Belenden Ker and the Palmerston National Park all include large tracts of upland rainforest. But most of the land within these parks and most of the State Forest of the uplands are on lesser quality soils. Little of the upland rainforest growing on the deep, rich basalt soils remains. Our observations suggest that many of the unique upland marsupials occur almost solely in rainforests on basalt soils. These animals are even further specialised; they live at the higher altitudes. The areas which satisfy both these conditions were only small to begin with and are constantly shrinking. The animals concerned are the Herbert River Ringtail, the Brush-tipped Ringtail and the Lumholtz Tree Kangaroo. In their chosen habitat they are often very common, in dense but isolated populations. These conditions constitute a danger, for as a dense population they are more prone to disease and can be wiped out by it, and because of isolation the habitat cannot be restocked by healthy animals further away.

A detailed study, followed by action based on the findings seems to be imperative for the long term survival of these three unique marsupials.

The drastic decline of another north Queensland animal, the Torres Strait Pigeon, is only in a minor way the result of the destruction of rain-forest. Large-scale illicit hunting is the main cause. This spectacular bird which adds so much to the charm and interest of north Queensland needs rigid, active protection to survive. It is protected by a law which is rarely enforced.

In the days before settlement the numbers of Torres Strait Pigeons must have been awe inspiring. Indeed 'the coming of the white birds' was a major event on the Aboriginal calendar.

The first figures of some accuracy were not recorded until 1908 when E. J. Banfield took a rough census on his beloved Dunk Island. He used the numbers of birds returning to their nests from feeding trips to the mainland as the basis for his estimate. He concluded that 10,000 pigeons nested on his island that year. Many islands to the north and south harboured similar if not greater numbers. But even in 1908 Banfield remarked that the numbers were 'small compared with the myriads that favoured the island in the years gone by'. In November 1967 at the height of the breeding season we could not find more than 30 pairs of birds nesting on Dunk Island. A reliable eye-witness on a nesting island to the south reported a pile of Torres Strait Pigeon feathers three feet high beneath a sign declaring the island a sanctuary.

The pigeons' decline is continuing. More and more fast speedboats equipped with freezers and ice boxes visit the unpatrolled islands. Automatic shotguns are used to shoot the birds as they return to their nests, heavy and slow with food for their young. The mature birds are killed or maimed, the next generation perishes on the nest.

North of Cairns the pigeons survive in moderate numbers but the increased activities of fishermen, always equipped with rifles and shot-guns, in the north Queensland waters, makes their future precarious as well.

As early as the 1920's and the 1930's there are reports of trochus and bêche-de-mer fishermen killing the pigeons off Cape York Peninsula. One report states that a fishing boat took shelter at a nesting island from rough weather. For three days the fishermen killed pigeons and collected their eggs. They did not even stop at night, using flares and torches to light their way to kill more of the birds. The fact that shooting pigeons is illegal does not seem to make any difference.

Almost every rainforest, including National Parks, to which a car can be driven is prey to the activities of orchid and fern collectors. Every tree to a climbable height is stripped of epiphytes. In the Mossman Gorge National Park for instance the only orchids visitors can see flowering are forty to fifty feet up in the trees, all others have been stripped.

Selling orchids and ferns is a lucrative business and their collection is often highly organised. Chain saws are used to cut down trees. An open woodland near Cooktown has been laid waste by chain saw-wielding orchid collectors.

The main target, of course, is the showy Cooktown Orchid which has completely disappeared from the place from which it derives its name. Not even the remotest areas of Cape York are safe from this kind of depredation.

Now and again a particular species of orchid becomes popular, prices rise, and the orchids disappear from places where once they were common. This happened in 1968 in two small areas of rainforest where a subspecies of *Dendrobium fusiforme*, having extra large flowers, was known to occur. Both places were completely denuded of this subspecies

—only weeks before members of an international orchid conference were to visit the area in order to be shown these beautiful plants in full flower.

In Australia tropical rainforests cover only a fraction of the total land area: most of the constituent plants and animals cannot survive outside this specialised environment. Should a particular kind of rainforest or a particular rainforest species become extinct from north Queensland it will disappear from the face of the earth forever. For this reason the conservation of a tropical rainforest, particularly in the lowlands, is perhaps the most urgent case of wildlife conservation in Australia. It receives little public attention. Apart from Webb's 1966 survey and efforts within the Queensland Forestry Department it also receives little scientific or official attention. Most attention is focused on the larger, well-known animals, the kangaroos, koalas, waterfowl and others. It is not denied that the need for preservation of these animals is urgent but most are species occurring over large tracts of land. If they disappear from one area it is possible to restock from another. Usually the animals find a retreat somewhere. The retreats for north Queensland's rainforest animals are few or non-existent.

CAPE YORK PENINSULA is one of the great wilderness areas of Australia. It has great potential attraction for the constantly increasing tourist industry. Yet there are no National Parks at all on Cape York. Neither its magnificent monsoon forests, nor the last strongholds of Queensland's floral emblem, the Cooktown Orchid, are protected in National Parks. For some time now part of the monsoon rainforests have been under consideration to be made into National Parks but to date there has been no action. Cattle grazing and mineral development between them could obliterate these areas, so uniquely different from the rest of Australia, in a matter of years. This is one case where only determined and prompt Government action can save an area; no action is in sight and destruction of the rainforests seems imminent.

Despite Cape York's isolation, great plunder of its wildlife resources is going on; because of its isolation the plunder is unchecked. The Freshwater Crocodile is virtually shot out, Cooktown Orchids are taken off in car loads. The Golden-shouldered Parrot, the bird which is moving most rapidly to extinction in Australia, lives not near any smog-ridden big city but in the remote vastness of Cape York Peninsula.

Because of the Golden-shouldered Parrot's great beauty and gentle disposition it is in great demand as a cage bird. This in itself does not constitute a threat to its survival, for many other parrots, still numerous, are similarly attractive. A combination of a restricted habitat and the easy location of its nest are the main factors against its survival. It is a comparatively simple matter to ride through the termite hill plains, inspect each termitarium and if a nesting hole is located to dig out the four to six young. There is even some competition amongst the collectors. If a nest containing eggs is found the hole dug to inspect its contents is plastered over again and the finder stakes his claim by scratching his name on the termite mound. In this way virtually every nest can be found. With other parrots, which nest mostly in hollow trees, this is not so simple and sufficient get through to ensure survival.

The finder of the nest of a Golden-shouldered Parrot usually receives a bottle of beer for a clutch of young from a travelling bird dealer or station manager. The birds are sold in Brisbane and Sydney for $100 or more. Bird dealers make extra profits on the way by trapping finches. But the really big profits on Golden-shouldered Parrots are made by people who manage to smuggle them out of the country. In Europe a Golden-shouldered Parrot will fetch anything up to $3,000. Smuggling these birds out from Cape York is not very difficult; the coastline is not patrolled. Air travellers sometimes try to smuggle the birds out and are occasionally caught. Often the birds are drugged and put in fake bottoms of suitcases, in a coat pocket or, in one case, a box camera. Some bird smugglers are caught because alert customs officials could smell the drugs or hear the birds scratching by using a stethoscope. As with pigeon hunting and orchid collecting the fact that the parrots are protected does not slow the traffic. The people of Cape York make no secret of it. They seem even proud of 'making a few extra quid' out of the country.

Of all the many threats to the wildlife we have seen over the years none is more outrageous or more tragic than the future facing the bats at Mt Etna near Rockhampton in Queensland. As already mentioned Mt Etna contains significant breeding caves of Bent-winged and Ghost Bats. In the case of the Bent-winged Bats *all* female members of the species for this district congregate at one cave, Bat Cleft. Mt Etna also supports the largest colony of the rare Ghost Bat in the world. Besides this the limestone caves of Mt Etna and neighbouring Limestone Ridge are the only significant caverns of this type remaining in the southern three-quarters of the state. They are of outstanding aesthetic value.

A cement company began mining Mt Etna's limestone in 1966 in the full knowledge of the irreplaceable biological and aesthetic assets of the caves. Other accessible limestone deposits, without caves, were not considered by the mining company. The mining company promised the Queensland Government not to mine within 66 feet of known caves. At the time of writing this promise has been breached, a breach ignored by the government. It has been established that blasting of the mine has seriously affected the breeding of bats at Bat Cleft. Neither mining company nor government can plead ignorance. Both the value of the wildlife resources and the easily accessible alternative sources of limestone have been forcefully pointed out to them by the University of Queensland Speleological Society since 1962. This society has done all that was humanly possible to save the caves and the bats. But they were no match for the insensitive, shortsighted but powerful mining interests. Mt Etna and all its inhabitants are doomed.

Similar powerful forces are at work in Tasmania. There they are working towards the destruction of the world's tallest hardwoods. It may be 50, 60 or even 70 years before these forests will have disappeared, but disappear they will. Each tree will be cut to provide Australia with newsprint. The unspoilt Mountain Ash forests of the Styx and Florentine River valleys are among the world's wonders. Smooth, glistening eucalypt trunks rise sheer and straight to heights of over 300 feet. Only the Californian Redwoods are taller. These eucalypt forests generate awe-inspring feelings and provide scenes of unique and incredible beauty. But not many Australians will be able to experience these uplifting emotions for these forests will not survive. The company controlling them has reserved the patches of tallest trees, but these reserves are mere 40, 50 and 60-acre plots. Once the surrounding forest is cleared the 'reserves' will succumb to wind damage and soil debilitation. The long-term harvesting programmes for these valleys ensures that trees will never again reach their majestic maximum heights.

Destruction on an even wider scale and of equal irresponsibility to that at Mt Etna and the Styx River valley is taking place along the coastline. The largest scale operations are carried out along the coast of northeast Tasmania, New South Wales and in southern Queensland. Whole complexes of integrated habitats are disappearing—beaches, dunes, coastal heaths, rainforests and eucalypt forests are destroyed for establishing pasture, mining for rutile and related minerals, tree planting of exotic pines and the export of wood-chips. No one could object to these operations if they were carried out to an integrated plan which would also take into account the values of the natural environment and its wildlife. But this is not the case. Mining leases are granted and vast parcels of land handed to grazing and wood-chip industries without anyone in control of these lands as much as looking at their natural values. Only when vigilant conservationists make representation are small areas sometimes grudgingly reserved by governments. This transfers the obligation

of watchfulness from government to conservationists and places conservationists in a false position.

Of all the destroyers of the coastlands, the sand-miners and those
government agencies that allow and encourage their activities, have been
most irresponsible. They have destroyed for all time huge tracts of our
beaches, dunes and heaths. Their destructive activities are expanding on
a staggering scale.

Already the sand dunes, including their heaths and rainforests, have
disappeared from most of the coastline of northern New South Wales
and southern Queensland. There are no significant coastal national parks
north of Sydney to preserve any of this outstanding coastline. Coastal
areas that are threatened, and for which mining leases have been applied
for or already granted, include three areas of particular interest. These are
the Myall Lakes district of New South Wales and Cooloola and Fraser
Island in southern Queensland. In any considerations of land use of these
areas there is no doubt that the resources of wildlife and landscape should
receive precedence over all others. The case for conserving these areas
becomes even more urgent when it is realised that most of the remainder
of the northern coast is already despoiled in one way or another. After a
bitter, six-year battle between conservationists on the one hand and sand-
mining companies and the government of Queensland on the other, the
government promised to dedicate part of Cooloola as a national park.
Five months after the government's promise, no Cooloola National Park
had come into being. At the time of writing it appears that part of the
Myall Lakes area may become national park. All three regions, Myall
Lakes, Cooloola and Fraser Island are vital assets to Australia as native,
natural areas of land. They are mosaics of lakes, heaths, rainforests,
eucalypt forests, sand dunes (including Mt. Tempest, the tallest sand dune
in the world) and beaches of outstanding interest. For reasons of science,
aesthetics, culture, commerce, education and national health, not just for
Australians but for the people of the world, it is vital that they be
preserved intact.

Each of the three coastal regions mentioned has items of major
significance unique to itself. Cooloola and Fraser Island, for example,
have luxuriant rainforests growing in pure sand. This phenomenon is of
great scientific interest as rainforests are usually only found on fertile soils.
Sand is one of the least fertile soils and yet, in these areas, supports
luxuriant plant growth. How this is possible is not yet known in detail.
When the reason is found it could conceivably lead to the discovery of
more productive agricultural practices. Should this type of rainforest
disappear, as in New South Wales and in Queensland south of Brisbane,

their secrets disappear with them. The rainforest is only one of numerous unique features of the eastern coastline. Space does not permit us to elaborate on the many other outstanding qualities.

Sand-mining, whereby minerals such as zircon, ilmenite and titanium are won from sand, totally destroys the landscape. Not only is the vegetation completely removed but the whole structure of fore-dunes, high dunes, lakes and infrequently beaches are flattened to one featureless, sterile plain. A few she-oaks, hardy grasses and bracken ferns are sometimes coaxed to live there. Gone forever are the wildflower areas as described in the heathland chapter. Few birds remain along the beaches. A stable, dynamic and uniquely Australian scene is turned into a desert. No one would deny that sand-mining is of importance but in the long term interest of the people, at least some of our coastal complexes of habitats must be preserved in their natural state. This is not being done. It must be remembered that natural land is of value for all time, for all people. Sand-mining benefits a few people for a short period.

These are just a few of the more serious threats to the natural environment. There are many others. The Loggerhead Turtle colony near Bundaberg; Tasmania's last remaining colony of Forester Kangaroos; the inundation of Lake Pedder in Tasmania; the Colong Caves in the Blue Mountains of New South Wales and other unique habitats face the possibility of complete destruction.

Nature conservation in Australia presents a depressing picture. The unfortunate situation exists that the people who have power over the environment have exploitation, often short term exploitation, as their sole, all-consuming aim. Other values are not just swept aside, they are not even considered at the outset. In Australia there is an all-pervading antagonism towards and lack of sympathy and understanding for the country's natural environment. This basic hostility can be traced to the first beginnings of European settlement.

People came here against their will, the environment was alien, it was different. Extremely hard work was needed merely to survive. There was neither time nor inclination to view the indigenous land and its plants and animals with sympathy and affection. The natural environment was rejected. Only those features reminiscent of home were admired. The birds, for instance, were given English names—robins, wagtails, magpies. The things which were different, the eucalypts with grey-green foliage, were dismissed as drab. The heaths with their prickly foliage were actively rejected as hostile. There was no appreciation of the eucalypts' clean trunks and profuse honey flow, or of the heath's brilliant flowering.

The first disastrous result of this antagonism was that the new settlers imported animals more familiar to them. They brought rabbits, foxes, starlings, sparrows and many others. They preferred these more familiar animals to the Koala, Platypus, wallaby, butcherbird and parrots. This preference cost them dearly—particularly their preference for the rabbit which made countless settlers destitute. But so deeply ingrained was their antipathy and their misguided feelings about the inferior quality of the Australian environment and its wildlife, that they compounded their mistakes when trying to eradicate the rabbit. They introduced and spread over the country mongooses, ferrets, foxes and domestic cats to combat the rabbit. At the same time they continued to trap, snare, shoot and poison quolls, devils, eagles and other native animals which were the equal or superior of the introduced rabbiters.

The result of the antagonism and ignorance about the environment can be seen most dramatically in the capital cities. Most streets are lined with foreign trees; gardens and parks are planted with trees, shrubs and flowers developed in other countries; the majority of birds and mammals in the cities were introduced from overseas. It is not that these importations are more attractive, or in the case of plants, easier to grow. To the contrary native species are in the main more attractive.

What land—land that retains all that is essentially Australian—that can be saved, must be saved during the 1970's and 1980's. The pace of destruction is such that it will be too late after that. There are hopeful signs. More and more people are becoming aware of the significance and value of large nature reserves and are becoming more sympathetic towards the wildlife native to their country. More and more Australian plants are appearing in gardens and parks. The high country in the Snowy Mountains area is slowly recovering as a national park after decades of abuse by grazing and burning. It is gradually being realised that values other than material ones are to be found in the unspoilt bush. These people with a sensitive appreciation of the environment are still small in number but their united efforts are becoming increasingly effective in saving remnants of native land.

In the early seventies the Australians are beginning to shake off their antagonism and hostility towards what for a long time they considered their enemy. It is to be hoped that the belated overtures of friendship will save the old 'enemy'.

Bibliography

TROPICAL QUEENSLAND

Bailey, F. M. *The Queensland Flora*. Vol. 1–6, Queensland Govt. Brisbane, 1899–1902.

Banfield, E. J. *Confessions of a Beachcomber*. Angus & Robertson, Sydney, 1968.

Blake, S. T. 'A Revision of *Melaleuca leucadendron* and its Allies (Myrtaceae).' *Contrib. Qld. Herbarium*, No. 1, 1968.

Brass, L. J. 'Summary of the 1948 Cape York (Australia) Expedition'. *Bull. Amer. Mus. Nat. Hist.*, Vol. 102, 1953.

Campbell, A. J. 'New and Strange Scavenger Moth'. *The Emu*, Vol. 24, 1924.

Christian, C. S., Crocker, R. L., Keast, A. (eds.). *Biogeography and Ecology in Australia*. Dr W. Junk, Den Haag, 1959.

Clausen, C. P. *Entomophagous Insects*. Hafner Publishing Co., New York, 1962.

Collett, R. 'On Some Apparently New Marsupials from Queensland.' *Proc. Zool. Soc. Lond.*, 1884.

Common, I. F. B. *Australian Moths*. Jacaranda Press, Brisbane, 1963.

Common, I. F. B. *Australian Butterflies*. Jacaranda Press, Brisbane, 1964.

Fleay, D. H. 'The Northern Quoll, *Satanellus hallucatus*.' *Vic. Nat.*, Vol. 78, 1962.

Francis, W. D. *Australian Rainforest Trees*. Forestry & Timber Bureau, Canberra, 1951.

Frith, H. J. *Waterfowl in Australia*. Angus & Robertson, Sydney, 1967.

Garrett, S. D. *Soil Fungi and Soil Fertility*. Pergamon Press, London, 1963.

Harrison, J. L. 'Mammals of Innisfail.' *Aust. J. Zool.* Vol. 10, 1962.

Hosmer, W. 'A New Leptodactylid Frog of the genus *Notaden* from Northern Australia.' *Amer. Mus. Novitates*, No. 2077, 1962.

Lavery, H. J., Seton, D., and Bravery, J. A. 'Breeding Seasons of Birds in North-eastern Australia.' *The Emu*, Vol. 68, 1968.

Lumholtz, C. *Among Cannibals*. John Murray, London, 1889.

Macnae, W. 'Mangroves in Eastern and Southern Australia'. *Aust. J. Bot.*, Vol. 16, 1966.

Ovington, J. D. *Woodlands*. English Universities Press, London, 1965.

Richards, P. W. *The Tropical Rainforest*. Cambridge University Press, London, 1952.

Russel, E. J. *The World of Soil*. Fontana Library, Collins, London, 1961.

Tate, G. H. H. 'The Marsupial Genus *Phalanger*.' *Amer. Mus. Novitates*, No. 1283, 1945.

Tate, G. H. H. 'The Marsupail Genus *Pseudocheirus* and its Subgenera.' *Amer. Mus. Novitates*, No. 1287, 1945.

Tate, G. H. H. 'The Rodents of Australia and New Guinea.' *Bull. Amer. Mus. Nat. Hist.*, Vol. 97, 1951.

Tate, G. H. H. 'Mammals of Cape York Peninsula, with Notes on the Occurrence of Rain Forest in Queensland.' *Bull. Amer. Mus. Nat. Hist.*, Vol. 98, 1952.

Thomson, D. F. *Birds of Cape York Peninsula*. Govt. Printer, Melbourne, 1935.

Tillyard, R. J. *The Insects of Australia and New Zealand*. Angus & Robertson, Sydney, 1926.

Urquhart, F. A. *The Monarch Butterfly.* University of Toronto Press, Toronto, 1960.
Van Deusen, H. M. and Stearns, E. I. 'Source of Colour in the Fur of the Green Ring-tailed Possum.' *J. of Mammalogy*, Vol. 42, 1961.
Waterhouse, G. A. *What Butterfly is That?* Angus & Robertson, Sydney, 1932.
Webb, L. J. 'Cyclones as an Ecological Factor in Tropical Lowland Rainforest, North Queensland.' *Aust. J. Bot.*, Vol. 6, 1958.
Webb, L. J. 'The Identification and Conservation of Habitat-types in the Wet Tropical Lowlands of North Queensland.' *Proc. R. Soc. Qld.*, Vol. 78, 1966.
Whitley, G. *Freshwater Fishes.* Jacaranda Press, Brisbane, 1960.

SOUTHEAST AUSTRALIA

Anderson, R. H. *The Trees of New South Wales.* Government Printer, Sydney, 1968.
Barrow, M. D., Costin, A. B., and Luke, P. 'Cyclical Changes in an Australian Fjaeldmark Community'. *J. Ecol.*, Vol. 56, 1968.
Bartholomew, G. A. and Hudson, J. W. 'Hibernation, Estivation, Temperature Regulation, Evaporative Water Loss, and Heart Rate of the Pygmy Possom *Cercaertus nanus.*' *Physiol. Zool.*, Vol 35, 1962.
Baur, G. N. (ed.). 'Forest Types in New South Wales'. *Forestry Comm. of N.S.W. Research Note* No. 17, 1965.
Beadle, N. C. W. 'Soil Temperatures During Forest Fires and their Effect on the Survival of Vegetation'. *J. Ecol.*, Vol. 28, 1940.
Beadle, N. C. W. 'Soil Phosphate and its Role in Molding Segments of the Australian Flora and Vegetation, with Special Reference to Xeromorphy and Sclerophylly'. *Ecology*, Vol. 47, 1966.
Beadle, N. C. W. 'Some Aspects of the Ecology and Physiology of Australian Xeromorphic Plants'. *Aust. J. Sci.*, Vol. 30, March 1968.
Beadle, N. C. W. and Costin, A. B. 'Ecological Classification and Nomenclature'. *Proc. Linn. Soc. N.S.W.*, Vol 77, 1952.
Blakely, W. F. *A Key to the Eucalypts.* Forestry and Timber Bureau, Canberra 1955.
Breeden, S. and K. *The Life of the Kangaroo.* Angus & Robertson, Sydney, 1966.
Breeden, S. and K. *Tropical Queensland.* Collins, Sydney, 1970.
Breeden, S. and K. *Living Marsupials.* Collins, Sydney, 1970.
Calaby, J. H. 'Mammals of the Upper Richmond and Clarence Rivers, N.S.W.' *CSIRO Div. of Wildlife Res. Technical Paper*, No. 10, 1966.
Calaby, J. H. and Wimbush, D. J. 'Observations on the Broad-toothed Rat, *Mastacomys fuscus*'. *CSIRO Wildlife Res.*, Vol. 9, 1964.
Cheney, N. P. 'Predicting Fire Behaviour with Fire Danger Tables'. *Aust. Forestry.* Vol. 32, 1968.
Chisholm, A. H. 'The Story of Scrub Birds'. *The Emu*, Vol. 51, 1951.
Churchill, D. M. and Christensen, P. 'Observations on Pollen Harvesting by Brush-tongued Lorikeets'. *Aust. J. Zool.*, Vol. 18, 1970.
Coaldrake, J. E. 'The Coastal Sand Dunes of Southern Queensland'. *Proc. Roy. Soc. Qld.*, Vol. 72, 1960.
Coaldrake, J. E. 'The Ecosystem of the Coastal Lowlands ("Wallum") of Southern Queensland'. *CSIRO Bulletin*, No. 283, 1961.
Cochrane, G. R., Fuhrer, B. A., Rotherham, E. R., and Willis, J. H. *Flowers and Plants of Victoria.* A. H. & A. W. Reed, Sydney, 1968.
Coleman, E. 'The Pollination of *Corysanthes bicalcarata*'. *Vic. Nat.*, Vol. 48, Sept. 1931.

Coleman, E. 'The Pollination of *Pterostylis acuminata and Pt. falcata*'. *Vic. Nat.*, Vol. 50, March, 1934.

Common, I. F. B. 'A Study of the Ecology of the Adult Bogong Moth, *Agrotis infusa*'. *Aust. J. Zool.*, Vol. 2, 1954.

Costin, A. B. *A Study of the Ecosystems of the Monaro Region of New South Wales*. Govt. Printer, Sydney, 1954.

Cremer, K. W. 'Eucalypts in Rainforest'. *Aust. Forestry*, Vol. 24, 1960.

Cremer, K. W. 'Dissemination of Seed from *Eucalyptus regnans*'. *Aust. Forestry*, Vol. 30, 1966.

CSIRO. 'An Index of Australian Bird Names'. *CSIRO Div. of Wildlife Res. Tech. Paper*, No. 20, 1969.

CSIRO. *The Insects of Australia*, Melbourne Univ. Press, Carlton, 1970.

Dorward, D. F. 'The Status of the Cape Barren Goose *Cereopsis novae-hollandiae*'. *International Council for Bird Preservation Bulletin*, No. 10, 1967.

Dwyer, P. D. 'The Biology, Origin and Adaptation of *Miniopterus australis* in New South Wales'. *Aust. J. Zool.*, Vol. 16, 1968.

Dwyer, P.D. 'Population Ranges of *Miniopterus schreibersii* in South-eastern Australia'. *Aust. J. Zool.*, Vol. 17, 1969.

Dwyer, P. D. 'Mammals' *Mount Etna Caves*. Univ. Qld. Speleological Soc., 1970.

Erickson, R. *Orchids of the West*. Paterson Brokensha, Perth, 1965.

Fleay, D. H. 'Breeding of *Dasyurus viverrinus* and General Observations of the Species'. *Jour. of Mammal.*, Vol. 16, 1935.

Fleay, D. H. *Gliders of the Gum Trees*. Bread & Cheese Club, Melbourne, 1947.

Fleay, D. H. 'Australia's "Needle-in-a-Haystack" Marsupial'. *Vic. Nat.*, Vol. 82 (7), Nov. 1965.

Fleay, D. H. *Nightwatchmen of Bush and Plain*, Jacaranda Press, Brisbane, 1968.

Florence, R. G. 'Edaphic Control of Vegetational Pattern in East Coast Forests'. *Proc. Linn. Soc. N.S.W.*, Vol. 89, 1964.

Florence, R. G. 'Some Vegetation-Soil Relationships in the Blackall Range Forests'. *Aust. Forestry*, Vol. 29, 1965.

Florence, R. G. 'The Application of Ecology to Forest Management with Particular References to Eucalypt Forests'. *Proc. Ecol. Soc. Aust.*, Vol. 4, 1969.

Frith, H. J. (ed) *Birds in the Australian High Country*. A. H. & A. W. Reed, Sydney, 1969.

Geehi Club. *Snowy Mountains Walks*. Geehi Club, Cooma, 1966.

Gilbert, J. M. 'Fire as a Factor in the Development of Vegetational Types'. *Aust. Forestry*, Vol. 27, 1963.

Grant, V. 'The Fertilisation of Flowers'. *Scientific American*, June, 1951.

Green, R. H. 'Notes on the Devil (*Sarcophilus harrisi*) and the Quoll (*Dasyurus viverrinus*) in North-eastern Tasmania'. *Rec. Queen Vict. Mus.*, No. 27, 1967.

Green, R. H. 'The Murids and Small Dasyurids in Tasmania Part 1 & 2'. *Rec. Queen Vict. Mus.*, No. 28, 1967.

Green, R. H. 'The Murids and Small Dasyurids in Tasmania Part 3 & 4'. *Rec. Queen Vict. Mus.*, No. 32, 1968.

Groves, R. H. 'Physiology of Sclerophyll Shrubs in South-eastern Australia'. *Proc. Ecol. Soc. Aust.*, Vol. 3, 1968.

Groves, R. H. and Specht, R. L. 'Growth of Heath Vegetation'. *Aust. J. Bot.*, Vol. 13, 1965.

Hall, N., Johnston, R. D., and Chippendale, G. M. *Forest Trees of Australia*. Forestry & Timber Bureau, Canberra, 1970.

Hickman, V. V. and Hickman, J. L. 'Notes on the Habits of the Tasmanian Dormouse Phalangers *Cercaertus nanus* and *Eudromecia lepida*'. *Proc. Zool. Soc. Lond.*, Vol. 135, 1960.

Jacobs, M. R. *Growth Habits of the Eucalypts*. Forestry and Timber Bureau, Canberra, 1955.

Jarrett, P. H. and Petrie, H. K. 'The Vegetation of the Black's Spur Region; II Pyric Succession'. *J. Ecol.*, Vol. 17, 1929.

Johnston, R. D. and Marryatt, R. 'Taxonomy and Nomenclature of Eucalypts'. *Dept. National Development Forestry & Timber Bureau Leaflet*, No. 92, 1965.

Keast, A., Crocker, R. L., and Christian, C. S. (eds.). *Biogeography and Ecology in Australia*. Dr. W. Junk, Den Haag, 1959.

King, H. J. and Burns, T. E. *Wildflowers of Tasmania*. Jacaranda Press, Brisbane, 1969.

King, J. E. *Seals of the World*. British Mus. (Nat. Hist.), 1964.

Lyne, A. G. 'Vibrissae in Marsupialia'. *Proc. Zool. Soc. Lond.*, Vol. 133, 1959.

McArthur, A. G. 'Fire Behaviour in Eucalypt Forests'. *Dept. National Development Forestry & Timber Bureau Leaflet*, No. 107, 1967.

McArthur, A. G. 'The Fire Resistance of Eucalypts'. *Proc. Ecol. Soc. Aust.*, Vol. 3, 1968.

McElroy, W. D. and Seliger, H. H. 'Biological Luminescence', *Scientific American*, Dec. 1962.

Main, B. 'Adaptive Radiation of Trapdoor Spiders'. *Aust. Mus. Mag.*, Vol. 12, No. 5, 1957.

Moore, J. A. 'The Frogs of Eastern New South Wales'. *Amer. Mus. Nat. Hist.. Bulletin*, Vol. 121, Art. 3, 1961.

Mount, A. B. 'The Interdependence of the Eucalypts and Forest Fires in Southern Australia'. *Aust. Forestry*, Vol. 28, 1964.

Nelson, J. E. 'Vocal Communication in Australian Flying Foxes'. *Zeitschrift für Tierpsychologie*, Vol. 21, 1964.

Nelson, J. E. 'Behaviour of Australian Pteropodidae'. *Animal Behaviour*, Vol. 13, 1965.

Nelson, J. E. 'Movements of Australian Flying Foxes'. *Aust. J. Zool.*, Vol. 13, 1965.

Nicholls, W. H. *Orchids of Australia*. Nelson, 1969.

Penfold, A. R. and Willis, J. L. *The Eucalypts*. Leonard Hill (Books), London, 1961.

Readshaw, J. L. 'The Distribution, Abundance, and Seasonal Movements of the Pied Currawong, *Strepera graculina*, an Important Bird Predator of Phasmitadae in eastern Australia'. *Aust. J. Zool.*, Vol. 16, 1968.

Recher, H. F. and Abbott, I. J. 'Some Differences in use of Habitat by White-eared and White-cheeked Honeyeaters'. *The Emu*, Vol. 70 (3), 1970.

Ride, W. D. L. *A Guide to the Native Mammals of Australia*. Oxford Univ. Press, Melbourne, 1970.

Rolls, E. C. *They All Ran Wild*. Angus & Robertson, 1969.

Rotherham, E. R. 'Pollination of *Spiculaea huntiana*'. *Vic. Nat.*, Vol. 85, 1968.

Slater, P. *A Field Guide to Australian Birds*. Rigby, 1970.

Smith, L. H. *The Lyrebird*. Lansdowne Press, 1968.

Sprent, J. K., (ed.) *Mount Etna Caves*. Univ. Qld. Speleological Soc., 1970.

Straughan, I. R. and Main, A. R. 'Speciation and Polymorphism in the Genus *Crinia* in Queensland'. *Proc. Roy. Soc. Qld.*, Vol. 78, 1966.

Thom, B. G. 'Late Quaternary Coastal Morphology of the Port Stephens-Myall Lakes Area, New South Wales'. *Proc. Roy. Soc. N.S.W.*, Vol. 98, 1965.

Thomson, J. A., and Owen W. H. 'A Field Study of the Australian Ringtail Possum *Pseudocheirus peregrinus*'. *Ecological Monographs*, Vol. 34, 1964.

Thomson, J. A. and Owen, W. H. 'Notes on the Comparative Ecology of the Common Bushtail and Mountain Possums of Eastern Australia'. *Vic. Nat.*, Vol. 82, 1965.

Van der Pyl, L. and Dodson, C. H. *Orchid Flowers, Their Pollination and Evolution*. Univ. of Miami Press, Miami, 1966.

Webb, L. J. 'A Physiognomic Classification of Australian Rain Forests'. *J. Ecol.*, Vol. 47, 1959.

Webb, L. J. 'Environmental Relationships of the Structural Types of Australian Rain Forest Vegetation'. *Ecology*, Vol. 49, 1968.

Webb, L. J., Whitelock, D., and Brereton, J. Le Gay. (eds.). *The Last of Lands*. Jacaranda Press, Brisbane, 1969.

Wimbush, D. J. 'Studies on the Pied Currawong, *Strepera graculina* in the Snowy Mountains'. *The Emu*, Vol. 69, 1969.

Wood, D. H. 'An Ecological Study of *Antechinus stuartii* in a Southeast Queensland Rain Forest'. *Aust. J. Zool.*, Vol. 18, 1970.

Index